The
Economist

Pocket
World in
Figures

2014 Edition

THE ECONOMIST IN ASSOCIATION WITH
PROFILE BOOKS LTD

Published by Profile Books Ltd,
3A Exmouth House, Pine Street, London EC1R OJH

This edition published by Profile Books in association with
The Economist, 2013

Material researched and compiled by
Andrea Burgess, Mark Doyle, Ian Emery, James Fransham,
Andrew Gilbert, Conrad Heine, Carol Howard, David McKelvey,
Jane Shaw, Roxana Willis, Christopher Wilson

The greatest care has been taken in compiling this book. However,
no responsibility can be accepted by the publishers or compilers
for the accuracy of the information presented.

Typeset in Officina by MacGuru Ltd
info@macguru.org.uk

Printed in Italy by
L.E.G.O Spa. Lavis

A CIP catalogue record for this book is available
from the British Library

ISBN 978 1 78125 104 1

Contents

CONTENTS

CONTENTS

Notes

This 2014 edition of *The Economist Pocket World in Figures* includes new rankings on such diverse topics as ages of mothers, slum dwellings, household debt, youth unemployment, sovereign-wealth funds, Olympics and environment data. The world rankings consider 198 countries, all those with a population of at least 1m or a GDP of at least $1bn, they are listed on pages 250–54. The country profiles cover 67 major countries. Also included are profiles of the euro area and the world. The extent and quality of the statistics available varies from country to country. Every care has been taken to specify the broad definitions on which the data are based and to indicate cases where data quality or technical difficulties are such that interpretation of the figures is likely to be seriously affected. Nevertheless, figures from individual countries may differ from standard international statistical definitions. The term "country" can also refer to territories or economic entities.

Some country definitions
Macedonia is officially known as the Former Yugoslav Republic of Macedonia. Data for Cyprus normally refer to Greek Cyprus only. Data for China do not include Hong Kong or Macau. Bosnia includes Herzegovina. Data for Sudan are largely for the country before it became two countries, Sudan and South Sudan, in July 2011. For countries such as Morocco they exclude disputed areas. Congo-Kinshasa refers to the Democratic Republic of Congo, formerly known as Zaire. Congo-Brazzaville refers to the other Congo. The Netherlands Antilles was dissolved in 2011 but continues to appear in some data; Curaçao qualifies for inclusion but there are few data as yet. Data for the EU refer to the 27 members as at January 1 2007, unless otherwise noted. Euro area data normally refer to the 17 members that had adopted the euro as at December 31 2012: Austria, Belgium, Cyprus, Estonia, France, Finland, Germany, Greece, Ireland, Italy, Luxembourg, Malta, Netherlands, Portugal, Slovakia, Slovenia and Spain. For more information about the EU and the euro area see the glossary on pages 248–9.

Statistical basis
The all-important factor in a book of this kind is to be able to make reliable comparisons between countries. Although this is never quite possible for the reasons stated above, the best route, which this book takes, is to compare data for the same

year or period and to use actual, not estimated, figures
wherever possible. In some cases, only OECD members are
considered. Where a country's data is excessively out of date,
it is excluded. The research for this edition of *The Economist
Pocket World in Figures* was carried out in 2013 using the
latest available sources that present data on an
internationally comparable basis.

Data in the country profiles, unless otherwise indicated,
refer to the year ending December 31 2011. Life expectancy,
death and fertility rates are based on 2010–15 projected
averages; human development indices for 2012, crude birth
rates for 2011, energy and religion data for 2010; marriage
and divorce, employment, health and education, consumer
goods and services data refer to the latest year for which
figures are available; internet hosts are as at January 2013.

Other definitions

Data shown in country profiles may not always be consistent
with those shown in the world rankings because the
definitions or years covered can differ.

Statistics for principal exports and principal imports are
normally based on customs statistics. These are generally
compiled on different definitions to the visible exports and
imports figures shown in the balance of payments section.

Definitions of the statistics shown are given on the relevant
page or in the glossary on pages 248–9. Figures may not add
exactly to totals, or percentages to 100, because of rounding or,
in the case of GDP, statistical adjustment. Sums of money have
generally been converted to US dollars at the official
exchange rate ruling at the time to which the figures refer.

Energy consumption data are not always reliable,
particularly for the major oil producing countries;
consumption per head data may therefore be higher than in
reality. Energy exports can exceed production and imports
can exceed consumption if transit operations distort trade
data or oil is imported for refining and re-exported.

Abbreviations

bn	billion (one thousand million)	ha	hectare
EU	European Union	m	million
kg	kilogram	PPP	Purchasing power parity
km	kilometre	TOE	tonnes of oil equivalent
GDP	Gross domestic product	trn	trillion (one thousand billion)
GNI	Gross national income	...	not available

World rankings

Countries: natural facts

Countries: *the largest*[a]
'000 sq km

1	Russia	17,075	31	Tanzania	945
2	Canada	9,971	32	Nigeria	924
3	China	9,561	33	Venezuela	912
4	United States	9,373	34	Namibia	824
5	Brazil	8,512	35	Pakistan	804
6	Australia	7,682	36	Mozambique	799
7	India	3,287	37	Turkey	779
8	Argentina	2,767	38	Chile	757
9	Kazakhstan	2,717	39	Zambia	753
10	Algeria	2,382	40	Myanmar	677
11	Congo-Kinshasa	2,345	41	Afghanistan	652
12	Saudi Arabia	2,200	42	South Sudan	644
13	Greenland	2,176	43	Somalia	638
14	Mexico	1,973	44	Central African Rep.	622
15	Indonesia	1,904	45	Ukraine	604
16	Sudan	1,862	46	Madagascar	587
17	Libya	1,760	47	Kenya	583
18	Iran	1,648	48	Botswana	581
19	Mongolia	1,565	49	France	544
20	Peru	1,285	50	Yemen	528
21	Chad	1,284	51	Thailand	513
22	Niger	1,267	52	Spain	505
23	Angola	1,247	53	Turkmenistan	488
24	Mali	1,240	54	Cameroon	475
25	South Africa	1,226	55	Papua New Guinea	463
26	Colombia	1,142	56	Sweden	450
27	Ethiopia	1,134	57	Morocco	447
28	Bolivia	1,099		Uzbekistan	447
29	Mauritania	1,031	59	Iraq	438
30	Egypt	1,000	60	Paraguay	407

Mountains: *the highest*[b]

	Name	Location	Height (m)
1	Everest	China-Nepal	8,848
2	K2 (Godwin Austen)	China-Jammu and Kashmir	8,611
3	Kangchenjunga	India-Nepal	8,586
4	Lhotse	China-Nepal	8,516
5	Makalu	China-Nepal	8,463
6	Cho Oyu	China-Nepal	8,201
7	Dhaulagiri	Nepal	8,167
8	Manaslu	Nepal	8,163
9	Nanga Parbat	Jammu and Kashmir	8,126
10	Annapurna I	Nepal	8,091
11	Gasherbrum I	China-Jammu and Kashmir	8,068
12	Broad Peak	China-Jammu and Kashmir	8,047
13	Gasherbrum II	China-Jammu and Kashmir	8,035
14	Xixabangma Feng	China	8,012

a Includes freshwater.
b Includes separate peaks which are part of the same massif.

Rivers: *the longest*

	Name	Location	Length (km)
1	Nile	Africa	6,695
2	Amazon	South America	6,516
3	Yangtze	Asia	6,380
4	Mississippi-Missouri system	North America	5,959
5	Ob'-Irtysh	Asia	5,568
6	Yenisey-Angara-Selanga	Asia	5,550
7	Huang He (Yellow)	Asia	5,464
8	Congo	Africa	4,667
9	Río de la Plata-Paraná	South America	4,500
10	Irtysh	Asia	4,440

Deserts: *the largest non-polar*

	Name	Location	Area ('000 sq km)
1	Sahara	Northern Africa	8,600
2	Arabian	South-western Asia	2,300
3	Gobi	Mongolia/China	1,166
4	Patagonian	Argentina	673
5	Great Victoria	Western and Southern Australia	647
6	Great Basin	South-western United States	492
7	Chihuahuan	Northern Mexico	450
8	Great Sandy	Western Australia	400

Lakes: *the largest*

	Name	Location	Area ('000 sq km)
1	Caspian Sea	Central Asia	371
2	Superior	Canada/United States	82
3	Victoria	East Africa	69
4	Huron	Canada/United States	60
5	Michigan	United States	58
6	Tanganyika	East Africa	33
7	Baikal	Russia	31
	Great Bear	Canada	31

Islands: *the largest*

	Name	Location	Area ('000 sq km)
1	Greenland	North Atlantic Ocean	2,176
2	New Guinea	South-west Pacific Ocean	809
3	Borneo	Western Pacific Ocean	746
4	Madagascar	Indian Ocean	587
5	Baffin	North Atlantic Ocean	507
6	Sumatra	North-east Indian Ocean	474
7	Honshu	Sea of Japan-Pacific Ocean	227
8	Great Britain	Off coast of north-west Europe	218

Notes: Estimates of the lengths of rivers vary widely depending on eg, the path to take through a delta. The definition of a desert is normally a mean annual precipitation value equal to 250ml or less. Australia is defined as a continent rather than an island.

Population: size and growth

Largest populations
Million, 2011

1	China	1,347.6	37	Sudan	33.6
2	India	1,241.5	38	Iraq	32.7
3	United States	313.1	39	Afghanistan	32.4
4	Indonesia	242.3	40	Morocco	32.3
5	Brazil	196.7	41	Nepal	30.5
6	Pakistan	176.7	42	Peru	29.4
7	Nigeria	162.5		Venezuela	29.4
8	Bangladesh	150.5	44	Malaysia	28.9
9	Russia	142.8	45	Saudi Arabia	28.1
10	Japan	126.5	46	Uzbekistan	27.8
11	Mexico	114.8	47	Ghana	25.0
12	Philippines	94.9	48	Yemen	24.8
13	Vietnam	88.8	49	North Korea	24.5
14	Ethiopia	84.7	50	Mozambique	23.9
15	Egypt	82.5	51	Taiwan	23.2
16	Germany	82.2	52	Australia	22.6
17	Iran	74.8	53	Romania	21.4
18	Turkey	73.6	54	Madagascar	21.3
19	Thailand	69.5	55	Sri Lanka	21.0
20	Congo-Kinshasa	67.8	56	Syria	20.8
21	France	63.1	57	Côte d'Ivoire	20.2
22	United Kingdom	62.4	58	Cameroon	20.0
23	Italy	60.8	59	Angola	19.6
24	South Africa	50.5	60	Chile	17.3
25	South Korea	48.4	61	Burkina Faso	17.0
26	Myanmar	48.3	62	Netherlands	16.7
27	Colombia	46.9	63	Kazakhstan	16.2
28	Spain	46.5	64	Niger	16.1
29	Tanzania	46.2	65	Mali	15.8
30	Ukraine	45.2	66	Malawi	15.4
31	Kenya	41.6	67	Guatemala	14.8
32	Argentina	40.8	68	Ecuador	14.7
33	Poland	38.3	69	Cambodia	14.3
34	Algeria	36.0	70	Zambia	13.5
35	Uganda	34.5	71	Senegal	12.8
36	Canada	34.3		Zimbabwe	12.8

Largest populations
Million, 2050

1	India	1,692.0	11	Ethiopia	145.2
2	China	1,295.6	12	Mexico	143.9
3	United States	403.1	13	Tanzania	138.3
4	Nigeria	389.6	14	Russia	126.2
5	Indonesia	293.5	15	Egypt	123.5
6	Pakistan	274.9	16	Japan	108.6
7	Brazil	222.8	17	Vietnam	104.0
8	Bangladesh	194.4	18	Kenya	96.9
9	Philippines	154.9	19	Uganda	94.3
10	Congo-Kinshasa	148.5	20	Turkey	91.6

Note: Populations include migrant workers.

Fastest growing populations
Total % change, 2000–10

1	Qatar	197.6	25	Iraq	32.8
2	United Arab Emirates	147.6	26	Malawi	32.7
3	Bahrain	97.7	27	Tanzania	31.7
4	Eritrea	43.2	28	Burundi	31.5
5	Niger	42.0	29	Andorra	31.3
6	Sierra Leone	41.6	30	Rwanda	31.2
7	Kuwait	41.0	31	Mauritania	30.9
8	Liberia	40.3	32	Senegal	30.8
9	French Guiana	40.1	33	Singapore	29.8
10	Cayman Islands	39.9	34	Kenya	29.6
11	Uganda	38.0	35	Congo-Brazzaville	28.9
12	Afghanistan	37.4	36	Mozambique	28.5
13	Angola	37.0	37	Zambia	28.3
14	Saudi Arabia	36.9	38	Jordan	28.2
15	Chad	36.5	39	Nigeria	28.1
16	Mali	36.1	40	Guatemala	28.0
17	Benin	35.8	41	Syria	27.7
18	Yemen	35.7	42	Papua New Guinea	27.5
19	Timor-Leste	35.4	43	Sudan	27.4
20	Madagascar	34.8	44	Ghana	27.3
21	Equatorial Guinea	34.6	45	Bhutan	27.1
22	Burkina Faso	34.0	46	Ethiopia	26.5
23	Gambia	33.3	47	West Bank & Gaza	26.3
24	Congo-Kinshasa	32.9	48	Somalia	26.1

Slowest growing populations
Total % change, 2000–10

1	Moldova	-13.0	24	Cuba	1.4
2	Georgia	-8.3	25	Uruguay	1.5
3	Ukraine	-7.0	26	Bosnia	1.8
4	Bulgaria	-6.4	27	Greenland	2.0
5	Latvia	-5.6	28	Barbados	2.2
6	Lithuania	-5.0		Slovenia	2.2
7	Belarus	-4.6	30	Czech Republic	2.4
8	Romania	-3.2	31	Macedonia	2.6
9	Serbia	-2.7	32	Guyana	2.9
10	Russia	-2.6	33	Portugal	3.3
11	Croatia	-2.3	34	Bermuda	3.4
12	Estonia	-2.2		Greece	3.4
	Hungary	-2.2	36	Finland	3.7
14	Puerto Rico	-1.7	37	Trinidad & Tobago	3.8
15	Montenegro	-0.2	38	Denmark	3.9
16	Germany	-0.1	39	Hong Kong	4.0
	Poland	-0.1	40	Albania	4.3
18	Armenia	0.5		El Salvador	4.3
	Virgin Islands (US)	0.5	42	Netherlands	4.7
	Zimbabwe	0.5	43	Malta	4.8
21	Japan	0.6		South Korea	4.8
22	Monaco	0.8	45	Austria	4.9
23	Slovakia	1.1	46	Belgium	5.3

Population: matters of breeding and sex

Crude birth rates
Births per 1,000 population, 2011

Highest			Lowest		
1	Niger	48.2	1	Germany	8.1
2	Mali	45.9	2	Japan	8.3
	Zambia	45.9	3	Bosnia	8.4
4	Uganda	44.7	4	Hungary	8.8
5	Malawi	44.4	5	Hong Kong	9.0
6	Chad	44.2		Italy	9.0
7	Somalia	43.3		Serbia	9.0
8	Afghanistan	43.1		Taiwan	9.0
9	Burkina Faso	42.9	9	Latvia	9.1
	Congo-Kinshasa	42.9	10	Channel Islands	9.2
11	Tanzania	41.2		Portugal	9.2
12	Rwanda	40.9		Romania	9.2
13	Angola	40.8	13	Austria	9.3
14	Nigeria	39.7	14	Greece	9.4
15	Benin	39.1	15	Croatia	9.5
16	Liberia	38.5		Singapore	9.5
17	Guinea	38.4		South Korea	9.5
18	Timor-Leste	38.1	18	Bulgaria	9.6
19	Guinea-Bissau	37.9	19	Cuba	9.7
20	Sierra Leone	37.8	20	Macau	9.9
	Yemen	37.8	21	Poland	10.1
22	Gambia, The	37.6		Spain	10.1
23	Kenya	37.4	23	San Marino	10.2
24	Mozambique	37.1		Switzerland	10.2
25	Senegal	36.8	25	Malta	10.3

Average age of mothers during the years they give birth to children, 2010

Highest			Lowest		
1	Libya	32.5	1	India	25.3
2	Djibouti	31.6	2	Armenia	25.6
	Saudi Arabia	31.6		Nepal	25.6
4	Burundi	31.5	4	Dominican Republic	25.7
5	Oman	31.3	5	Brazil	26.1
6	Ireland	31.2		Georgia	26.1
	Tunisia	31.2	7	China	26.2
8	Algeria	31.0		Moldova	26.2
	Italy	31.0	9	Bangladesh	26.3
10	Rwanda	30.9		Cuba	26.3
	Timor-Leste	30.9		Panama	26.3
12	Mauritania	30.8	12	Azerbaijan	26.4
	Morocco	30.8		Bulgaria	26.4
	Netherlands	30.8		Ukraine	26.4
	Spain	30.8	15	Puerto Rico	26.5
	Switzerland	30.8	16	Costa Rica	26.6
17	Hong Kong	30.7		Nicaragua	26.6
18	Somalia	30.6	18	Jamaica	26.7
	Sweden	30.6		Venezuela	26.7
			20	Belarus	26.8
				El Salvador	26.8
				Russia	26.8

Fertility rates, 2015–20
Average number of children per woman

Highest			Lowest		
1	Niger	6.7	1	Bosnia	1.1
2	Zambia	6.3		Taiwan	1.1
3	Somalia	6.2	3	Hong Kong	1.3
4	Malawi	5.9		Italy	1.3
5	Mali	5.8		Macau	1.3
6	Burkina Faso	5.5		Malta	1.3
7	Afghanistan	5.4		Portugal	1.3
	Tanzania	5.4	8	Andorra	1.4
	Uganda	5.4		Austria	1.4
10	Chad	5.3		Cuba	1.4
	Timor-Leste	5.3		Cyprus	1.4
12	Nigeria	5.2		Macedonia	1.4
13	Congo-Kinshasa	4.9		Moldova	1.4
	Rwanda	4.9			
15	Benin	4.7			
	Liberia	4.7			
17	Guinea	4.6			
	Guinea-Bissau	4.6			
19	Angola	4.5			
	Equatorial Guinea	4.5			

Women[a] who use modern methods of contraception

Highest, 2011 or latest, %			Lowest, 2011 or latest, %		
1	China	83.4	1	South Sudan	2.0
2	United Kingdom	80.8	2	Somalia	3.5
3	Costa Rica	78.2	3	Chad	3.6
4	Thailand	77.3	4	Congo-Kinshasa	6.3
5	Brazil	75.7	5	Guinea	6.9
6	Hong Kong	75.6	6	Sierra Leone	7.2
7	Uruguay	74.1	7	Niger	7.5
8	France	73.0	8	Mali	8.9
9	Norway	72.9		Nigeria	8.9
10	Finland	72.4	10	Guinea-Bissau	9.1
11	Colombia	71.7	11	Angola	9.3
	Portugal	71.7	12	Benin	9.7
13	Switzerland	71.5	13	Sudan	10.4
14	Canada	71.3	14	Mauritania	10.9
15	United States	71.0	15	Eritrea	11.9
16	Cuba	70.2		Mozambique	11.9
17	Réunion	69.3	17	Côte d'Ivoire	12.0
18	Belgium	69.1	18	Central African Rep.	12.3
19	Nicaragua	69.0	19	Equatorial Guinea	12.5
20	South Korea	68.9	20	Senegal	12.6
21	Puerto Rico	68.8	21	Liberia	12.8
22	New Zealand	68.4	22	Cameroon	14.3
23	Hungary	68.3	23	Togo	14.8
24	Paraguay	67.5	24	Albania	15.2

a Married women aged 15–49; excludes traditional methods of contraception, such as the rhythm method.

Population: age

Median age[a]

Highest, 2011			Lowest, 2011		
1	Monaco	45.0	1	Niger	15.5
2	Japan	44.7	2	Uganda	15.7
3	Germany	44.3	3	Mali	16.3
4	Italy	43.2	4	Afghanistan	16.6
5	Channel Islands	42.6		Angola	16.6
6	Bermuda	42.4		Timor-Leste	16.6
7	Finland	42.0	7	Congo-Kinshasa	16.7
	San Marino	42.0		Zambia	16.7
9	Austria	41.8	9	Malawi	16.9
	Hong Kong	41.8	10	Burkina Faso	17.1
11	Slovenia	41.7		Chad	17.1
12	Bulgaria	41.6	12	Yemen	17.4
13	Croatia	41.5	13	Somalia	17.5
14	Greece	41.4		Tanzania	17.5
	Switzerland	41.4	15	Gambia, The	17.8
16	Belgium	41.2		Mozambique	17.8
17	Portugal	41.0		Senegal	17.8
18	Netherlands	40.7	18	Benin	17.9
	Sweden	40.7	19	South Sudan	18.0
20	Denmark	40.6	20	West Bank & Gaza	18.1
21	Latvia	40.2	21	Liberia	18.2
22	Spain	40.1		Madagascar	18.2
23	Andorra	40.0	23	Guinea	18.3
24	Canada	39.9		Iraq	18.3
	France	39.9	25	Sierra Leone	18.4
26	Hungary	39.8	26	Kenya	18.5
	United Kingdom	39.8		Nigeria	18.5
28	Estonia	39.7	28	Ethiopia	18.7
29	Malta	39.5		Rwanda	18.7
30	Bosnia	39.4	30	Guatemala	18.9
	Czech Republic	39.4	31	Eritrea	19.0
	Martinique	39.4		Guinea-Bissau	19.0
33	Lithuania	39.3	33	Côte d'Ivoire	19.2
	Ukraine	39.3	34	Cameroon	19.3
35	Luxembourg	38.9		Zimbabwe	19.3

Highest, 2050			Lowest, 2050		
1	Bosnia	53.2	1	Zambia	17.9
2	Japan	52.3	2	Malawi	19.6
3	Portugal	52.1		Niger	19.6
4	Cuba	52.0	4	Somalia	19.7
5	South Korea	51.8	5	Tanzania	20.9
6	Macau	51.6	6	Uganda	22.0
7	Singapore	51.4	7	Mali	22.1
8	Netherlands Antilles	51.3	8	Burkina Faso	22.2
9	Hong Kong	50.7	9	Nigeria	23.1
10	Malta	50.6	10	Chad	23.9

a Age at which there are an equal number of people above and below.

City living

Biggest cities[a]
Population, m, 2020

1	Tokyo, Japan	38.7	48	Hangzhou, China	7.7
2	Delhi, India	29.3		Nanjing, China	7.7
3	Shanghai, China	26.1	50	Luanda, Angola	7.6
4	Mumbai, India	23.7	51	Harbin, China	7.5
5	Mexico City, Mexico	23.2	52	Riyadh, Saudi Arabia	7.3
6	New York, US	22.5	53	Chittagong, Bangladesh	7.0
7	São Paulo, Brazil	22.2	54	Miami, US	6.8
8	Beijing, China	20.1		Shenyang, China	6.8
	Dhaka, Bangladesh	20.1	56	Philadelphia, US	6.7
10	Karachi, India	17.7		Santiago, Chile	6.7
11	Kolkata, India	16.7	58	Pune, India	6.6
12	Lagos, Nigeria	15.8		Surat, India	6.6
13	Buenos Aires, Argentina	14.9	60	Toronto, Canada	6.3
	Los Angeles, US	14.9		Xi'an, China	6.3
15	Manila, Philippines	14.4	62	Barcelona, Spain	6.2
16	Guangzhou, China	14.2		Belo Horizonte, Brazil	6.2
	Shenzhen, China	14.2	64	Khartoum, Sudan	6.0
18	Istanbul, Turkey	13.8	65	Abidjan, Côte d'Ivoire	5.9
19	Cairo, Egypt	13.3		Dallas, US	5.9
20	Rio de Janeiro, Brazil	13.0	67	Dar es Salaam, Tanzania	5.7
21	Chongqing, China	12.5	68	Atlanta, US	5.6
	Moscow, Russia	12.5		Singapore	5.6
23	Kinshasa, Congo-Kins.	12.3		Yangon, Myanmar	5.6
24	Osaka, Japan	12.0	71	Alexandria, Egypt	5.5
25	Paris, France	11.7		Boston, US	5.5
26	Bangalore, India	11.6		Houston, US	5.5
	Jakarta, Indonesia	11.6		Zhengzhou, China	5.5
	Wuhan, China	11.6	75	Guadalajara, Mexico	5.3
29	Chennai, India	11.3		Shantou, China	5.3
30	Tianjin, China	10.9		Suzhou, China	5.3
31	Chicago, US	10.8		Sydney, Australia	5.3
32	Lima, Peru	10.7		Washington, DC, US	5.3
33	Bogotá, Colombia	10.6	80	Ankara, Turkey	5.2
34	Bangkok, Thailand	10.3	81	Monterrey, Mexico	5.1
	Hyderabad, India	10.3		St Petersburg, Russia	5.1
36	Lahore, Pakistan	9.8	83	Detroit, US	5.0
	London, UK	9.8	84	Nairobi, Kenya	4.9
	Seoul, South Korea	9.8		Qingdao, China	4.9
39	Chengdu, China	9.1		Salvador, Brazil	4.9
40	Foshan, China	8.9	87	Jinan, China	4.8
41	Dongguan, China	8.8	88	Brasília, Brazil	4.7
42	Ahmadabad, India	8.5		Changchun, China	4.7
	Ho Chi Minh City, Vietnam	8.5		Jeddah, Saudi Arabia	4.7
44	Tehran, Iran	8.1		Kano, Nigeria	4.7
45	Baghdad, Iraq	7.8		Wuxi, China	4.7
	Hong Kong	7.8	93	Melbourne, Australia	4.6
	Madrid, Spain	7.8		Ürümqi, China	4.6

---

a Urban agglomerations. Data may change from year-to-year based on reassessments of agglomeration boundaries.

Biggest populations living in urban areas

Million, 2011

1	China	660.3
2	India	378.8
3	United States	255.0
4	Brazil	164.4
5	Indonesia	119.7
6	Japan	114.6
7	Russia	105.3
8	Mexico	88.3
9	Nigeria	77.6
10	Pakistan	62.3
11	Germany	60.8
12	France	53.5
13	Turkey	51.3
14	Iran	51.0
15	United Kingdom	49.3
16	Philippines	45.4
17	Bangladesh	41.5
18	Italy	41.3
19	South Korea	40.0
20	Argentina	37.3
21	Spain	35.6
22	Egypt	35.2
23	Colombia	34.7
24	Ukraine	31.2
25	South Africa	31.0
26	Canada	27.4
27	Venezuela	27.0
28	Vietnam	26.7
29	Algeria	25.5
30	Poland	23.3
	Thailand	23.3
32	Saudi Arabia	22.5
33	Peru	22.4
34	Congo-Kinshasa	22.3
35	Iraq	21.1
36	Malaysia	20.5
37	Australia	19.8
38	Morocco	18.1
39	Myanmar	15.4
40	Chile	15.2
41	North Korea	14.7
42	Ethiopia	13.9
43	Netherlands	13.7
44	Ghana	12.5
45	Tanzania	11.7
46	Syria	11.4
47	Romania	11.3
48	Angola	11.1
	Sudan	11.1
50	Belgium	10.4

Highest, %, 2011

1	Bermuda	100.0
	Cayman Islands	100.0
	Hong Kong	100.0
	Macau	100.0
	Monaco	100.0
	Singapore	100.0
7	Puerto Rico	98.9
8	Qatar	98.8
9	Guadeloupe	98.4
10	Kuwait	98.3
11	Belgium	97.5
12	Virgin Islands (US)	95.5
13	Malta	94.8
14	Réunion	94.3
15	San Marino	94.1
16	Iceland	93.7
17	Venezuela	93.5
18	Netherlands Antilles	93.4
19	Guam	93.2
20	Uruguay	92.5

Lowest, %, 2011

1	Burundi	10.9
2	Papua New Guinea	12.5
3	Trinidad & Tobago	13.7
4	Liechtenstein	14.4
5	Sri Lanka	15.1
6	Uganda	15.6
7	Malawi	15.7
8	Ethiopia	17.0
	Nepal	17.0
10	St Lucia	17.5
11	Niger	17.8
12	South Sudan	18.0
13	Rwanda	19.1
14	Cambodia	20.0
15	Swaziland	21.2
16	Eritrea	21.3
17	Chad	21.8
18	Afghanistan	23.5
19	Kenya	24.0
20	Burkina Faso	26.5

Single city importance
% of total population, 2015

1	Hong Kong	100.0
	Singapore	100.0
3	Kuwait City, Kuwait	88.9
4	Khartoum, Sudan	81.5
5	Lomé, Togo	68.6
6	San Juan, Puerto Rico	66.6
7	Ulan Bator, Mongolia	64.4
8	Brazzaville, Congo-Braz.	61.6
9	Dakar, Senegal	56.7
	Yerevan, Armenia	56.7
11	Beirut, Lebanon	56.2
12	Phnom Penh, Cambodia	55.3
13	Nouakchott, Mauritania	54.9
14	Montevideo, Uruguay	54.3
15	Panama City, Panama	54.0
16	Asunción, Paraguay	53.7
17	San José, Costa Rica	51.4
18	Mogadishu, Somalia	50.6
19	Tbilisi, Georgia	50.3
20	Conakry, Guinea	50.2
21	Athens, Greece	49.5
22	Tel Aviv, Israel	49.1
23	Kigali, Rwanda	48.3
24	Ouagadougou, Burk. Faso	47.2
25	Niamey, Niger	46.9
26	Luanda, Angola	45.5
27	Baku, Azerbaijan	44.5
28	N'Djaména, Chad	44.4
29	Bishkek, Kyrgyzstan	43.9
30	Lisbon, Portugal	43.5
31	Abidijan, Côte d'Ivoire	41.3
32	San Salvador, El Salvador	40.9
33	Freetown, Sierra Leone	40.8
34	Lima, Peru	40.7
35	Auckland, New Zealand	40.4
36	Freetown, Sierra Leone	39.9
37	Dublin, Ireland	39.8
38	San Salvador, El Salvador	39.5
39	Santiago, Chile	39.1
40	Kinshasa, Congo-Kins.	37.8

Fastest growing cities
Average annual change in population, 2015–20, %

1	Ouagadougou, Burk. F.	6.13
2	Niamey, Niger	5.74
3	Kampala, Uganda	5.68
4	Aden, Yemen	5.14
5	Dar es Salaam, Tanzania	5.12
6	Lilongwe, Malawi	5.07
7	Antananarivo, Madag.	4.94
	Sanaa, Yemen	4.94
9	Lusaka, Zambia	4.77
10	Yamoussoukro, Côte d'Ivoire	4.73
11	Mogadishu, Somalia	4.71
12	Samut Prakan, Thailand	4.61
13	Can Tho, Vietnam	4.50
14	Mombasa, Kenya	4.49
15	Nairobi, Kenya	4.43
16	Vientiane, Laos	4.42
17	Conakry, Guinea	4.29
	Kigali, Rwanda	4.29
19	Huambo, Angola	4.28
20	Onitsha, Nigeria	4.25
21	Enugu, Nigeria	4.23
22	Abu Dhabi, UAE	4.21
	Abuja, Nigeria	4.21
24	Jos, Nigeria	4.20
25	Aba, Nigeria	4.19
	Ilorin, Nigeria	4.19
27	Maiduguri, Nigeria	4.16
28	Ogbomosho, Nigeria	4.15
29	Port Harcourt, Nigeria	4.12
30	Benin City, Nigeria	4.11
31	Bamako, Mali	4.10
	Kathmandu, Nepal	4.10
33	Kaduna, Nigeria	4.07
34	Kisangani, Congo-Kins.	4.02
35	Kananga, Congo-Kins.	4.01
	Luanda, Angola	4.01
37	Sharjah, UAE	3.96
38	Dubai, UAE	3.95
	Ibadan, Nigeria	3.95
40	Kano, Nigeria	3.92
41	Kabul, Afghanistan	3.90
	Lubumbashi, Congo-Kins	3.90
	Mbuji-Mayi, Congo-Kins.	3.90
44	Batam, Indonesia	3.85
45	Guatemala City, Guatemala	3.83
	Wuhu, China	3.83
	Yinchuan, China	3.83
48	Matola, Mozambique	3.82
	N'Djaména, Chad	3.82
	Tiruppur, India	3.82

City liveability[a]
January 2013

Best

1	Melbourne, Australia	97.5
2	Vienna, Austria	97.4
3	Vancouver, Canada	97.3
4	Toronto, Canada	97.2
5	Adelaide, Australia	96.6
	Calgary, Canada	96.6
7	Sydney, Australia	96.1
8	Helsinki, Finland	96.0
9	Perth, Australia	95.9
10	Auckland, New Zealand	95.7
11	Zurich, Switzerland	95.6
12	Geneva, Switzerland	95.2
	Osaka, Japan	95.2
14	Hamburg, Germany	95.0
	Stockholm, Sweden	95.0
16	Montreal, Canada	94.8
	Paris, France	94.8
18	Frankfurt, Germany	94.7
	Tokyo, Japan	94.7
20	Brisbane, Australia	94.2
21	Berlin, Germany	94.0
22	Copenhagen, Denmark	93.8
	Wellington, New Zealand	93.8
24	Oslo, Norway	93.4

Worst

1	Damascus, Syria	38.4
2	Dhaka, Bangladesh	38.7
3	Lagos, Nigeria	38.9
	Port Moresby, Papua NG	38.9
5	Harare, Zimbabwe	39.4
6	Algiers, Algeria	40.9
	Karachi, Pakistan	40.9
8	Tripoli, Libya	42.8
9	Douala, Cameroon	43.3
10	Tehran, Iran	45.8
11	Abidjan, Côte d'Ivoire	45.9
12	Dakar, Senegal	48.3
13	Colombo, Sri Lanka	48.5
14	Kathmandu, Nepal	51.0
15	Phnom Penh, Cambodia	51.4
16	Lusaka, Zambia	51.7
17	Nairobi, Kenya	51.9
18	Ho Chi Minh City, Vietnam	52.7
19	Cairo, Egypt	53.9
20	Hanoi, Vietnam	54.2
	Khobar, Saudi Arabia	54.2
22	Jakarta, Indonesia	54.6
23	Caracas, Venezuela	55.2
24	Tashkent, Uzbekistan	55.9

Slum dwellings[b]
% of urban population living in a slum, 2007

1	Sierra Leone	97
2	Central African Rep.	94
	Sudan	94
4	Chad	91
5	Angola	87
6	Guinea-Bissau	83
7	Ethiopia	82
	Niger	82
9	Madagascar	81
10	Mozambique	80
11	Cambodia	79
	Laos	79
13	Congo-Kinshasa	76
14	Somalia	74
15	Benin	72
	Rwanda	72
17	Bangladesh	71
18	Haiti	70
19	Uganda	67

	Yemen	67
21	Equatorial Guinea	66
	Malawi	66
	Mali	66
	Nigeria	66
	Tanzania	66
26	Burundi	64
27	Togo	62
28	Jamaica	61
	Nepal	61
30	Burkina Faso	60
31	Mongolia	58
32	Zambia	57
33	Côte d'Ivoire	56
34	Kenya	55
35	Congo-Brazzaville	53
	Iraq	53
	Lebanon	53
38	Bolivia	50

a EIU liveability index, based on a range of factors including stability, health care, culture, education, infrastructure, climate.
b Lack of basic services and/or substandard dwellings.

Refugees[a] and asylum seekers

Refugees[a], country of origin
'000, 2011

1	Afghanistan	2,664.4	11	Central African Rep.	162.9
2	Iraq	1,428.3	12	Serbia[b]	161.7
3	Somalia	1,077.1	13	Côte d'Ivoire	154.8
4	Sudan	500.0	14	Turkey	139.8
5	Congo-Kinshasa	491.5	15	Sri Lanka	136.6
6	Myanmar	414.6	16	Angola	128.7
7	Colombia	395.9	17	Russia	109.8
8	Vietnam	337.8	18	Rwanda	106.8
9	Eritrea	252.0	19	Burundi	101.3
10	China	190.4	20	West Bank & Gaza	94.2

Countries with largest refugee[a] populations
'000, 2011

1	Pakistan	1,702.7	11	Bangladesh	229.7
2	Iran	886.5	12	Yemen	214.7
3	Syria	755.4	13	France	210.2
4	Germany	571.7	14	Venezuela	200.0
5	Kenya	566.5	15	United Kingdom	193.5
6	Jordan	451.0	16	India	185.1
7	Chad	366.5	17	Canada	164.9
8	China	301.0	18	Congo-Kinshasa	152.7
9	Ethiopia	288.8	19	Congo-Brazzaville	141.2
10	United States	264.8	20	Uganda	139.5

Origin of asylum applications to industrialised countries
'000, 2011

1	Afghanistan	35.7	11	Mexico	8.9
2	China	24.4	12	Sri Lanka	8.5
3	Iraq	23.5	13	Syria	8.4
4	Serbia[b]	21.2	14	Tunisia	7.9
5	Iran	18.1	15	Bangladesh	7.6
	Pakistan	18.1	16	India	6.8
7	Russia	17.0	17	Georgia	6.7
8	Somalia	15.5		Turkey	6.7
9	Eritrea	10.6	19	Congo-Kinshasa	6.6
10	Nigeria	10.5	20	Armenia	6.2

Asylum applications in industrialised countries
'000, 2011

1	United States	74.0	9	Switzerland	19.4
2	France	51.9	10	Turkey	16.0
3	Germany	45.8	11	Austria	14.4
4	Italy	34.1	12	Netherlands	11.6
5	Sweden	29.7	13	Australia	11.5
6	Belgium	26.0	14	Greece	9.3
7	Canada	25.4	15	Norway	9.1
	United Kingdom	25.4	16	Poland	5.2

a According to UNHCR. Includes people in "refugee-like situations".
b Including Kosovo.

The world economy

Biggest economies
GDP, $bn, 2011

1	United States	14,991	24	Norway	486
2	China	7,318	25	Taiwan	464
3	Japan	5,867	26	Argentina	446
4	Germany	3,601	27	Iran[b]	429
5	France[a]	2,773	28	Austria	418
6	Brazil	2,477	29	South Africa	408
7	United Kingdom	2,445	30	United Arab Emirates	360
8	Italy	2,194	31	Thailand	346
9	India	1,873	32	Denmark	334
10	Russia	1,858	33	Colombia	333
11	Canada	1,736	34	Venezuela	316
12	Spain	1,477	35	Greece	290
13	Australia	1,379	36	Malaysia	288
14	Mexico	1,153	37	Finland	263
15	South Korea	1,116	38	Chile	249
16	Indonesia	847		Hong Kong	249
17	Netherlands	836	40	Nigeria	244
18	Turkey	775	41	Israel	243
19	Switzerland	659	42	Singapore	240
20	Saudi Arabia	577	43	Portugal	237
21	Sweden	540	44	Egypt	230
22	Belgium	514	45	Philippines	225
	Poland	514			

Biggest economies by purchasing power
GDP PPP, $bn, 2011

1	United States	14,991	23	Saudi Arabia	682
2	China	11,291	24	Thailand	601
3	India	4,532	25	South Africa	554
4	Japan	4,303	26	Egypt	518
5	Germany	3,227	27	Pakistan	485
6	Russia	3,134	28	Colombia	471
7	France	2,306	29	Malaysia	463
8	Brazil	2,289	30	Belgium	427
9	United Kingdom	2,234	31	Nigeria	412
10	Italy	1,984	32	Switzerland	405
11	Mexico	1,904	33	Sweden	392
12	South Korea	1,485	34	Philippines	391
13	Spain	1,482	35	United Arab Emirates	378
14	Canada	1,394	36	Venezuela	373
15	Turkey	1,260	37	Hong Kong	357
16	Indonesia	1,123	38	Austria	355
17	Australia	937	39	Romania	342
18	Taiwan	872	40	Ukraine	329
19	Iran[c]	842	41	Singapore	315
20	Poland	812	42	Algeria	311
21	Netherlands	714	43	Peru	301
22	Argentina	712	44	Vietnam	300

Note: For a list of 198 countries with their GDPs, see pages 250–254.
a Includes overseas departments. b 2010 c 2009 d IMF definitions.

Regional GDP

$bn, 2012		*% annual growth 2007–12*	
World	71,707	World	2.9
Advanced economies	44,417	Advanced economies	0.5
G7	33,932	G7	0.3
Euro area (17)	12,198	Euro area (17)	-0.3
Developing Asia	12,325	Developing Asia	7.9
Latin America & Caribbean	5,766	Latin America & Caribbean	3.2
Central & E. Europe & CIS	4,504	Central & E. Europe & CIS	2.2
Middle East, N. Africa,		Middle East, N. Africa,	
Afghanistan & Pakistan	3,423	Afghanistan & Pakistan	4.4
Sub-Saharan Africa	1,273	Sub-Saharan Africa	4.8

Regional purchasing power

GDP, % of total, 2012		*$ per head, 2012*	
World	100.0	World	11,990
Advanced economies	50.1	Advanced economies	40,390
G7	37.8	G7	42,120
Euro area (17)	13.7	Euro area (17)	34,120
Developing Asia	25.1	Developing Asia	6,140
Latin America & Caribbean	8.7	Latin America & Caribbean	12,330
Central & E. Europe & CIS	7.7	Central & E. Europe & CIS	13,870
Middle East, N. Africa,		Middle East, N. Africa,	
Afghanistan & Pakistan	5.8	Afghanistan & Pakistan	7,980
Sub-Saharan Africa	2.5	Sub-Saharan Africa	2,470

Regional population

% of total (7.2bn), 2012		*No. of countries[d], 2012*	
World	100.0	World	188
Advanced economies	14.9	Advanced economies	35
G7	10.7	G7	7
Euro area (17)	4.8	Euro area (17)	17
Developing Asia	49.0	Developing Asia	28
Latin America & Caribbean	8.4	Latin America & Caribbean	32
Central & E. Europe & CIS	6.7	Central & E. Europe & CIS	26
Middle East, N. Africa,		Middle East, N. Africa,	
Afghanistan & Pakistan	8.8	Afghanistan & Pakistan	22
Sub-Saharan Africa	12.3	Sub-Saharan Africa	45

Regional international trade

Exports of goods & services		*Current-account balances*	
% of total, 2012		*$bn, 2012*	
World	100.0	World	336
Advanced economies	61.2	Advanced economies	-58
G7	33.9	G7	-404
Euro area (17)	24.9	Euro area (17)	221
Developing Asia	16.7	Developing Asia	130
Latin America & Caribbean	5.6	Latin America & Caribbean	-100
Central & E. Europe & CIS	7.4	Central & E. Europe & CIS	6
Middle East, N. Africa,		Middle East, N. Africa,	
Afghanistan & Pakistan	7.1	Afghanistan & Pakistan	393
Sub-Saharan Africa	2.1	Sub-Saharan Africa	-36

Living standards

Highest GDP per head
$, 2011

1	Monaco	171,465	31	Brunei	40,301
2	Liechtenstein[a]	134,915	32	British Virgin Islands	39,015
3	Luxembourg	114,232	33	United Kingdom	38,974
4	Norway	98,081	34	New Caledonia	38,690
5	Qatar	92,501	35	New Zealand	36,254
6	Bermuda[b]	89,739	36	Italy	36,130
7	Switzerland	83,326	37	Hong Kong	35,156
8	Macau	65,550	38	Spain	31,985
9	San Marino	64,480	39	Israel	31,281
10	Kuwait	62,664	40	Cyprus	30,670
11	Australia	61,789	41	Guam[bd]	28,700
12	Denmark	59,889	42	Martinique[b]	28,513
13	Cayman Islands	57,610	43	Equatorial Guinea	27,478
14	Sweden	57,114	44	French Polynesia	26,290
15	Channel Islands[cd]	51,958	45	Puerto Rico[b]	25,863
16	Canada	50,344	46	Greece	25,630
17	Netherlands	50,085	47	Réunion[b]	25,269
18	Austria	49,581	48	Oman	25,221
19	Finland	48,812	49	Aruba	24,753
20	United States	48,112	50	Slovenia	24,132
21	Ireland	47,478	51	Guadeloupe[b]	23,242
22	Belgium	46,608	52	Greenland[a]	22,508
23	Singapore	46,241	53	Portugal	22,485
24	Japan	45,903	54	Bahamas	22,431
25	United Arab Emirates	45,653	55	South Korea	22,424
26	Faroe Islands[a]	45,206	56	Malta	21,380
27	Germany	44,021	57	Czech Republic	20,677
28	Iceland	43,967	58	Saudi Arabia	20,540
29	France	42,379	59	Taiwan	19,980
30	Andorra	41,517	60	French Guiana[b]	19,864

Lowest GDP per head
$, 2011

1	Somalia	112	17	Mozambique	533
2	Congo-Kinshasa	231	18	Afghanistan	543
3	Burundi	271	19	Rwanda	583
4	Ethiopia	357	20	Togo	588
5	Malawi	365	21	Burkina Faso	613
6	Liberia	374	22	Nepal	619
	Niger	374	23	Guinea-Bissau	626
8	Madagascar	465	24	Mali	684
9	Eritrea	482	25	Haiti	726
10	Uganda	487	26	Bangladesh	743
11	Central African Rep.	489	27	Zimbabwe	757
12	Sierra Leone	496	28	Benin	802
13	Guinea	498	29	Kenya	808
14	Gambia, The	506	30	Timor-Leste	896
	North Korea	506	31	Cambodia	897
16	Tanzania	532	32	Chad	918

a 2009 b 2010 c Latest available year. d Estimate.

Highest purchasing power
GDP per head in PPP (US = 100), 2011

1	Liechtenstein[ab]	185.8	35	United Kingdom	74.0
2	Luxembourg	184.6	36	France	73.3
3	Qatar	183.6	37	Japan	70.0
4	Bermuda[b]	175.2	38	Italy	67.9
5	Macau	160.2	39	Cyprus	67.0
6	Monaco[b]	144.0	40	Spain	66.7
7	Singapore	126.1	41	Bahamas	66.5
8	Norway	125.5	42	New Zealand	64.6
9	Kuwait	112.8	43	Faroe Islands[ab]	63.4
10	Channel Islands[ab]	108.0	44	South Korea	62.0
11	Brunei	107.6	45	Israel	59.9
12	Switzerland	106.5	46	Oman	59.6
13	Hong Kong	105.1	47	Guam[bc]	58.5
14	United States	100.0	48	Malta	57.2
15	United Arab Emirates	99.5	49	Slovenia	56.0
16	Cayman Islands[ab]	91.0	50	Czech Republic	54.7
17	Netherlands	88.9	51	Greece	53.7
18	Austria	87.7	52	Seychelles	53.6
19	Australia	87.2	53	Portugal	53.1
20	British Virgin Islands[ab]	86.2	54	Trinidad & Tobago	52.1
	Sweden	86.2	55	Martinique[c]	51.7
22	Denmark	85.1	56	Aruba[b]	51.5
23	Ireland	84.9	57	Saudi Arabia	50.4
24	Canada	84.0	58	Slovakia	50.1
25	Germany	82.0	59	Bahrain[c]	49.1
26	Belgium	80.5	60	Réunion[c]	45.9
27	New Caledonia[ab]	78.4	61	Estonia	45.7
28	Taiwan	78.1		French Polynesia[ab]	45.7
29	Finland	77.9	63	Russia	45.6
30	Greenland[ab]	77.7	64	Hungary	45.0
31	Andorra[b]	75.8	65	Lithuania	44.6
	Iceland	75.8	66	Poland	43.8
33	Equatorial Guinea	75.2	67	Guadeloupe[c]	42.0
	San Marino[ab]	75.2	68	Croatia	40.5

Lowest purchasing power
GDP per head in PPP (US = 100), 2011

1	Congo-Kinshasa	0.78	13	Mali	2.27
2	Zimbabwe[b]	1.10	14	Ethiopia	2.30
3	Eritrea	1.22	15	Guinea	2.34
	Liberia	1.22	16	Sierra Leone	2.35
	Somalia[b]	1.22	17	Afghanistan	2.37
6	Burundi	1.26	18	Haiti	2.43
7	Niger	1.51	19	Nepal	2.60
8	Central African Rep.	1.68	20	Guinea-Bissau	2.64
9	Malawi	1.86	21	Rwanda	2.66
10	Madagascar	2.01	22	Burkina Faso	2.71
11	Mozambique	2.03	23	Myanmar[b]	2.75
12	Togo	2.18	24	Uganda	2.80

a Latest available year.   b Estimate.   c 2010

The quality of life

Human development index[a]
Highest, 2012

1	Norway	95.5	31	Cyprus	84.8
2	Australia	93.8	32	Malta	84.7
3	United States	93.7	33	Andorra	84.6
4	Netherlands	92.1		Estonia	84.6
5	Germany	92.0	35	Slovakia	84.0
6	New Zealand	91.9	36	Qatar	83.4
7	Ireland	91.6	37	Hungary	83.1
	Sweden	91.6	38	Barbados	82.5
9	Switzerland	91.3	39	Poland	82.1
10	Japan	91.2	40	Chile	81.9
11	Canada	91.1	41	Lithuania	81.8
12	South Korea	90.9		United Arab Emirates	81.8
13	Hong Kong	90.6	43	Portugal	81.6
	Iceland	90.6	44	Latvia	81.4
15	Denmark	90.1	45	Argentina	81.1
16	Israel	90.0	46	Seychelles	80.6
17	Belgium	89.7	47	Croatia	80.5
18	Austria	89.5	48	Bahrain	79.6
	Singapore	89.5	49	Bahamas	79.4
20	France	89.3	50	Belarus	79.3
21	Finland	89.2	51	Uruguay	79.2
	Slovenia	89.2	52	Montenegro	79.1
23	Spain	88.5	53	Kuwait	79.0
24	Liechtenstein	88.3	54	Russia	78.8
25	Italy	88.1	55	Romania	78.6
26	Luxembourg	87.5	56	Bulgaria	78.2
	United Kingdom	87.5		Saudi Arabia	78.2
28	Czech Republic	87.3	58	Cuba	78.0
29	Greece	86.0		Panama	78.0
30	Brunei	85.5	60	Mexico	77.5

Human development index[a]
Lowest, 2012

1	Congo-Kinshasa	30.4	13	Afghanistan	37.4
	Niger	30.4	14	Liberia	38.8
3	Mozambique	32.7	15	Ethiopia	39.6
4	Chad	34.0	16	Zimbabwe	39.7
5	Burkina Faso	34.3	17	Sudan	41.4
6	Mali	34.4	18	Malawi	41.8
7	Eritrea	35.1	19	Côte d'Ivoire	43.2
8	Central African Rep.	35.2	20	Rwanda	43.4
9	Burundi	35.5	21	Benin	43.6
	Guinea	35.5	22	Gambia, The	43.9
11	Sierra Leone	35.9	23	Djibouti	44.5
12	Guinea-Bissau	36.4	24	Zambia	44.8

a GDP or GDP per head is often taken as a measure of how developed a country is, but its usefulness is limited as it refers only to economic welfare. The UN Development Programme combines statistics on average and expected years of schooling and life expectancy with income levels (now GNI per head, valued in PPP US$). The HDI is shown here scaled from 0 to 100; countries scoring over 80 are considered to have very high human development, 67–79 high, 50–66 medium and those under 50 low.

Inequality-adjusted human development index[a]
Highest, 2012

1	Norway	89.4	13	Canada	83.2
2	Australia	86.4	14	Czech Republic	82.6
3	Sweden	85.9	15	Belgium	82.5
4	Netherlands	85.7	16	United States	82.1
5	Germany	85.6	17	Luxembourg	81.3
6	Ireland	85.0	18	France	81.2
7	Switzerland	84.9	19	United Kingdom	80.2
8	Iceland	84.8	20	Spain	79.6
9	Denmark	84.5	21	Israel	79.0
10	Slovenia	84.0	22	Slovakia	78.8
11	Finland	83.9	23	Malta	77.8
12	Austria	83.7	24	Italy	77.6

Gini coefficient[b]

Highest 2000–12			*Lowest 2000–12*		
1	Seychelles	65.8	1	Sweden	25.0
2	Namibia	63.9	2	Norway	25.8
3	South Africa	63.1	3	Slovakia	26.0
4	Haiti	59.2	4	Ukraine	26.4
5	Angola	58.6	5	Finland	26.9
6	Honduras	57.0	6	Belarus	27.2
7	Bolivia	56.3	7	Afghanistan	27.8
	Central African Rep.	56.3		Serbia	27.8
9	Colombia	55.9	9	Bulgaria	28.2
	Guatemala	55.9	10	Germany	28.3
11	Brazil	54.7	11	Kazakhstan	29.0
12	Zambia	54.6	12	Austria	29.2
13	Rwanda	53.1	13	Ethiopia	29.8

Economic freedom index[c]
2013

1	Hong Kong	89.3	14	United Kingdom	74.8
2	Singapore	88.0	15	Luxembourg	74.2
3	Australia	82.6	16	Finland	74.0
4	New Zealand	81.4	17	Netherlands	73.5
5	Switzerland	81.0	18	Sweden	72.9
6	Canada	79.4	19	Germany	72.8
7	Chile	79.0	20	Taiwan	72.7
8	Mauritius	76.9	21	Georgia	72.2
9	Denmark	76.1	22	Iceland	72.1
10	United States	76.0		Lithuania	72.1
11	Ireland	75.7	24	Austria	71.8
12	Bahrain	75.5		Japan	71.8
13	Estonia	75.3	26	Macau	71.7

a When there is inequality in the distribution of health, education and income, the IHDI of an average person in society is less than the ordinary HDI.
b The lower its value, the more equally household income is distributed.
c Ranks countries on the basis of indicators of how government intervention can restrict the economic relations between individuals, published by the Heritage Foundation. Scores are from 80–100 (free) to 0–49.9 (repressed) (see Glossary).

Economic growth

Highest economic growth
Average annual % increase in real GDP, 2001–11

#	Country		#	Country	
1	Azerbaijan	14.0		Vietnam	7.2
2	Qatar	13.9	29	Tanzania	7.0
3	Macau	13.5	30	Ghana	6.9
4	Equatorial Guinea	12.2	31	Nigeria	6.8
5	Angola	11.2		Sudan	6.8
6	China	10.6	33	Timor-Leste	6.7
7	Myanmar	9.7	34	Georgia	6.5
8	Turkmenistan	8.7	35	Peru	6.3
9	Afghanistan[a]	8.6	36	Singapore	6.2
10	Bhutan	8.4		Sri Lanka	6.2
	Chad	8.4	38	Bahrain[b]	6.1
12	Ethiopia	8.3		Kuwait	6.1
	Sierra Leone	8.3	40	Bangladesh	6.0
14	Tajikistan	8.1		Cape Verde	6.0
15	Rwanda	8.0		Jordan	6.0
16	Cambodia	7.9		Liberia	6.0
	Mongolia	7.9	44	Congo-Kinshasa	5.8
18	Kazakhstan	7.7		Zambia	5.8
19	India	7.6	46	Argentina	5.7
	Uganda	7.6		Burkina Faso	5.7
21	Belarus	7.5	48	Dominican Republic	5.6
22	Armenia	7.4	49	Indonesia	5.5
	Laos	7.4	50	Cuba[b]	5.4
	Panama	7.4		Libya[c]	5.4
25	Mozambique	7.3		Malawi	5.4
	Uzbekistan	7.3	53	Mauritania	5.3
27	Maldives	7.2		Turkey	5.3

Lowest economic growth
Average annual % change in real GDP, 2001–11

#	Country		#	Country	
1	Zimbabwe	-4.2		Germany	1.1
2	Puerto Rico[b]	-0.5	20	Channel Islands[d]	1.2
3	Italy	0.2	21	Brunei	1.3
4	Portugal	0.3		Central African Rep.	1.3
5	Bahamas	0.4		Fiji	1.3
6	Barbados[c]	0.5		Netherlands	1.3
7	Côte d'Ivoire	0.6	25	Belgium	1.5
	Jamaica	0.6		Norway	1.5
	Japan	0.6	27	Antigua & Barbuda	1.6
10	Denmark	0.7		United Kingdom	1.6
	Haiti	0.7		United States	1.6
	Iraq	0.7	30	Austria	1.7
13	Eritrea	0.9		Spain	1.7
	Greece	0.9	32	Finland	1.8
15	Bermuda[b]	1.0		Guinea-Bissau	1.8
	Greenland[c]	1.0		Hungary	1.8
17	Euro area	1.1		Switzerland	1.8
	France	1.1			

a 2002–11 b 2001–10 c 2001–09 d 2001–07

Highest economic growth
Average annual % increase in real GDP, 1991–2001

1	Equatorial Guinea	25.8	10	Cambodia	7.0
2	Bosnia[a]	23.1	11	Eritrea[b]	6.7
3	China	10.3	12	Uganda	6.5
4	Myanmar	8.4	13	Singapore	6.4
5	Qatar	7.9	14	Laos	6.3
6	Vietnam	7.7		Liberia	6.3
7	Cape Verde	7.3	16	Dominican Republic	6.2
	Ireland	7.3		Malaysia	6.2
9	Maldives	7.1	18	Mozambique	6.1

Lowest economic growth
Average annual % change in real GDP, 1991–2001

1	Moldova	-7.7	11	Burundi	-2.2
2	Tajikistan	-7.6	12	Lithuania	-2.0
3	Georgia	-6.7	13	Armenia	-1.7
4	Ukraine	-6.4	14	Turkmenistan	-1.5
5	Congo-Kinshasa	-5.0	15	Libya	-1.4
6	Azerbaijan	-4.2	16	Djibouti	-1.2
	Serbia	-4.2		Kazakhstan	-1.2
8	Sierra Leone	-3.2	18	Latvia	-0.7
9	Russia	-2.9		Macedonia	-0.7
10	Kyrgyzstan	-2.7	20	Belarus	-0.6

Highest services growth
Average annual % increase in real terms, 2003–11

1	Angola	15.3	10	Rwanda	10.2
2	Azerbaijan	13.7	11	Bhutan	9.8
3	Afghanistan	13.3		India	9.8
4	Equatorial Guinea[c]	12.6		Namibia	9.8
5	Liberia	12.4	14	Burundi	9.4
6	Ethiopia	12.0		Moldova	9.4
7	China	11.3		Mongolia	9.4
8	Uzbekistan	10.8	17	Panama	9.2
9	Kyrgyzstan	10.4	18	Sudan	8.8

Lowest services growth
Average annual % change in real terms, 2003–11

1	Trinidad & Tobago	-2.7	10	Denmark[d]	1.0
2	Zimbabwe	-1.2	11	Eritrea[e]	1.1
3	Antigua & Barbuda	0.1		Togo	1.1
4	Bahamas	0.5	13	Bermuda[d]	1.2
5	Jamaica	0.7		Finland[d]	1.2
	Japan[d]	0.7	15	Fiji	1.5
7	Haiti	0.8		France[e]	1.5
8	Hungary[d]	0.9		Guinea	1.5
	Italy[d]	0.9		United Kingdom	1.5

a 1994–2001   b 1992–2001   c 2003–08   d 2003–10   e 2003–09
Note: Rankings of highest and lowest industrial growth 2003–11 can be found on page 46 and highest and lowest agricultural growth 2003–11 on page 49.

Trading places

Biggest exporters
% of total world exports (goods, services and income), 2011

1	Euro area (17)	16.02	22	Sweden	1.30
2	United States	11.42	23	Ireland	1.24
3	China	8.94	24	Brazil	1.22
4	Germany	8.16	25	United Arab Emirates	1.18
5	Japan	4.62	26	Malaysia	1.12
6	United Kingdom	4.34	27	Austria	1.09
7	France	4.17	28	Thailand	1.07
8	Netherlands	3.08	29	Luxembourg	1.03
9	Italy	2.77	30	Hong Kong	1.00
10	South Korea	2.66	31	Norway	0.97
11	Canada	2.45	32	Poland	0.96
	Russia	2.45	33	Indonesia	0.86
13	Switzerland	2.09	34	Denmark	0.83
14	Spain	2.02	35	Turkey	0.75
15	Belgium	1.99	36	Czech Republic	0.64
16	India	1.79	37	Hungary	0.54
17	Singapore	1.64	38	Iran	0.53
18	Saudi Arabia	1.58	39	Finland	0.51
19	Taiwan	1.51		Qatar	0.51
20	Mexico	1.50	41	Kuwait	0.50
21	Australia	1.46	42	South Africa	0.49

Most trade dependent
Trade[a] as % of GDP, 2011

1	Aruba	206.8
2	Singapore	89.1
3	Liberia	87.8
4	Slovakia	79.9
5	Vietnam	78.6
6	Belarus	77.2
7	Panama	74.4
8	Malaysia	70.7
9	Hungary	69.3
10	Bahrain	69.2
11	Lesotho	68.6
12	Estonia	67.2
13	United Arab Emirates	67.1
14	Lithuania	66.2
15	Belgium	64.3
16	Seychelles	64.1
17	Mauritania	63.3
18	Taiwan	63.2
19	Zimbabwe	62.4
20	Netherlands	61.3
21	Slovenia	60.9
	Thailand	60.9

Least trade dependent
Trade[a] as % of GDP, 2011

1	Bermuda	8.0
2	Brazil	9.7
3	Central African Rep.	12.3
4	United States	12.5
5	Japan	13.5
6	Macau	13.6
7	Myanmar	13.7
8	Burundi	14.5
9	French Polynesia	14.7
10	Sudan	14.8
11	Cuba	15.4
12	Pakistan	15.5
13	Greece	16.2
14	Colombia	16.4
	Egypt	16.4
16	Afghanistan	17.3
	Argentina	17.3
18	Nepal	17.6
	Rwanda	17.6
20	Australia	18.6
21	Ethiopia	18.8
	Euro area (17)	18.8

Notes: The figures are drawn wherever possible from balance of payment statistics so have differing definitions from statistics taken from customs or similar sources. For Hong Kong and Singapore, only domestic exports and retained imports are used. Euro area data exclude intra-euro area trade.

a Average of imports plus exports of goods.

Biggest traders of goods[a]
% of world, 2012

Exports				Imports	
1	China	11.2	1	United States	12.6
2	United States	8.4	2	China	9.8
3	Germany	7.7	3	Germany	6.3
4	Japan	4.4	4	Japan	4.8
5	Netherlands	3.6	5	United Kingdom	3.7
6	France	3.1	6	France	3.6
7	South Korea	3.0	7	Netherlands	3.2
8	Russia	2.9	8	South Korea	2.8
9	Italy	2.7	9	Canada	2.6
10	United Kingdom	2.6		India	2.6
11	Canada	2.5		Italy	2.6
12	Belgium	2.4	12	Belgium	2.3
13	Saudi Arabia[b]	2.1	13	Mexico	2.0
14	Mexico	2.0	14	Russia	1.8
15	India	1.6		Spain	1.8
	Spain	1.6	16	Taiwan	1.5
	Taiwan	1.6	17	Australia	1.4
	United Arab Emirates[b]	1.6	18	Brazil	1.3
19	Australia	1.4		Thailand	1.3
20	Brazil	1.3		Turkey	1.3
	Thailand	1.3	21	United Arab Emirates[b]	1.2

Biggest earners from services and income
% of world exports of services and income, 2011

1	Euro area (17)	19.80	24	Australia	1.22
2	United States	17.46	25	Norway	1.07
3	United Kingdom	7.80	26	Taiwan	0.91
4	Germany	7.01	27	Malaysia	0.68
5	France	5.79	28	Brazil	0.63
6	China	5.46		Thailand	0.63
7	Japan	4.70	30	Finland	0.59
8	Luxembourg	3.06		Poland	0.59
9	Hong Kong	2.95	32	Greece	0.58
10	Netherlands	2.90	33	Turkey	0.55
11	Spain	2.60	34	Macau	0.53
12	Italy	2.45	35	Portugal	0.50
13	Ireland	2.35	36	Hungary	0.46
14	Singapore	2.34	37	Israel	0.44
15	Switzerland	2.29	38	Saudi Arabia	0.40
16	Belgium	2.22	39	Czech Republic	0.37
17	Canada	1.96	40	Ukraine	0.34
18	India	1.90	41	Mexico	0.33
19	Sweden	1.76	42	Indonesia	0.31
20	South Korea	1.46	43	Philippines	0.30
21	Austria	1.29	44	Kuwait	0.28
	Russia	1.29		Lebanon	0.28
23	Denmark	1.24			

a Individual countries only.   b Estimate.

Balance of payments: current account

Largest surpluses
$m, 2011

1	Germany	203,640		26	Kazakhstan	14,110
2	China	201,714		27	Oman	10,263
3	Saudi Arabia	158,545		28	Nigeria	8,689
4	Japan	119,060		29	Austria	7,988
5	Russia	98,834		30	Angola	7,421
6	Netherlands	81,323		31	Philippines	6,988
7	Kuwait	70,762		32	Thailand	5,918
8	Norway	66,694		33	Brunei	5,294
9	Iran	59,382		34	Luxembourg	4,199
10	Singapore	56,989		35	South Sudan	3,310
11	Qatar	51,978		36	Bahrain	3,247
12	Sweden	41,703		37	Gabon[a]	2,676
13	Taiwan	41,270		38	Trinidad & Tobago	2,623
14	Switzerland	35,900		39	Uzbekistan	2,612
15	Malaysia	31,770		40	Ireland	2,514
16	United Arab Emirates	30,700		41	Timor-Leste	2,385
17	Venezuela	27,325		42	Indonesia	2,070
18	Iraq	26,203		43	Israel	1,905
19	South Korea	26,068		44	Hungary	1,320
20	Algeria	19,393		45	Sudan	711
21	Denmark	18,887		46	Bermuda[b]	671
22	Azerbaijan	17,145		47	Turkmenistan	569
23	Macau	16,967		48	Bolivia	537
24	Euro area (17)	15,710		49	Estonia	477
25	Hong Kong	14,139		50	Côte d'Ivoire[b]	465

Largest deficits
$m, 2011

1	United States	-465,920		22	Czech Republic	-6,349
2	Turkey	-76,986		23	Egypt	-5,484
3	Italy	-67,366		24	Belarus	-5,121
4	India	-60,038		25	Lebanon	-4,866
5	France	-54,440		26	Sri Lanka	-4,675
6	Canada	-52,993		27	Tanzania	-4,561
7	Brazil	-52,480		28	Dominican Republic	-4,499
8	Spain	-51,919		29	Serbia	-4,157
9	United Kingdom	-34,260		30	Panama	-3,874
10	Australia	-33,752		31	Ghana	-3,501
11	Greece	-28,583		32	Jordan	-3,470
12	Poland	-25,023		33	Tunisia	-3,386
13	Portugal	-16,814		34	Peru	-3,341
14	South Africa	-13,683		35	Kenya	-3,333
15	Ukraine	-10,233		36	Chile	-3,220
16	Colombia	-9,955		37	Zimbabwe[a]	-3,217
17	Mexico	-9,166		38	Equatorial Guinea[b]	-2,918
18	Romania	-8,344		39	Libya	-2,799
19	Morocco	-8,337		40	Mongolia	-2,760
20	Belgium	-7,102		41	Mozambique	-2,438
21	New Zealand	-6,686		42	Uganda	-2,276

Note: Euro area data exclude intra-euro area trade. a Estimate. b 2010

Largest surpluses as % of GDP
2011

1	Timor-Leste	226.3	26	Angola	7.1
2	Macau	46.6		Luxembourg	7.1
3	Kuwait	40.1	28	Suriname	5.8
4	Brunei	32.4		Uzbekistan	5.8
5	Qatar	30.0	30	Denmark	5.7
6	Saudi Arabia	27.5		Germany	5.7
7	Azerbaijan	27.0		Hong Kong	5.7
8	Singapore	23.8	33	Switzerland	5.4
9	Iraq	22.7	34	Russia	5.3
10	South Sudan	17.3	35	Nigeria	3.6
11	Gabon[a]	15.7	36	Philippines	3.1
12	Oman	14.3	37	China	2.8
13	Bahrain	14.2	38	Gambia, The	2.3
14	Iran	13.8		South Korea	2.3
15	Norway	13.7	40	Bolivia	2.2
16	Trinidad & Tobago	11.7		Estonia	2.2
17	Bermuda[b]	11.6	42	Afghanistan[a]	2.1
18	Malaysia	11.0	43	Côte d'Ivoire[b]	2.0
19	Algeria	10.3		Japan	2.0
20	Netherlands	9.7		Turkmenistan	2.0
21	Taiwan	8.9	46	Austria	1.9
22	United Arab Emirates	8.5	47	Thailand	1.7
23	Venezuela	8.6	48	Ireland	1.2
24	Sweden	7.7	49	Sudan	1.1
25	Kazakhstan	7.5	50	Hungary	0.9

Largest deficits as % of GDP
2011

1	Liberia	-61.7	22	Panama	-14.5
2	Sierra Leone	-40.8	22	Jamaica	-14.3
3	Zimbabwe[a]	-33.3	24	Bahamas	-14.0
4	Mongolia	-31.5		Nicaragua	-14.0
5	Guinea	-23.9	26	Malawi	-13.6
	Maldives	-23.9	27	Uganda	-13.5
7	Haiti	-23.8	28	Djibouti	-13.4
8	St Lucia	-22.5		Guyana	-13.4
9	Lesotho	-21.4	30	Georgia	-13.3
10	Seychelles	-21.3	31	Mauritius	-12.6
11	Equatorial Guinea[b]	-20.8	31	Moldova	-12.4
12	Bhutan	-20.5	33	Albania	-12.3
	Niger[b]	-20.5	34	Tajikistan	-12.2
14	Montenegro	-19.6	34	Lebanon	-12.1
15	Netherlands Antilles[c]	-19.5	36	Jordan	-12.0
16	Mozambique	-19.1	37	Fiji[b]	-11.3
	Tanzania	-19.1	37	Armenia	-11.1
17	New Caledonia	-16.8	39	Antigua & Barbuda	-10.7
19	Burundi	-16.5	40	Swaziland[b]	-10.5
20	Cape Verde	-16.0	41	Barbados	-10.2
21	Kosovo	-15.9			

a Estimate.   b 2010   c 2009

Official reserves[a]
$m, end-2012

1	China	3,387,530	16	France	184,522
2	Japan	1,268,081	17	Italy	181,672
3	Euro area (17)	909,246	18	Thailand	181,482
4	Saudi Arabia	681,475	19	Mexico	167,076
5	United States	574,266	20	Malaysia	139,693
6	Russia	537,817	21	Libya[b]	122,981
7	Switzerland	531,303	22	Turkey	119,184
8	Taiwan	403,164	23	Indonesia	112,797
9	Brazil	373,160	24	Poland	108,902
10	South Korea	327,725	25	United Kingdom	105,207
11	Hong Kong	317,336	26	Denmark	89,699
12	India	300,426	27	Philippines	83,788
13	Singapore	265,750	28	Israel	75,868
14	Germany	248,865	29	Iraq	70,331
15	Algeria	200,582	30	Canada	68,548

Official gold reserves
Market prices, $m, end-2012

1	Euro area (17)	576,892	14	Turkey	19,241
2	United States	435,136	15	Saudi Arabia	17,276
3	Germany	181,443	16	United Kingdom	16,607
4	Italy	131,173	17	Lebanon	15,342
5	France	130,291	18	Spain	15,059
6	China	56,410	19	Austria	14,976
7	Switzerland	55,644	20	Belgium	12,164
8	Russia	51,240	21	Philippines	10,310
9	Japan	40,934	22	Algeria	9,285
10	Netherlands	32,764	23	Thailand	8,154
11	India	29,839	24	Sweden	6,726
12	Portugal	20,467	25	South Africa	6,689
13	Venezuela	19,569	26	Mexico	6,663

Workers' remittances
Inflows, $m, 2011

1	India	63,011	16	Poland	7,641
2	China	61,365	17	Lebanon	7,612
3	Mexico	23,588	18	Morocco	7,256
4	Philippines	23,065	19	Italy	7,025
5	Nigeria	20,619	20	Indonesia	6,924
6	France	19,483	21	Ukraine	6,716
7	Egypt	14,324	22	Russia	5,667
8	Germany	13,393	23	United States	5,437
9	Pakistan	12,263	24	Sri Lanka	5,193
10	Bangladesh	12,068	25	Brazil	4,793
11	Spain	11,543	26	Guatemala	4,508
12	Belgium	10,912	27	Nepal	4,217
13	South Korea	10,576	28	Colombia	4,205
14	Vietnam	8,600	29	Thailand	3,994
15	United Kingdom	8,078	30	Portugal	3,836

a Foreign exchange, SDRs, IMF position and gold at market prices.   b November 2012.

Exchange rates

The Economist's Big Mac index

		Big Mac prices		Implied	Actual $	Under (-)/
		in local currency	in $	PPP[a] of the $	exchange rate	over (+) valuation against $, %
Countries with the most under-valued currencies, January 2013						
1	India[b]	89.00	1.67	20.38	53.40	-62
2	South Africa	18.33	2.03	4.20	9.05	-54
3	Hong Kong	17.00	2.19	3.89	7.76	-50
4	Ukraine	19.00	2.33	4.35	8.14	-47
5	Egypt	16.00	2.39	3.66	6.69	-45
6	Russia	72.88	2.43	16.69	30.05	-44
7	Taiwan	75.00	2.54	17.17	29.50	-42
8	China[c]	16.00	2.57	3.66	6.22	-41
	Malaysia	7.95	2.58	1.82	3.08	-41
10	Sri Lanka	350.00	2.77	80.14	126.45	-37
11	Indonesia	27,939.00	2.86	6,397.18	9,767.50	-35
12	Mexico	37.00	2.90	8.47	12.74	-33
	Philippines	118.00	2.91	27.02	40.60	-33
	Poland	9.10	2.94	2.08	3.09	-33
	Saudi Arabia	11.00	2.93	2.52	3.75	-33
	Thailand	87.00	2.92	19.92	29.76	-33
17	Pakistan	290.00	2.97	66.40	97.67	-32
18	Lithuania	7.80	3.07	1.79	2.54	-30
19	Latvia	1.69	3.28	0.39	0.52	-25
	UAE	12.00	3.27	2.75	3.67	-25
21	South Korea	3,700.00	3.41	847.19	1085.48	-22
22	Japan	320.00	3.51	73.27	91.07	-20
23	Singapore	4.50	3.64	1.03	1.23	-17
24	Czech Republic	70.33	3.72	16.10	18.89	-15
25	Argentina	19.00	3.82	4.35	4.98	-13
	Hungary	830.00	3.82	190.04	217.47	-13
27	Peru	10.00	3.91	2.29	2.56	-11
28	Israel	14.90	4.00	3.41	3.72	-8
29	United Kingdom	2.69	4.25	1.62[d]	1.58[d]	-3
Countries with the most over-valued currencies, January 2013						
1	Venezuela	39.00	9.08	8.93	4.29	108
2	Norway	43.00	7.84	9.85	5.48	80
3	Switzerland	6.50	7.12	1.49	0.91	63
4	Sweden	40.56	6.39	9.29	6.35	46
5	Brazil	11.25	5.64	2.58	1.99	29
6	Uruguay	105.00	5.45	24.04	19.28	25
7	Canada	5.41	5.39	1.24	1.00	24
8	Denmark	28.50	5.18	6.53	5.50	19
9	Australia	4.70	4.90	1.08	0.96	12
	Euro area[e]	3.59	4.88	1.21[f]	1.36[f]	12
11	Colombia	8,600.00	4.85	1,969.14	1,773.18	11
12	Turkey	8.45	4.78	1.93	1.77	9

a Purchasing-power parity: local price in the 41 countries listed divided by United States price ($4.37, average of four cities).
b Maharaja Mac.   c Average of five cities.   d Dollars per pound.
e Weighted average of prices in euro area.   f Dollars per euro.

Public finance

Government debt
As % of GDP, 2012

1	Japan	219.1		16	Austria	84.9
2	Greece	165.6		17	Netherlands	82.6
3	Italy	140.2		18	Israel	72.9
4	Portugal	138.8		19	Finland	63.3
5	Iceland	131.8		20	Poland	62.6
6	Ireland	123.3		21	Slovenia	61.0
7	France	109.7		22	Denmark	58.9
8	United States	106.3		23	Slovakia	56.6
9	Belgium	104.1		24	Czech Republic	55.9
10	Euro area (15)	103.9		25	Sweden	48.7
	United Kingdom	103.9		26	New Zealand	44.3
12	Spain	90.5		27	Switzerland	43.8
13	Germany	89.2		28	South Korea	35.1
14	Hungary	89.0		29	Norway	34.6
15	Canada	85.5		30	Australia	32.4

Government spending
As % of GDP, 2012

1	Denmark	59.5		16	Iceland	46.5
2	France	56.9		17	Germany	45.0
3	Finland	56.0			New Zealand	45.0
4	Belgium	54.9		19	Czech Republic	44.6
5	Greece	54.8			Israel	44.6
6	Sweden	52.0		21	Japan	43.2
7	Austria	51.2			Norway	43.2
8	Italy	50.6		23	Luxembourg	43.0
9	Netherlands	50.3		24	Poland	42.3
10	Euro area (15)	50.0		25	Ireland	42.1
11	Slovenia	49.0		26	Canada	41.2
12	United Kingdom	48.5		27	Estonia	40.5
13	Hungary	48.4		28	United States	40.3
14	Portugal	47.4		29	Slovakia	37.4
15	Spain	47.0		30	Australia	36.1

Tax revenue
As % of GDP, 2011

1	Denmark	48.1		14	Hungary	35.7
2	Sweden	44.5		15	United Kingdom	35.5
3	France	44.2		16	Czech Republic	35.3
4	Belgium	44.0		17	Estonia	32.8
5	Finland	43.4		18	Israel	32.6
6	Norway	43.2		19	New Zealand	31.7
7	Italy	42.9			Poland[a]	31.7
8	Austria	42.1		21	Spain	31.6
9	Netherlands[a]	38.7		22	Portugal[a]	31.3
10	Germany	37.1		23	Greece	31.2
	Luxembourg	37.1		24	Canada	31.0
12	Slovenia	36.8		25	Slovakia	28.8
13	Iceland	36.0		26	Switzerland	28.5

Note: Includes only OECD countries.   a 2010

Democracy

Democracy index
Most democratic = 10, 2012

Most			Least		
1	Norway	9.93	1	North Korea	1.08
2	Sweden	9.73	2	Guinea-Bissau	1.43
3	Iceland	9.65	3	Chad	1.62
4	Denmark	9.52	4	Syria	1.63
5	New Zealand	9.26	5	Saudi Arabia	1.71
6	Australia	9.22	6	Turkmenistan	1.72
7	Switzerland	9.09		Uzbekistan	1.72
8	Canada	9.08	8	Equatorial Guinea	1.83
9	Finland	9.06	9	Congo-Kinshasa	1.92
10	Netherlands	8.99	10	Iran	1.98
11	Luxembourg	8.88	11	Central African Rep.	1.99
12	Austria	8.62	12	Laos	2.32
13	Ireland	8.56	13	Myanmar	2.35
14	Germany	8.34	14	Sudan	2.38
15	Malta	8.28	15	Eritrea	2.40
16	United Kingdom	8.21	16	Afghanistan	2.48
17	Czech Republic	8.19	17	Tajikistan	2.51
18	Mauritius	8.17	18	Bahrain	2.53
	Uruguay	8.17	19	United Arab Emirates	2.58
20	South Korea	8.13	20	Zimbabwe	2.67

Parliamentary seats
Lower or single house, seats per 100,000 population, May 2013

Most			Least		
1	San Marino	187.5	1	India	0.04
2	Monaco	77.4	2	United States	0.14
3	Liechtenstein	69.4	3	Pakistan	0.19
4	Seychelles	36.0	4	China	0.22
5	Andorra	32.9		Nigeria	0.22
6	Maldives	25.7	6	Bangladesh	0.23
7	Antigua & Barbuda	21.6		Indonesia	0.23
8	Iceland	21.0	8	Brazil	0.26
9	Malta	17.5	9	Philippines	0.31
10	Cape Verde	14.4	10	Russia	0.32

Women in parliament
Lower or single house, women as % of total seats, May 2013

1	Rwanda	56.3	12	Mozambique	39.2
2	Andorra	50.0	13	Denmark	39.1
3	Cuba	48.9	14	Netherlands	38.7
4	Sweden	44.7	15	Costa Rica	38.6
5	Seychelles	43.8	16	Timor-Leste	38.5
6	Senegal	42.7	17	Belgium	38.0
7	Finland	42.5	18	Argentina	37.4
8	South Africa	42.3	19	Mexico	36.8
9	Nicaragua	40.2	20	Spain	36.0
10	Iceland	39.7		Tanzania	36.0
11	Norway	39.6	22	Uganda	35.0

Inflation

Consumer price inflation

Highest, 2012, %	
1 Belarus	59.2
2 South Sudan	54.8
3 Iran	27.3
4 Ethiopia	22.9
5 Malawi	21.3
6 Venezuela	21.1
7 Burundi	18.0
8 Suriname[a]	17.7
9 Yemen	17.3
10 Tanzania	16.0
11 Guinea	15.2
12 Uganda	14.0
13 Sudan[b]	13.0
14 Sierra Leone	12.9
15 Eritrea	12.3
16 Nigeria	12.2
17 Timor-Leste	11.8
18 Maldives	10.9
19 Congo-Kinshasa	10.4
Mozambique[a]	10.4
21 Angola	10.3
22 Chad	10.2

Lowest, 2012, %	
1 Belize[a]	-2.5
2 Georgia	-0.9
3 Switzerland	-0.7
4 Bahrain[a]	-0.4
5 Japan	0.0
6 Niger	0.5
7 Aruba	0.6
Ukraine	0.6
9 New Zealand	0.7
Norway	0.7
United Arab Emirates	0.7
12 Sweden	0.9
13 Central African Rep.[a]	1.3
Côte d'Ivoire	1.3
Morocco	1.3
16 Senegal	1.4
17 Canada	1.5
Greece	1.5
19 El Salvador	1.7
Ireland	1.7
Israel	1.7
Malaysia	1.7

Highest average annual consumer price inflation, 2007–12, %	
1 Belarus	27.8
2 Venezuela	27.4
3 Ethiopia	22.6
4 Congo-Kinshasa	22.1
5 Iran	19.2
6 Eritrea	18.0
7 South Sudan	17.9
8 Guinea	14.9
9 Pakistan	13.8
10 Burundi	13.7
Yemen	13.7
12 Vietnam	13.2
13 Angola	12.9
14 Ghana	12.8
Sudan[c]	12.8
16 Mongolia[d]	12.5
17 Kenya	12.3
18 Uganda	12.2
19 Nigeria	12.0
20 Sierra Leone	11.9
21 Egypt	11.6
Jamaica	11.6
23 Ukraine	11.5

Lowest average annual consumer price inflation, 2007–12, %	
1 Japan	-0.2
2 Switzerland	0.4
3 Ireland	0.5
4 Belize[d]	0.9
5 Brunei[d]	1.4
Taiwan	1.4
7 Germany	1.6
Morocco	1.6
Sweden	1.6
10 France	1.7
11 Canada	1.8
12 Netherlands	1.9
Portugal	1.9
14 Bahrain[d]	2.0
15 Norway	2.1
Qatar	2.1
Senegal	2.1
United States	2.1
19 Australia	2.2
Spain	2.2
21 Austria	2.3
Finland	2.3
Italy	2.3

a 2011 b 2010 c 2007–10 d 2007–11

Commodity prices

End 2012, % change on a year earlier		*2005–12, % change*	
1 Timber	46.7	1 Gold	276.0
2 Soya meal	41.3	2 Corn	235.1
3 Wheat	23.1	3 Tin	185.9
4 Soyabeans	20.0	4 Soyabeans	144.2
5 Tin	19.7	5 Wheat	138.5
6 Hides	17.3	6 Palm oil	135.9
7 Tea	16.1	7 Soya meal	135.3
8 Lead	15.7	8 Soya oil	132.6
9 Zinc	11.3	9 Sugar	116.8
10 Corn	11.2	10 Copper	116.0
11 Cocoa	7.1	11 Lead	110.4
12 Beef (Aus)	5.0	12 Rubber	106.0
13 Gold	3.3	13 Tea	105.6
14 Aluminium	2.7	14 Rice	96.7
15 Copper	2.5	15 Coconut oil	76.6
16 Beef (US)	0.9	16 Coffee	72.0
17 Rice	-1.8	17 Oil[a]	65.5
18 Soya oil	-5.6	18 Cotton	62.4
19 Rubber	-7.0	19 Cocoa	56.6
20 Nickel	-8.7	20 Beef (Aus)	54.1
21 Cotton	-9.2	21 Wool (Aus)	52.8
22 Wool (Aus)	-9.8	22 Lamb	42.7
23 Oil[a]	-12.3	23 Zince	40.9
24 Palm oil	-13.3	24 Beef (US)	32.6
25 Sugar	-17.2	25 Hides	26.2
26 Lamb	-21.2	26 Wool (NZ)	20.7

The Economist's house-price indicators

Q1 2013[b], % change on a year earlier		*Q1 2008–Q1 2013[b], % change*	
1 Hong Kong	24.5	1 Hong Kong	89.6
2 South Africa	11.1	2 Austria	24.3
3 United States	9.3	3 Switzerland	23.2
3 Austria	8.5	4 Singapore	20.3
5 New Zealand	6.4	5 Canada	18.2
6 Switzerland	3.6	6 China	17.5
7 Singapore	3.5	7 South Africa	16.8
8 Germany	3.4	8 Belgium	13.4
9 China	3.3	9 Australia	11.5
10 Sweden	3.0	10 Sweden	11.3
11 Australia	2.6	11 Germany	7.5
12 Belgium	2.0	12 New Zealand	3.8
Canada	2.0	13 France	1.8
14 United Kingdom	0.9	14 United Kingdom	-9.2
15 Denmark	0.4	15 Italy	-12.2
16 France	-1.7	16 Japan	-14.0
17 Japan	-2.6	17 United States	-15.1
18 Ireland	-3.0	18 Denmark	-17.2
19 Italy	-4.0	19 Netherlands	-17.4
20 Netherlands	-7.0	20 Spain	-27.1

a West Texas Intermediate.   b Or latest.

Debt

Highest foreign debt[a]

$bn, 2011

1	China	685.4		24	Colombia	76.9
2	Russia	543.0		25	Philippines	76.0
3	South Korea	449.6		26	Venezuela	67.9
4	Brazil	404.3		27	Hong Kong	67.3
5	India	334.3		28	Pakistan	60.2
6	Poland	320.6		29	Vietnam	57.8
7	Turkey	307.0		30	Iraq	50.8
8	Mexico	287.0		31	Peru	44.9
9	Indonesia	213.6		32	Bulgaria	39.9
10	Hungary	184.7		33	Latvia	38.3
11	United Arab Emirates	156.3		34	Egypt	35.0
12	Ukraine	134.5		35	Serbia	31.6
13	Qatar	133.6		36	Lithuania	30.0
14	Romania	129.8		37	Kuwait	29.9
15	Kazakhstan	124.4		38	Belarus	29.1
16	Taiwan	122.5		39	Morocco	29.0
17	Argentina	114.7		40	Bangladesh	27.0
18	South Africa	113.5		41	Estonia	25.0
19	Israel	103.9		42	Lebanon	24.8
20	Chile	96.2		43	Sri Lanka	24.0
21	Malaysia	94.5		44	Singapore	23.6
22	Czech Republic	93.9		45	Tunisia	22.3
23	Thailand	80.0		46	Cuba	21.9

Highest foreign debt burden[a]

Present value of foreign debt as % of GDP, 2011

1	Seychelles	184.8		22	Lebanon	61.6
2	Hungary	133.2		23	Jordan	61.2
3	Latvia	132.1		24	Macedonia	60.2
4	Poland	128.9		25	Armenia	59.0
5	Estonia	112.5		26	Bhutan	58.5
6	Jamaica	101.0		27	Côte d'Ivoire	55.4
7	Papua New Guinea	99.5		28	Belarus	51.9
8	Ukraine	88.0		29	Bahrain	51.5
9	Georgia	80.1		30	Bosnia	48.8
10	Kazakhstan	80.0		31	El Salvador	48.6
11	Kyrgyzstan	78.3		32	Montenegro	48.1
12	Qatar	77.1		33	United Arab Emirates	46.2
13	Belize	76.8		34	Guinea	45.3
14	Bulgaria	75.8		35	Tunisia	45.2
15	Lithuania	72.2		36	Chile	43.4
16	Mauritania	71.2		37	Czech Republic	43.3
17	Moldova	71.0		38	Panama	42.8
18	Zimbabwe	68.5		39	Israel	42.6
19	Serbia	67.7		40	Tajikistan	42.4
20	Laos	65.7		41	Sudan	42.0
21	Romania	65.6		42	Maldives	41.5

a Foreign debt is debt owed to non-residents and repayable in foreign currency; the figures shown include liabilities of government, public and private sectors. Developed countries have been excluded.

Highest foreign debt[a]
As % of exports of goods and services, 2011

1	Eritrea	321.2	14	Ukraine	167.2
2	Jamaica	307.6	15	Burkina Faso	166.0
3	Latvia	246.8	16	Papua New Guinea	161.6
4	Sudan	217.9	17	Sri Lanka	160.4
5	El Salvador	206.6	18	Moldova	160.2
6	Georgia	203.3	19	Seychelles	156.5
7	Armenia	201.5	20	Pakistan	155.9
8	Romania	192.4	21	Zimbabwe	153.5
9	Serbia	190.4	22	Brazil	147.1
10	Tajikistan	187.9		Kazakhstan	147.1
11	Laos	182.3	24	Macedonia	141.5
12	Turkey	170.4	25	Kyrgyzstan	140.2
13	Burundi	168.7	26	Guinea	137.3

Highest debt service ratio[b]
Average, %, 2011

1	Latvia	47.0	15	Brazil	19.4
2	Jamaica	36.5	16	Macedonia	18.9
3	Kazakhstan	34.6	17	Philippines	17.6
4	Serbia	31.5	18	Israel	17.0
5	Ukraine	30.8	19	Honduras	16.0
6	Turkey	30.2	20	Papua New Guinea	15.8
7	Hungary	28.9	21	Colombia	15.6
8	Romania	27.5		Guatemala	15.6
9	Georgia	26.9	23	Argentina	15.3
10	Poland	26.6	24	Chile	15.2
11	Armenia	25.4	25	Nicaragua	14.8
12	El Salvador	21.7	26	Indonesia	14.5
13	Lithuania	20.1	27	Belize	13.9
14	Lebanon	19.9	28	Costa Rica	13.5

Household debt[c]
As % of gross disposable income, 2011

1	Denmark	301.5	15	United States	114.3
2	Netherlands	280.5	16	Finland	112.0
3	Ireland	225.6	17	Estonia	97.7
4	Norway	200.6	18	France	97.3
5	Switzerland[d]	186.4	19	Greece	95.8
6	Australia[d]	168.0	20	Belgium	91.2
7	Sweden	167.8	21	Austria	89.7
8	South Korea	156.3	22	Germany	88.5
9	United Kingdom	151.2	23	Italy	85.2
10	Canada[d]	146.5	24	Hungary	68.6
11	Luxembourg	143.4	25	Czech Republic	62.6
12	Portugal	140.1	26	Poland	59.3
13	Spain	134.0	27	Slovenia	52.9
14	Japan	122.9	28	Slovakia	46.5

b Debt service is the sum of interest and principal repayments (amortisation) due on outstanding foreign debt. The debt service ratio is debt service expressed as a percentage of the country's exports of goods and services.   c OECD countries.   d 2010

Aid

Largest recipients of bilateral and multilateral aid[a]
$m, 2011

1	Afghanistan	6,711	24	Somalia	1,096
2	Congo-Kinshasa	5,522	25	South Sudan	1,087
3	Ethiopia	3,563	26	Zambia	1,073
4	Vietnam	3,514	27	Senegal	1,052
5	Pakistan	3,509	28	Burkina Faso	990
6	India	3,220	29	Jordan	959
7	Kenya	2,474	30	Nepal	892
8	Tanzania	2,445	31	Mexico	882
9	West Bank & Gaza	2,444	32	Brazil	870
10	Mozambique	2,047	33	Turkey	839
11	Iraq	1,904	34	Malawi	798
12	Ghana	1,815	35	Cambodia	792
13	Nigeria	1,813	36	Liberia	765
14	Haiti	1,712	37	Bolivia	759
15	Uganda	1,580	38	Ukraine	750
16	Bangladesh	1,498	39	Zimbabwe	718
17	Côte d'Ivoire	1,437	40	Nicaragua	695
18	Rwanda	1,278	41	Benin	677
19	South Africa	1,274	42	Kosovo	657
20	Mali	1,271		Tunisia	657
21	Morocco	1,237	44	Niger	649
22	Sudan	1,138	45	Libya	642
23	Colombia	1,130	46	Honduras	624

Largest recipients of bilateral and multilateral aid[a]
$ per head, 2011

1	West Bank & Gaza	607.9	23	Lesotho	120.8
2	Cape Verde	491.3	24	Armenia	120.7
3	Kosovo	367.1	25	Nicaragua	118.4
4	Timor-Leste	240.5	26	Montenegro	117.0
5	Seychelles	237.0	27	Rwanda	116.8
6	Guyana	209.8	28	Somalia	114.6
7	St Lucia	205.2	29	Bosnia	113.2
8	Bhutan	194.4	30	South Sudan	105.4
9	Afghanistan	190.0	31	Mauritania	104.6
10	Liberia	185.3	32	Lebanon	101.5
11	Suriname	178.5	33	Libya	100.0
12	Antigua & Barbuda	170.0	34	Albania	95.4
13	Haiti	169.2	35	Kyrgyzstan	94.9
14	Djibouti	155.6	36	Togo	90.6
15	Jordan	155.2	37	Papua New Guinea	87.3
16	Mauritius	148.5	38	Fiji	86.5
17	Maldives	143.8	39	Mozambique	85.5
18	Moldova	126.7	40	Belize	82.8
19	Namibia	122.7	41	Senegal	82.4
20	Georgia	122.4	42	Serbia	82.1
21	Mongolia	121.4	43	Congo-Kinshasa	81.5
22	Swaziland	121.3	44	Honduras	80.5

a Israel also receives aid, but does not disclose amounts.

Largest bilateral and multilateral donors[a]
$m, 2011

1	United States	30,924	15	Denmark	2,931
2	Germany	14,093	16	Belgium	2,807
3	United Kingdom	13,832	17	Finland	1,406
4	France	12,997	18	South Korea	1,328
5	Japan	10,831	19	Turkey	1,273
6	Netherlands	6,344	20	Austria	1,111
7	Sweden	5,603	21	Ireland	914
8	Canada	5,457	22	United Arab Emirates	737
9	Saudia Arabia	5,095	23	Portugal	708
10	Australia	4,983	24	Russia	479
11	Norway	4,934	25	Greece	425
12	Italy	4,326	26	New Zealand	424
13	Spain	4,173	27	Poland	417
14	Switzerland	3,076	28	Luxembourg	409

Largest bilateral and multilateral donors[a]
% of GDP, 2011

1	Sweden	1.02	15	Portugal	0.31
2	Norway	1.00	16	Spain	0.29
3	Luxembourg	0.97	17	New Zealand	0.28
4	Denmark	0.85	18	Austria	0.27
5	Netherlands	0.75	19	Malta	0.25
6	United Kingdom	0.56	20	United Arab Emirates	0.22
7	Belgium	0.54	21	Iceland	0.21
8	Finland	0.53	22	Italy	0.20
9	Ireland	0.51		United States	0.20
10	France	0.46	24	Japan	0.18
11	Switzerland	0.45	25	Cyprus	0.16
12	Germany	0.39		Turkey	0.16
13	Australia	0.34	27	Greece	0.15
14	Canada	0.32	28	Slovenia	0.13

Largest financial resource donors[b]
% of GNI, 2011

1	Netherlands	2.62	12	Australia	1.02
2	United Kingdom	1.91		Japan	1.02
3	Switzerland	1.77	14	Norway	1.00
4	Germany	1.54	15	Luxembourg	0.99
5	Austria	1.47	16	Denmark	0.82
6	Spain	1.38	17	Canada	0.79
7	Ireland	1.37	18	Italy	0.55
8	France	1.21	19	Finland	0.38
9	Sweden	1.20	20	New Zealand	0.35
10	United States	1.09	21	Belgium	0.23
11	South Korea	1.03	22	Greece	0.17

a China also provides aid, but does not disclose amounts.
b Including other financial resources to developing countries and multinational organisations.

Industry and services

Largest industrial output
$bn, 2011

1	China	3,411		23	Thailand	142
2	United States[a]	2,690		24	Switzerland[a]	135
3	Japan[a]	1,496		25	Poland[a]	131
4	Germany[a]	822		26	Argentina	126
5	Russia	583		27	Malaysia	116
6	Brazil	581		28	Colombia	114
7	India	466		29	South Africa	113
8	Italy[a]	462		30	Sweden[a]	106
9	Canada	461		31	Austria[a]	99
10	France[b]	451		32	Algeria[a]	95
11	United Kingdom[a]	435		33	Belgium[a]	91
12	Mexico	406		34	Chile	89
13	Indonesia	399		35	Egypt	81
14	South Korea	394		36	Kazakhstan	71
15	Spain[a]	328			Philippines	71
16	Saudi Arabia[a]	269		38	Romania	68
17	Australia[a]	209		39	Angola	65
18	Venezuela[a]	191			Czech Republic[a]	65
19	Turkey	189		41	Ireland[b]	64
20	Netherlands[a]	165		42	Finland[a]	60
	United Arab Emirates[a]	165			Singapore	60
22	Norway[a]	149				

Highest growth in industrial output
Average annual % increase in real terms, 2003–11

1	Liberia	20.6			Bhutan	9.5
2	Azerbaijan	18.7			Cambodia	9.5
3	Laos	13.6		13	Congo-Kinshasa	9.0
4	China	11.7		14	Tanzania	8.7
5	Belarus	11.6			Uganda	8.7
6	Rwanda	10.8		16	Malawi	8.5
7	Ethiopia	10.0			Romania	8.5
8	Angola	9.9		18	India	8.4
	Togo	9.9			Vietnam	8.4
10	Afghanistan	9.5		20	Tajikistan	8.3

Lowest growth in industrial output
Average annual % change in real terms, 2003–11

1	Moldova	-2.8			New Zealand[c]	-1.2
2	Malta[d]	-1.9		12	United Kingdom[d]	-1.1
3	Brunei	-1.7		13	Portugal[d]	-1.0
	Chad	-1.7		14	France	-0.7
5	Bermuda[d]	-1.4		15	Luxembourg	-0.6
	Eritrea[c]	-1.4			Spain[d]	-0.6
	Italy[d]	-1.4		17	Canada[d]	-0.4
	Jamaica	-1.4		18	Hong Kong	-0.2
9	Norway[d]	-1.3		19	Swaziland	0.0
10	Denmark[d]	-1.2				

a 2010   b 2009   c 2003–09   d 2003–10

Largest manufacturing output
$bn, 2011

1	United States[a]	1,771	21	Poland[a]	76
2	China[a]	1,757	22	Malaysia	70
3	Japan[a]	1,064	23	Sweden[a]	66
4	Germany[a]	610	24	Austria[a]	65
5	South Korea	313	25	Belgium[b]	59
6	Brazil	308	26	Venezuela[a]	51
7	Italy[a]	306	27	Ireland[b]	49
8	France[b]	254		South Africa	49
9	Russia	252	29	Philippines	47
10	India	251		Singapore	47
11	United Kingdom[a]	230	31	Puerto Rico[a]	45
12	Indonesia	206	32	Saudi Arabia[a]	44
13	Canada	205	33	Colombia	42
14	Mexico	203		Czech Republic[a]	42
15	Spain[b]	172	35	Finland[a]	39
16	Turkey	126	36	Pakistan	37
17	Thailand[a]	114	37	Egypt	34
18	Australia[a]	98		Norway[a]	34
19	Netherlands[a]	92	39	Denmark[a]	33
20	Argentina	84	40	United Arab Emirates[a]	29

Largest services output
$bn, 2011

1	United States[a]	10,574	27	Hong Kong[a]	204
2	Japan[a]	3,904	28	Saudi Arabia[a]	170
3	China	3,172	29	Colombia	169
4	Germany[a]	2,096	30	Singapore	165
5	France[b]	1,871	31	Thailand	161
6	United Kingdom[a]	1,564	32	Venezuela[a]	154
7	Brazil	1,414	33	Portugal[a]	148
8	Italy[a]	1,335	34	Finland[a]	139
9	India	971	35	Malaysia	138
10	Canada[c]	934	36	Ireland[b]	135
11	Russia	926	37	Chile	131
12	Spain[a]	898	38	United Arab Emirates[a]	130
13	Australia[a]	822	39	Philippines	125
14	Mexico	664	40	Czech Republic[a]	110
15	South Korea	584	41	Egypt	109
16	Netherlands[a]	513	42	Pakistan	106
17	Turkey	426	43	Kazakhstan	95
18	Belgium[a]	325	44	Peru	92
19	Indonesia	323	45	Romania	86
20	Sweden[a]	290	46	Ukraine	84
21	Poland[a]	268	47	Hungary	71
22	South Africa	246	48	Bangladesh	58
23	Argentina	239	49	Morocco	50
24	Austria[a]	237	50	Slovakia	49
25	Norway[a]	216	51	Algeria	47
26	Denmark[a]	208		Puerto Rico	47

a 2010   b 2009   c 2008

Agriculture

Largest agricultural output
$bn, 2011

1	China	735		16	Malaysia	34
2	India	306			Spain[a]	34
3	United States[a]	159		18	Egypt	31
4	Indonesia	125		19	Philippines	29
5	Brazil	115		20	South Korea	27
6	Russia	67			Vietnam	27
7	Japan[a]	63		22	Germany[a]	26
8	Turkey	62		23	Australia[a]	24
9	Argentina	43		24	Colombia	21
	Pakistan	43			Venezuela[a]	21
	Thailand	43		26	Bangladesh	20
12	France[b]	42		27	Poland[a]	15
	Mexico	42			Sudan	15
14	Canada	37			United Kingdom[a]	15
15	Italy[a]	35				

Most economically dependent on agriculture
% of GDP from agriculture, 2011

1	Sierra Leone	57.6		13	Togo	31.9
2	Central African Rep.[b]	56.8		15	Nepal	31.8
3	Liberia	53.1		16	Laos	30.8
4	Ethiopia	46.4		17	Malawi	30.2
5	Congo-Kinshasa	45.6		18	Mozambique	29.8
6	Mali[b]	38.9		19	Madagascar[b]	29.1
7	Cambodia	36.7		20	Kenya	28.5
8	Myanmar	36.4		21	Tanzania	27.7
9	Papua New Guinea	35.9		22	Ghana	25.6
10	Burundi	35.2		23	Sudan	24.5
11	Burkina Faso	33.8		24	Côte d'Ivoire	24.3
12	Benin[a]	32.4		25	Paraguay	23.5
13	Rwanda	31.9		26	Uganda	23.4

Least economically dependent on agriculture
% of GDP from agriculture, 2011

1	Macau[a]	0.0		14	Ireland[b]	1.0
	Singapore	0.0		15	Denmark[a]	1.2
3	Hong Kong[a]	0.1			Japan[a]	1.2
4	Luxembourg	0.3			United States[a]	1.2
5	Brunei	0.6		18	Austria[a]	1.5
	Puerto Rico[a]	0.6		19	Norway[a]	1.6
7	Belgium[a]	0.7		20	Canada	1.7
	Switzerland	0.7		21	France[b]	1.8
	Trinidad & Tobago	0.7			Sweden[a]	1.8
	United Kingdom[a]	0.7		23	Italy[a]	1.9
11	Bermuda[a]	0.8			Malta[a]	1.9
12	Germany[a]	0.9		25	Netherlands[a]	2.0
	United Arab Emirates[a]	0.9		26	Bahamas	2.2

a 2010   b 2009

Highest growth in agriculture
Average annual % increase in real terms, 2003–11

1	Angola	13.7	10	Tajikistan	6.0
2	Chad	11.9	11	Paraguay	5.6
3	Ethiopia	9.3		Ukraine	5.6
4	Mozambique	7.4	13	Cambodia	5.4
5	Jordan	7.1	14	Belarus	5.3
6	Cape Verde[a]	6.9	15	Bosnia & Herzegovina	5.1
7	Liberia	6.8	16	Australia	4.9
8	Sierra Leone	6.7		Kazakhstan	4.9
9	Uzbekistan	6.1			

Lowest growth in agriculture
Average annual % change in real terms, 2003–11

1	United Arab Emirates[a]	-4.7	9	Belize	-3.1
	Zimbabwe	-4.7	10	St Lucia	-2.6
3	Ireland[b]	-4.4	11	Maldives	-2.5
4	Hong Kong	-4.2	12	Japan[a]	-2.2
5	Luxembourg	-3.7	13	Bahamas	-1.9
6	Malta[a]	-3.5	14	Gambia, The	-1.7
7	Bulgaria	-3.4	15	Guyana	-1.6
8	Trinidad & Tobago	-3.3	16	Seychelles	-1.5

Biggest producers
'000 tonnes, 2011

Cereals

1	China	520,812	6	Brazil	77,586
2	United States	386,788	7	France	65,688
3	India	285,520	8	Ukraine	56,256
4	Russia	91,825	9	Bangladesh	52,642
5	Indonesia	83,370	10	Argentina	50,946

Meat

1	China	80,971	6	India	6,228
2	United States	42,463	7	Mexico	6,001
3	Brazil	23,890	8	France	5,695
4	Germany	8,359	9	Spain	5,530
5	Russia	7,566	10	Argentina	4,555

Fruit

1	China	134,951	6	Indonesia	17,196
2	India	74,836	7	Philippines	16,139
3	Brazil	40,949	8	Mexico	16,117
4	United States	27,140	9	Spain	15,452
5	Italy	17,353	10	Turkey	14,388

Vegetables

1	China	561,745	5	Iran	25,961
2	India	105,795	6	Egypt	18,945
3	United States	34,670	7	Russia	16,275
4	Turkey	27,407	8	Italy	13,288

a 2003–10   b 2003–09

Commodities

Wheat

Top 10 producers, 2011–12 '000 tonnes		Top 10 consumers, 2011–12 '000 tonnes	
1 EU27	137,355	1 EU27	126,780
2 China	117,920	2 China	121,450
3 India	86,870	3 India	81,220
4 Russia	56,231	4 Russia	37,570
5 United States	54,413	5 United States	32,180
6 Australia	29,923	6 Pakistan	23,560
7 Canada	25,288	7 Egypt	19,220
8 Pakistan	24,200	8 Turkey	18,630
9 Kazakhstan	22,732	9 Iran	15,880
10 Ukraine	22,323	10 Ukraine	13,900

Rice[a]

Top 10 producers, 2011–12 '000 tonnes		Top 10 consumers, 2011–12 '000 tonnes	
1 China	140,700	1 China	139,600
2 India	105,310	2 India	93,334
3 Indonesia	36,500	3 Indonesia	39,550
4 Bangladesh	33,700	4 Bangladesh	34,300
5 Vietnam	27,075	5 Vietnam	19,650
6 Thailand	20,460	6 Philippines	12,850
7 Myanmar	10,816	7 Thailand	10,400
8 Philippines	10,700	8 Myanmar	10,200
9 Brazil	7,888	9 Brazil	8,050
10 Japan	7,646	Japan	8,050

Sugar[b]

Top 10 producers, 2011 '000 tonnes		Top 10 consumers, 2011 '000 tonnes	
1 Brazil	37,150	1 India	23,130
2 India	27,960	2 EU27	19,240
3 EU27	18,120	3 China	14,800
4 China	11,430	4 Brazil	13,300
5 Thailand	10,940	5 United States	10,370
6 United States	6,890	6 Russia	5,870
7 Mexico	5,380	7 Indonesia	5,430
8 Russia	5,130	8 Pakistan	4,760
9 Pakistan	4,710	9 Mexico	4,330
10 Australia	3,190	10 Egypt	3,040

Coarse grains[c]

Top 5 producers, 2011–12 '000 tonnes		Top 5 consumers, 2011–12 '000 tonnes	
1 United States	323,905	1 United States	290,053
2 China	201,080	2 China	203,040
3 EU27	147,133	3 EU27	147,920
4 Brazil	75,824	4 Brazil	54,949
5 India	41,760	5 Mexico	39,050

Tea

Top 10 producers, 2011		*Top 10 consumers, 2011*	
'000 tonnes		*'000 tonnes*	
1 China	1,640	1 China	1,305
2 India	967	2 India	875
3 Kenya	378	3 Russia	184
4 Sri Lanka	328	4 Turkey	151
5 Turkey	222	5 United Kingdom	129
6 Vietnam	207	6 Pakistan	126
7 Iran	163	7 United States	125
8 Indonesia	142	8 Japan	104
9 Argentina	97	9 Iran	80
10 Japan	95	10 Egypt	74

Coffee

Top 10 producers, 2011–12		*Top 10 consumers, 2011–12*	
'000 tonnes		*'000 tonnes*	
1 Brazil	2,609	1 United States	1,358
2 Vietnam	1,443	2 Brazil	1,183
3 Indonesia	517	3 Germany	544
4 Colombia	459	4 Japan	426
5 Ethiopia	360	5 France	353
6 Honduras	342	6 Italy	339
7 Peru	335	7 Russia	222
8 India	314	8 Canada	214
9 Mexico	273	9 Ethiopia	203
10 Guatemala	230	10 Indonesia	200

Cocoa

Top 10 producers, 2011–12		*Top 10 consumers, 2010–11*	
'000 tonnes		*'000 tonnes*	
1 Côte d'Ivoire	1,486	1 United States	763
2 Ghana	879	2 Germany	324
3 Indonesia	450	3 France	229
4 Nigeria	230	4 United Kingdom	229
5 Brazil	220	5 Russia	200
6 Cameroon	207	6 Brazil	178
7 Ecuador	190	7 Japan	155
8 Dominican Republic	72	8 Spain	105
9 Peru	58	9 Italy	89
10 Papua New Guinea	45	10 Canada	65

a Milled.
b Raw.
c Includes: maize (corn), barley, sorghum, oats, rye, millet, triticale and other.

Copper

Top 10 producers[a], 2011 *'000 tonnes*		*Top 10 consumers[b], 2011* *'000 tonnes*	
1 Chile	5,263	1 China	7,915
2 China	1,267	2 United States	1,745
3 Peru	1,235	3 Germany	1,247
4 United States	1,110	4 Japan	1,003
5 Australia	960	5 South Korea	784
6 Zambia	784	6 Russia	676
7 Russia	725	7 Italy	608
8 Canada	569	8 Taiwan	457
9 Indonesia	543	9 India	402
10 Congo-Kinshasa	480	10 Brazil	400

Lead

Top 10 producers[a], 2011 *'000 tonnes*		*Top 10 consumers[b], 2011* *'000 tonnes*	
1 China	2,358	1 China	4,662
2 Australia	621	2 United States	1,440
3 United States	346	3 South Korea	427
4 Peru	230	4 India	420
5 Mexico	224	5 Germany	374
6 Russia	113	6 Spain	263
7 Bolivia	100	7 Japan	236
8 India	94	8 Italy	233
9 Sweden	62	9 Brazil	218
10 Canada	59	10 United Kingdom	211

Zinc

Top 10 producers[a], 2011 *'000 tonnes*		*Top 10 consumers[c], 2011* *'000 tonnes*	
1 China	4,308	1 China	5,470
2 Australia	1,516	2 United States	939
3 Peru	1,256	3 India	556
4 United States	769	4 South Korea	519
5 India	733	5 Germany	515
6 Mexico	632	6 Japan	501
7 Canada	612	7 Italy	338
8 Bolivia	427	8 Belgium	256
9 Kazakhstan	350	9 Brazil	244
10 Ireland	344	10 Taiwan	221

Tin

Top 5 producers[a], 2011 *'000 tonnes*		*Top 5 consumers[b], 2011* *'000 tonnes*	
1 China	127.4	1 China	180.8
2 Indonesia	78.0	2 United States	31.9
3 Peru	29.0	3 Japan	26.9
4 Bolivia	20.4	4 Germany	20.1
5 Australia	15.4	5 South Korea	14.4

Nickel

Top 10 producers[a], 2011 '000 tonnes		Top 10 consumers[b], 2011 '000 tonnes	
1 Philippines	319.4	1 China	713.1
2 Russia	270.0	2 Japan	173.6
3 Indonesia	226.9	3 United States	133.9
4 Canada	219.6	4 South Korea	100.1
5 Australia	215.0	5 Germany	88.4
6 New Caledonia	131.1	6 Italy	65.8
7 China	89.8	7 Taiwan	53.2
8 Brazil	74.6	8 South Africa	33.6
9 Cuba	66.0	9 Belgium	29.8
10 South Africa	43.3	10 Sweden	29.7

Aluminium

Top 10 producers[d], 2011 '000 tonnes		Top 10 consumers[e], 2011 '000 tonnes	
1 China	18,062	1 China	17,629
2 Russia	3,992	2 United States	4,060
3 Canada	2,988	3 Germany	2,103
4 United States	1,983	4 Japan	1,946
5 Australia	1,945	5 India	1,569
6 United Arab Emirates	1,793	6 South Korea	1,233
7 India	1,660	7 Brazil	1,077
8 Brazil	1,440	8 Italy	982
9 Norway	1,202	9 Turkey	870
10 Bahrain	881	10 Russia	685

Precious metals

Gold [a] Top 10 producers, 2011 tonnes		Silver [a] Top 10 producers, 2011 tonnes	
1 China	361.0	1 Mexico	4,778
2 Australia	258.0	2 Peru	3,414
3 United States	233.6	3 China	3,232
4 South Africa	186.7	4 Australia	1,725
5 Russia	185.3	5 Chile	1,311
6 Peru	164.0	6 Russia	1,244
7 Canada	100.4	7 Bolivia	1,214
8 Mexico	88.7	8 Poland	1,167
9 Ghana	87.6	9 United States	1,120
10 Indonesia	74.4	10 Argentina	703

Platinum Top 3 producers, 2011 tonnes		Palladium Top 3 producers, 2011 tonnes	
1 South Africa	151.2	1 Russia	84.1
2 Russia	26.0	2 South Africa	79.6
3 United States/Canada	10.9	3 United States/Canada	28.0

a Mine production. b Refined consumption. c Slab consumption.
d Primary refined production. e Primary refined consumption.

Rubber (natural and synthetic)

Top 10 producers, 2011
'000 tonnes

1	China	4,217
2	Thailand	3,588
3	Indonesia	3,043
4	EU27	2,612
5	United States	2,498
6	Japan	1,611
7	Russia	1,447
8	South Korea	1,369
9	Malaysia	1,106
10	India	1,004

Top 10 consumers, 2011
'000 tonnes

1	China	8,286
2	EU27	3,779
3	United States	2,896
4	Japan	1,717
5	India	1,381
6	Brazil	896
7	Germany	895
8	Thailand	858
9	South Korea	759
10	Russia	755

Raw wool

Top 10 producers[a], 2011, '000 tonnes

1	China	393	7	Argentina	54
2	Australia	362	8	Russia	53
3	New Zealand	166	9	Turkey	47
4	United Kingdom	67	10	India	43
5	Iran	60		Pakistan	43
6	Morocco	55	12	South Africa	41

Cotton

Top 10 producers, 2011–12
'000 tonnes

1	China	7,400
2	India	6,001
3	United States	3,391
4	Pakistan	2,294
5	Brazil	1,877
6	Australia	1,198
7	Uzbekistan	880
8	Turkey	750
9	Turkmenistan	330
10	Greece	280

Top 10 consumers, 2011–12
'000 tonnes

1	China	8,635
2	India	4,358
3	Pakistan	2,163
4	Turkey	1,300
5	Brazil	888
6	United States	718
7	Bangladesh	700
8	Indonesia	448
9	Mexico	390
10	Vietnam	378

Major oil seeds[b]

Top 5 producers, 2011–12
'000 tonnes

1	United States	91,920
2	Brazil	69,850
3	Argentina	45,415
4	China	50,540
5	EU27	30,210

Top 5 consumers, 2011–12
'000 tonnes

1	China	112,265
2	United States	59,517
3	EU25	45,427
4	Brazil	43,406
5	Argentina	41,812

Oil[c]

Top 10 producers, 2012 '000 barrels per day		Top 10 consumers, 2012 '000 barrels per day	
1 Saudi Arabia[d]	11,530	1 United States	18,555
2 Russia	10,643	2 China	10,221
3 United States	8,905	3 Japan	4,714
4 China	4,155	4 India	3,652
5 Canada	3,741	5 Russia	3,174
6 Iran[d]	3,680	6 Saudi Arabia[d]	2,935
7 United Arab Emirates[d]	3,380	7 Brazil	2,805
8 Kuwait[d]	3,127	8 South Korea	2,458
9 Iraq[d]	3,115	9 Canada	2,412
10 Mexico	2,911	10 Germany	2,358

Natural gas

Top 10 producers, 2012 Billion cubic metres		Top 10 consumers, 2012 Billion cubic metres	
1 United States	681.4	1 United States	722.1
2 Russia	592.3	2 Russia	416.2
3 Iran[d]	160.5	3 Iran[d]	156.1
4 Qatar[d]	157.0	4 China	143.8
5 Canada	156.5	5 Japan	116.7
6 Norway	114.9	6 Saudi Arabia[d]	102.8
7 China	107.2	7 Canada	100.7
8 Saudi Arabia[d]	102.8	8 Mexico	83.7
9 Algeria[d]	81.5	9 United Kingdom	78.3
10 Indonesia	71.1	10 Germany	75.2

Coal

Top 10 producers, 2012 Million tonnes oil equivalent		Top 10 consumers, 2012 Million tonnes oil equivalent	
1 China	1,825.0	1 China	1,873.3
2 United States	515.9	2 United States	437.8
3 Australia	241.1	3 India	298.3
4 Indonesia	237.4	4 Japan	124.4
5 India	228.8	5 Russia	93.9
6 Russia	168.1	6 South Africa	89.8
7 South Africa	146.6	7 South Korea	81.8
8 Kazakhstan	58.8	8 Germany	79.2
Poland	58.8	9 Poland	54.0
10 Colombia	58.0	10 Indonesia	50.4

Oil reserves[c]

Top proved reserves, end 2012 % of world total			
1 Venezuela[d]	17.8	5 Iraq[d]	9.0
2 Saudi Arabia[d]	15.9	6 Kuwait[d]	6.1
3 Canada	10.4	7 United Arab Emirates[d]	5.9
4 Iran[d]	9.4	8 Russia	5.2

a Greasy basis. b Soybeans, sunflower seed, cottonseed, groundnuts and rapeseed.
c Includes crude oil, shale oil, oil sands and natural gas liquids. d Opec members.

Energy

Largest producers
Million tonnes of oil equivalent, 2010

1	China	2,209	16	Qatar	174
2	United States	1,725	17	South Africa	162
3	Russia	1,293	18	Kazakhstan	157
4	Saudi Arabia	538	19	Algeria	151
5	India	519	20	United Kingdom	149
6	Canada	398	21	France	136
7	Indonesia	381	22	Kuwait	134
8	Iran	349	23	Germany	131
9	Australia	311	24	Iraq	126
10	Nigeria	258	25	Colombia	105
11	Brazil	246	26	Angola	99
12	Mexico	226	27	Japan	97
13	Norway	206	28	Libya	89
14	Venezuela	193	29	Egypt	88
15	United Arab Emirates	176	30	Malaysia	86

Largest consumers
Million tonnes of oil equivalent, 2010

1	China	2,417	16	Saudi Arabia	169
2	United States	2,216	17	South Africa	137
3	Russia	702	18	Ukraine	130
4	India	693	19	Spain	128
5	Japan	497	20	Australia	125
6	Germany	327	21	Thailand	117
7	Brazil	266	22	Nigeria	113
8	France	262	23	Turkey	105
9	Canada	252	24	Poland	101
10	South Korea	250	25	Pakistan	85
11	Indonesia	208	26	Netherlands	83
	Iran	208	27	Venezuela	77
13	United Kingdom	203	28	Argentina	75
14	Mexico	178		Kazakhstan	75
15	Italy	170	30	Egypt	73

Energy efficiency[a]

Most efficient			Least efficient		
GDP per unit of energy use, 2010			*GDP per unit of energy use, 2010*		
1	Hong Kong	21.8	1	Congo-Kinshasa	0.9
2	Peru	12.8	2	Trinidad & Tobago	1.5
3	Colombia	12.2	3	Turkmenistan	1.7
4	Albania	11.8	4	Uzbekistan	1.8
	Panama	11.8	5	Iceland	1.9
6	Switzerland	11.7		Mozambique	1.9
7	Malta	11.3	7	Togo	2.0
8	Ireland	11.2	8	Ukraine	2.1
9	Botswana	11.1	9	Zambia	2.2
10	Congo-Brazzaville	10.5	10	Ethiopia	2.3
	Costa Rica	10.5	11	Kazakhstan	2.4

a 2005 PPP $ per kg of oil equivalent.

Net energy importers
% of commercial energy use, 2010

Highest			Lowest	
1	Hong Kong	100	1 Congo-Brazzaville	-1,078
	Malta	100	2 Qatar	-673
3	Singapore	99	3 Angola	-623
4	Lebanon	97	4 Gabon	-570
	Luxembourg	97	5 Norway	-533
6	Cyprus	96	6 Brunei	-460
	Jordan	96	7 Azerbaijan	-453
	Moldova	96	8 Libya	-362
9	Morocco	95	9 Mongolia	-357
10	Ireland	86	10 Kuwait	-301
11	Belarus	85	11 Algeria	-273
	Jamaica	85	12 Oman	-261

Largest consumption per head
Kg of oil equivalent, 2010

1	Iceland	16,882	12	Finland	6,787
2	Trinidad & Tobago	15,913	13	Norway	6,637
3	Qatar	12,799	14	Singapore	6,456
4	Kuwait	12,204	15	Saudi Arabia	6,168
5	Luxembourg	8,343	16	Australia	5,653
6	Brunei	8,308	17	Belgium	5,586
7	United Arab Emirates	8,271	18	Sweden	5,468
8	Bahrain	7,754	19	South Korea	5,060
9	Canada	7,380	20	Netherlands	5,021
10	Oman	7,188	21	Russia	4,927
11	United States	7,164	22	Kazakhstan	4,595

Sources of electricity
% of total, 2010

Oil			Gas		
1	Malta	100.0	1	Bahrain	100.0
2	Eritrea	99.4		Qatar	100.0
3	Benin	99.3		Turkmenistan	100.0
4	Cyprus	97.6	4	Trinidad & Tobago	99.7
5	Jamaica	93.6	5	Brunei	99.0

Hydropower			Nuclear power		
1	Albania	100.0	1	France	75.9
	Paraguay	100.0	2	Slovakia	53.1
3	Mozambique	99.9	3	Belgium	51.1
	Nepal	99.9	4	Ukraine	47.3
5	Zambia	99.7	5	Hungary	42.2

Coal		
1	Botswana	100.0
2	Kosovo	96.5
3	Mongolia	96.0
4	South Africa	94.2
5	Estonia	88.4

Workers of the world

Population in labour force
%, 2012 or latest

Highest			Lowest		
1	Qatar	76.5	1	West Bank & Gaza	23.8
2	Cayman Islands	68.4	2	Iraq	24.5
3	United Arab Emirates	67.5	3	Afghanistan	25.3
4	Macau	64.1	4	Syria	27.9
5	Azerbaijan	63.8	5	Jordan	28.0
6	Serbia	61.6	6	Yemen	28.3
7	Vietnam	60.9	7	Mali	29.0
8	Iceland	60.5	8	Timor-Leste	31.2
	North Korea	60.5	9	Somalia	32.1
10	China	60.4	10	Algeria	32.6
11	Myanmar	59.5	11	Nigeria	32.7
12	Bahamas	58.8	12	Mauritania	33.4
13	Barbados	58.4	13	Djibouti	34.2
14	Cambodia	58.1		Niger	34.2
15	Thailand	57.7	15	Egypt	34.4
16	Bahrain	57.6	16	Moldova	34.7
17	Latvia	56.4	17	Lebanon	35.3
18	Singapore	56.3	18	Iran	35.4
	Switzerland	56.3	19	Liberia	35.7
20	Canada	55.9	20	Pakistan	35.8
21	Nepal	55.7	21	Saudi Arabia	35.9
22	Lithuania	55.4	22	Puerto Rico	36.0
23	Zimbabwe	55.0	23	Morocco	36.4
24	New Zealand	54.8	24	Libya	36.7
25	Peru	54.7	25	Tunisia	36.9
26	Australia	54.5	26	South Africa	37.1
27	Equatorial Guinea	54.3	27	Turkey	38.0
28	Cyprus	53.5	28	Angola	38.8
	Sweden	53.5	29	Belize	39.3

Most male workforce
Highest % men in workforce
2012 or latest

1	Qatar	87.9
2	United Arab Emirates	85.1
3	Afghanistan	84.4
	Saudi Arabia	84.4
	Syria	84.4
6	Oman	82.2
7	Iraq	82.1
8	Iran	81.7
	Jordan	81.7
	West Bank & Gaza	81.7
11	Bahrain	80.7
12	Algeria	79.4
13	Pakistan	78.9
14	Kuwait	76.0
15	Egypt	75.5
16	India	74.7

Most female workforce
Highest % women in workforce
2012 or latest

1	Mozambique	53.2
2	Burundi	51.9
3	Rwanda	51.7
4	Malawi	51.2
	Martinique	51.2
6	Sierra Leone	50.5
7	Estonia	50.4
	Togo	50.4
9	Lithuania	49.9
10	Congo-Kinshasa	49.8
11	Tanzania	49.7
12	Cambodia	49.6
	Laos	49.6
14	Guadeloupe	49.5
	Latvia	49.5
	Netherlands Antilles	49.5

Highest rate of unemployment
% of labour force[a], 2011 or latest

1	Namibia	37.6	25	Ireland	14.4
2	Réunion	33.6	26	Bahrain	14.2
3	Macedonia	31.4	27	New Caledonia	14.0
4	Guadeloupe	28.9	28	Albania	13.8
5	Bosnia	27.6	29	Bahamas	13.7
6	Martinique	25.5	30	Iran	13.5
7	Lesotho	25.3		Slovakia	13.5
8	South Africa	24.7	32	Croatia	13.4
9	West Bank & Gaza	23.5	33	Zambia	13.2
10	Belize	23.3	34	Tunisia	13.0
11	Spain	21.6	35	Jordan	12.9
12	Guyana	21.0	36	Portugal	12.7
13	Gabon	20.4		Jamaica	12.7
14	Serbia	19.2	38	Estonia	12.5
15	Armenia	19.0	39	Dominican Republic	12.4
16	Ethiopia	18.9	40	Colombia	11.8
17	Botswana	17.8	41	French Polynesia	11.7
18	Greece	17.7		Maldives	11.7
19	Puerto Rico	15.7	43	Barbados	11.2
20	Latvia	15.4		Bulgaria	11.2
	Lithuania	15.4	45	Hungary	10.9
22	Iraq	15.3	46	Algeria	10.0
23	Georgia	15.1		Senegal	10.0
24	Yemen	14.6			

Highest rate of youth unemployment[b]
% of labour force aged 15–24[a], 2011 or latest

1	Bosnia	57.5	23	Poland	25.8
2	Macedonia	55.3	24	Egypt	24.8
3	South Africa	49.8	25	Romania	23.7
4	Spain	46.4	26	Sweden	22.9
5	Guyana	46.1	27	Estonia	22.4
	Serbia	46.1	28	Cyprus	22.3
7	Greece	44.4	29	France	22.1
8	West Bank & Gaza	38.8	30	Mauritius	21.7
9	Montenegro	37.0	31	Algeria	21.5
10	Croatia	36.1	32	United Kingdom	20.0
11	Georgia	35.6	33	Sri Lanka	19.4
12	Slovakia	33.2	34	Syria	19.2
13	Lithuania	32.9	35	Finland	18.9
14	Jamaica	30.1	36	Argentina	18.7
	Portugal	30.1		Belgium	18.7
16	Jordan	29.9	38	Ukraine	18.6
	Puerto Rico	29.9	39	Turkey	18.4
18	Ireland	29.4	40	Czech Republic	18.0
19	Italy	29.1	41	Morocco	17.9
	Latvia	29.1	42	Chile	17.5
21	Bulgaria	26.6		Venezuela	17.5
22	Hungary	26.1	44	Uruguay	17.4

a ILO definition.

The business world

Global competitiveness
2013

Overall	Government	Business
1 United States	United Arab Emirates	United States
2 Switzerland	Hong Kong	Hong Kong
3 Hong Kong	Singapore	Sweden
4 Sweden	Switzerland	Malaysia
5 Singapore	Qatar	Norway
6 Norway	Norway	Switzerland
7 Canada	Sweden	Canada
8 United Arab Emirates	Taiwan	Singapore
9 Germany	Canada	United Arab Emirates
10 Qatar	New Zealand	Taiwan
11 Taiwan	Denmark	Denmark
12 Denmark	Finland	Qatar
13 Luxembourg	Australia	Ireland
14 Netherlands	Netherlands	Netherlands
15 Malaysia	Malaysia	Germany
16 Australia	Chile	Luxembourg
17 Ireland	Ireland	Australia
18 United Kingdom	Luxembourg	Thailand
19 Israel	Germany	Philippines
20 Finland	South Korea	Finland
21 China	Israel	Japan
22 South Korea	Thailand	Austria
23 Austria	Kazakhstan	United Kingdom
24 Japan	United Kingdom	Israel
25 New Zealand	United States	China
26 Belgium	Indonesia	Lithuania
27 Thailand	Poland	New Zealand
28 France	Turkey	Belgium
29 Iceland	Mexico	Turkey
30 Chile	Estonia	Chile
31 Lithuania	Philippines	Indonesia
32 Mexico	South Korea	India
33 Poland	Peru	Mexico
34 Kazakhstan	Lithuania	South Korea
35 Czech Republic	Iceland	Poland
36 Estonia	Czech Republic	Iceland
37 Turkey	Austria	Brazil
38 Philippines	Belgium	Kazakhstan
39 Indonesia	Jordan	Estonia
40 India	China	Czech Republic
41 Russia	Colombia	Peru
42 Peru	Russia	France
43 Italy	France	South Africa
44 Spain	Japan	Colombia

Notes: Overall competitiveness of 60 economies is calculated by combining four factors: economic performance, government efficiency, business efficiency and infrastructure. Column 1 is based on over 300 criteria, using hard data and survey data. Column 2 looks at public finance, fiscal policy, institutional and societal frameworks and business legislation. Column 3 includes productivity, labour market, finance, management practices and attitudes and values.

The business environment

		2013–17 score	2008–12 score	2008–12 ranking
1	Singapore	8.61	8.52	1
2	Switzerland	8.49	8.42	2
3	Hong Kong	8.40	8.36	3
4	Australia	8.32	8.17	6
5	Canada	8.31	8.18	5
6	Sweden	8.30	8.20	4
7	New Zealand	8.24	7.94	12
	United States	8.24	8.01	9
9	Denmark	8.14	8.02	8
10	Norway	8.03	7.90	13
11	Chile	8.01	8.16	7
	Finland	8.01	7.80	14
13	Taiwan	7.98	7.66	17
14	Germany	7.92	7.95	11
15	Netherlands	7.73	7.97	10
16	Ireland	7.69	7.74	15
17	Belgium	7.66	7.72	16
18	Austria	7.64	7.58	18
19	Malaysia	7.56	7.14	23
20	Qatar	7.50	7.33	21
21	United Kingdom	7.46	7.38	20
22	Israel	7.45	7.21	22
23	France	7.40	7.47	19
24	South Korea	7.32	7.06	26
25	Czech Republic	7.31	7.01	28
	Estonia	7.31	7.11	24
27	United Arab Emirates	7.30	6.95	30
28	Japan	7.29	6.95	29
29	Spain	7.24	7.09	25
30	Poland	7.21	6.87	32
31	Slovakia	7.18	7.04	27
32	Mexico	6.96	6.82	33
33	Bahrain	6.85	6.87	31
34	Slovenia	6.79	6.62	37
35	Thailand	6.74	6.42	39
36	Cyprus	6.70	6.72	34
37	Costa Rica	6.66	6.46	38
	Kuwait	6.66	6.20	43
39	Latvia	6.65	6.11	45
40	Brazil	6.64	6.39	40
41	Lithuania	6.56	6.31	42
42	Portugal	6.54	6.72	35
43	Hungary	6.52	6.66	36
44	Turkey	6.51	5.96	50
45	Saudi Arabia	6.49	6.13	44
46	Colombia	6.48	5.86	53

Note: Scores reflect the opportunities for, and hindrances to, the conduct of business, measured by countries' rankings in ten categories including market potential, tax and labour-market policies, infrastructure, skills and the political environment. Scores reflect average and forecast average over given date range.

Business creativity and research

Innovation index[a]
2012

1	Switzerland	5.78	13	Austria	5.07
2	Finland	5.75	14	Taiwan	4.99
3	Israel	5.57	15	Norway	4.96
4	Sweden	5.56	16	South Korea	4.94
5	Japan	5.54	17	France	4.91
6	United States	5.50	18	Luxembourg	4.82
7	Germany	5.42	19	Qatar	4.71
8	Singapore	5.39	20	Iceland	4.68
9	Netherlands	5.31	21	Ireland	4.66
10	United Kingdom	5.17	22	Canada	4.64
11	Belgium	5.09	23	Australia	4.51
12	Denmark	5.08	24	New Zealand	4.43

Technological readiness index[b]
2012

1	Sweden	6.29	13	Norway	5.78
2	Luxembourg	6.21	14	France	5.72
3	Denmark	6.17	15	Germany	5.71
4	Hong Kong	6.16	16	Austria	5.70
5	Singapore	6.10		Japan	5.70
6	Switzerland	6.02		South Korea	5.70
7	United Kingdom	6.00	19	Australia	5.61
8	Iceland	5.99	20	Canada	5.60
9	Netherlands	5.98	21	Malta	5.59
10	Finland	5.92	22	Belgium	5.57
11	United States	5.84	23	New Zealand	5.47
12	Ireland	5.82	24	Taiwan	5.44

Brain drain[c]

	Highest, 2012			Lowest, 2012	
1	Algeria	1.54	1	Switzerland	6.29
2	Haiti	1.64	2	Singapore	5.72
3	Burundi	1.73	3	Qatar	5.67
4	Serbia	1.86	4	United Kingdom	5.62
5	Bosnia	1.92	5	United States	5.58
6	Kyrgyzstan	1.95	6	United Arab Emirates	5.51
7	Venezuela	2.05	7	Canada	5.49
8	Moldova	2.07	8	Hong Kong	5.44
	Romania	2.07	9	Norway	5.37
10	Macedonia	2.11	10	Netherlands	5.27
11	Lesotho	2.13	11	Sweden	5.16
12	Yemen	2.19	12	Finland	5.07

a The innovation index is a measure of the adoption of new technology, and the interaction between the business and science sectors. It includes measures of the investment into research institutions and protection of intellectual property rights.
b The technological readiness index measures the ability of the economy to adopt new technologies. It includes measures of information and communication technology (ICT) usage, the regulatory framework with regard to ICT, and the availability of new technology to business.
c Scores: 1=talented people leave for other countries, 7=they always remain in home country.

Total expenditure on R&D

% of GDP, 2011 or latest			$bn, 2011 or latest	
1	Israel	4.38	1 United States	415.2
2	Finland	3.78	2 Japan	178.8
3	South Korea	3.74	3 China	134.4
4	Sweden	3.37	4 Germany	102.4
5	Japan	3.25	5 France	62.4
6	Denmark	3.09	6 United Kingdom	43.1
7	Taiwan	3.02	7 South Korea	37.9
8	Switzerland	2.99	8 Canada	30.3
9	Germany	2.84	9 Australia	28.4
10	Austria	2.75	10 Italy	27.5
	United States	2.75	11 Brazil	24.9
12	Iceland	2.70	12 Russia	20.8
13	Slovenia	2.47	13 Spain	19.7
14	Estonia	2.38	14 Sweden	18.2
15	Venezuela	2.37	15 India	17.1
16	Australia	2.27	Netherlands	17.1
17	France	2.25	17 Switzerland	15.0
18	Singapore	2.23	18 Taiwan	14.0
19	Belgium	2.04	19 Austria	11.5
	Netherlands	2.04	20 Israel	10.7
21	China	1.84	21 Belgium	10.5
	Czech Republic	1.84	22 Denmark	10.3
23	United Kingdom	1.77	23 Finland	10.0
24	Ireland	1.72	24 Norway	8.1
25	Canada	1.70	25 Venezuela	7.8
26	Norway	1.67	26 Turkey	6.7

Patents

No. of patents granted by applicant's country of origin, average 2010–11			No. of patents in force by applicant's country of origin, per 100,000 people, 2011	
1	Japan	295,783	1 Japan	1,657
2	United States	196,394	2 South Korea	1,222
3	China	101,490	3 Switzerland	990
4	South Korea	86,867	4 Luxembourg	588
5	Germany	71,522	5 Sweden	493
6	France	34,126	6 Finland	484
7	Russia	22,906	7 United States	473
8	Italy	20,545	8 Netherlands	368
9	United Kingdom	17,552	9 Germany	332
10	Switzerland	17,063	10 Denmark	320
11	Netherlands	14,645	11 Israel	303
12	Sweden	10,765	12 Norway	251
13	Canada	10,299	13 Canada	213
14	Finland	6,145	14 Austria	210
15	Australia	5,943	15 France	180
16	Belgium	5,129	16 Belgium	177
17	Spain	4,920	17 New Zealand	159
18	Austria	4,727	18 Australia	157
19	Denmark	4,105	19 Iceland	155
20	Israel	3,869	20 Singapore	133

Business costs and FDI

Office rents

Rent, taxes and operating expenses, $ per sq. ft., Q1 2013

1	Hong Kong (Central)	235.23	9	London (City), UK	132.94
2	London (West End), UK	222.58	10	New York (Midtown Manhattan), US	120.65
3	Beijing (Finance Street), China	194.07	11	Mumbai (Bandra Kurla Complex), India	119.93
4	Beijing (Jianguomen-CBD), China	187.06	12	Paris, France	119.32
5	New Delhi (Connaught Place-CBD), India	178.96	13	Sydney, Australia	119.23
6	Hong Kong (West Kowloon)	173.90	14	São Paulo, Brazil	118.86
7	Moscow, Russia	165.05	15	Shanghai (Pudong), China	117.68
8	Tokyo (Marunouchi/Otemachi), Japan	161.16	16	Rio de Janeiro, Brazil	113.06
			17	Shanghai (Puxi), China	109.21
			18	Geneva, Switzerland	104.24

Minimum wage

Minimum wage as a ratio of the median wage of full-time workers, 2011

1	Turkey	0.71	11	Ireland	0.48
2	France	0.60		Lithuania	0.48
3	New Zealand	0.59	13	Romania	0.48
4	Slovenia	0.58	14	Netherlands	0.47
5	Latvia	0.57		United Kingdom	0.47
	Portugal	0.57	16	Slovakia	0.46
7	Australia	0.54	17	Canada	0.45
8	Greece	0.51		Poland	0.45
9	Belgium	0.50	19	Spain	0.44
	Hungary	0.50	20	Luxembourg	0.42

Foreign direct investment[a]

Inflows, $m, 2011

1	United States	226,937
2	China	123,985
3	Belgium	89,142
4	Hong Kong	83,156
5	Brazil	66,660
6	Singapore	64,003
7	United Kingdom	53,949
8	British Virgin Islands	53,717
9	Russia	52,878
10	Australia	41,317
11	France	40,945
12	Canada	40,932
13	Germany	40,402
14	India	31,554
15	Spain	29,476
16	Italy	29,059
17	Mexico	19,554
18	Indonesia	18,906
19	Luxembourg	17,530

Outflows, $m, 2011

1	United States	396,656
2	Japan	114,353
3	United Kingdom	107,086
4	France	90,146
5	Hong Kong	81,607
6	Belgium	70,706
7	Switzerland	69,612
8	Russia	67,283
9	China	65,117
10	British Virgin Islands	62,507
11	Germany	54,368
12	Canada	49,569
13	Italy	47,210
14	Spain	37,256
15	Netherlands	31,867
16	Austria	30,451
17	Sweden	26,850
18	Singapore	25,227
19	Denmark	23,413

Note: CBD is Central Business District.
a Investment in companies in a foreign country.

Business red tape, corruption and piracy

Number of days taken to register a new company

Lowest, 2012			Highest, 2012	
1	New Zealand	1	1	Suriname	694
2	Australia	2	2	Congo-Brazzaville	161
	Georgia	2	3	Venezuela	144
	Macedonia	2	4	Equatorial Guinea	135
5	Hong Kong	3	5	Brazil	119
	Rwanda	3	6	Haiti	105
	Singapore	3	7	Brunei	101
8	Albania	4	8	Timor-Leste	94
	Belgium	4	9	Laos	92
10	Belarus	5	10	Zimbabwe	90
	Canada	5	11	Cambodia	85
	Hungary	5	12	Eritrea	84
	Iceland	5	13	Iraq	74
	Netherlands	5	14	Angola	68
	Portugal	5	15	Namibia	66
	Senegal	5	16	Chad	62

Corruption perceptions index[a]

2012, 100 = least corrupt

Lowest			Highest	
1	Denmark	90	1	Afghanistan	8
	Finland	90		North Korea	8
	New Zeland	90		Somalia	8
4	Sweden	88	4	Sudan	13
5	Singapore	87	5	Myanmar	15
6	Switzerland	86	6	Turkmenistan	17
7	Australia	85		Uzbekistan	17
	Norway	85	8	Iraq	18
9	Canada	84	9	Burundi	19
	Netherlands	84		Chad	19
11	Iceland	82		Haiti	19
12	Luxembourg	80		Venezuela	19
13	Germany	79	13	Equatorial Guinea	20
14	Hong Kong	77		Zimbabwe	20
15	Barbados	76			
16	Belgium	75			

Business software piracy

% of software that is pirated, 2011

1	Zimbabwe	92		Belarus	87
2	Georgia	91	11	Indonesia	86
3	Bangladesh	90		Iraq	86
	Libya	90		Pakistan	86
	Moldova	90	14	Algeria	84
6	Yemen	89		Sri Lanka	84
7	Armenia	88		Ukraine	84
	Venezuela	88	17	Cameroon	83
9	Azerbaijan	87			

a This index ranks countries based on how much corruption is perceived by business
  people, academics and risk analysts to exist among politicians and public officials.

Businesses and banks

Largest non-financial companies
By market capitalisation, $bn
End December 2010

1	Exxon Mobil	United States	364.1
2	PetroChina	China	303.3
3	Apple	United States	267.8
4	Petrobras	Brazil	229.1
5	Royal Dutch Shell	United Kingdom/Netherlands	205.3
6	Walmart	United States	202.3
7	Microsoft	United States	199.5
8	China Mobile	China	199.3
9	Berkshire Hathaway	United States	198.3
10	General Electric	United States	194.2
11	Nestlé	Switzerland	190.9
12	Google	United States	190.8
13	Chevron	United States	183.2
14	IBM	United States	180.2
15	BHP Billiton	Australia/United Kingdom	177.4
	Johnson & Johnson	United States	177.4
17	Vale	Brazil	173.9
18	AT&T	United States	173.7
19	Rio Tinto	United Kingdom/Australia	171.6
20	Procter & Gamble	United States	170.6
21	Coca-Cola	United States	150.7
22	Gazprom	Russia	150.3
23	Pfizer	United States	140.3
24	BP	United Kingdom	136.4

End March 2013

1	Apple	United States	415.7
2	Exxon Mobil	United States	403.7
3	Google	United States	263.0
4	Berkshire Hathaway	United States	256.8
5	PetroChina	China	254.7
6	Walmart	United States	246.4
7	General Electric	United States	239.8
8	Microsoft	United States	239.6
9	IBM	United States	237.7
10	Nestlé	Switzerland	233.3
11	Chevron	United States	230.8
12	Johnson & Johnson	United States	227.9
13	China Mobile	China	212.8
14	Procter & Gamble	United States	210.5
15	Royal Dutch Shell	United Kingdom/Netherlands	209.1
16	Pfizer	United States	207.4
17	AT&T	United States	201.5
18	Roche	Switzerland	201.1
19	Samsung	South Korea	199.8
20	Novartis	Switzerland	192.4
21	Coca-Cola	United States	180.2
22	Toyota Motor	Japan	176.9
23	BHP Billiton	Australia/United Kingdom	171.2
24	Anheuser-Busch	United States	159.2

Largest banks
By loans outstanding, $bn
End December 2010

1	Industrial and Commerical Bank of China	China	1,030
2	Banco Santander	Spain	994
3	Bank of America Merrill Lynch	United States	975
4	Lloyds Banking Group	United Kingdom	948
5	HSBC	United Kingdom	932
6	BNP Paribas	France	929
7	Mitsubishi UFJ	Japan	920
8	China Construction Bank	China	860
9	Bank of China	China	859
10	Royal Bank of Scotland	United Kingdom	812
11	Wells Fargo	United States	810
12	UniCredit	Italy	774
13	Agricultural Bank of China	China	752
14	JPMorgan Chase	United States	693
15	Barclays	United Kingdom	687

End March 2013

1	Bank of China	China	1,101
2	Mitsubishi UFJ	Japan	985
3	HSBC	United Kingdom	974
4	Crédit Agricole	France	963
5	Banco Santander	Spain	961
6	Bank of America Merrill Lynch	United States	931
7	BNP Paribas	France	864
8	Wells Fargo	United States	847
9	Lloyds Banking Group	United Kingdom	773
10	Mizuho Financial	Japan	732
11	UniCredit	Italy	730
12	JPMorgan Chase	United States	729
13	Sumitomo Mitsui Financial Group	Japan	720
14	Barclays	United Kingdom	708
15	Royal Bank of Scotland	United Kingdom	689

Largest sovereign-wealth funds
By assets, $bn, May 2013

1	Government Pension Fund, Norway	716	7	Hong Kong Monetary Authority Investment Portfolio	299
2	Abu Dhabi Investment Authority	627	8	Government of Singapore Investment Corporation	248
3	SAFE Investment Company, China	568	9	National Welfare Fund, Russia	176
4	SAMA Foreign Holdings, Saudi Arabia	533	10	National Social Security Fund, China	161
5	China Investment Corporation	482			
6	Kuwait Investment Authority	342			

Stockmarkets

Largest market capitalisation
$bn, end 2012

1	United States	18,668	23	Singapore	414
2	China	3,697	24	Indonesia	397
3	Japan	3,681	25	Thailand	383
4	United Kingdom	3,019	26	Saudia Arabia	373
5	Canada	2,016	27	Chile	313
6	France	1,823	28	Turkey	309
7	Germany	1,486	29	Belgium	300
8	Australia	1,286	30	Philippines	264
9	India	1,263	31	Colombia	262
10	Brazil	1,230	32	Norway	253
11	South Korea	1,180	33	Denmark	225
12	Hong Kong	1,108	34	Poland	178
13	Switzerland	1,079	35	Finland	159
14	Spain	995	36	Israel	148
15	Russia	875	37	Iran	141
16	Taiwan	712	38	Qatar	126
17	Netherlands	651	39	Ireland	109
18	South Africa	612	40	Austria	106
19	Sweden	561	41	Kuwait	97
20	Mexico	525		Peru	97
21	Italy	480	43	New Zealand	80
22	Malaysia	476	44	Luxembourg	70

Largest gains in global stockmarkets
$ terms, % increase December 31st 2011 to January 2nd 2013

1	Turkey (ISE)	65.1	24	Euro area (DJ STOXX 50)	19.4
2	Egypt (Case 30)	46.8	25	South Africa (JSE AS)	19.0
3	Poland (WIG)	42.9	26	Australia (All Ord)	18.0
4	Thailand (SET)	42.7	27	Switzerland (SMI)	17.6
5	Greece (Athex Comp)	41.1	28	United States (S&P 500)	16.3
6	Germany (DAX)[a]	34.5	29	Chile (IGPA)	15.7
7	Pakistan (KSE)	34.2	30	Taiwan (TWI)	14.8
8	Austria (ATX)	33.5	31	Malaysia (KLSE)	14.3
9	Denmark (OMXCB)	31.6		Netherlands (AEX)	14.3
10	Mexico (IPC)	30.9	33	Italy (FTSE/MIB)	14.2
11	Singapore (STI)	28.5	34	China (SSEB, $ terms)	13.8
12	Colombia (IGBC)	28.1	35	United Kingdom (FTSE)	13.3
13	Hong Kong (Hang Seng)	26.7	36	Israel (TA-100)	12.9
14	India (BSE)	24.5	37	Russia (RTS, $ terms)	10.5
15	Belgium (BEL 20)	23.1	38	United States (DJIA)	9.8
16	Norway (OSEAX)	22.5	39	Saudi Arabia (Tadawul)	8.7
17	Sweden (OMXS30)	21.3	40	Canada (S&P TSX)	8.6
18	Czech Republic (PX)	20.8	41	Japan (Nikkei 225)	8.5
19	France (CAC 40)	20.5	42	Indonesia (JSX)	6.9
	South Korea (KOSPI)	20.5	43	Argentina (MERV)	4.8
21	Hungary (BUX)	20.1	44	China (SSEA)	4.2
22	Euro area (FTSE Euro 100)	19.8		Japan (Topix)	4.2
23	United States (NAScomp)	19.5	46	Spain (Madrid SE)	1.4

a Total return index.

Largest value traded, $bn
$bn, 2012

1	United States	21,375	23	Thailand	229
2	China	5,327	24	Singapore	156
3	Japan	3,605	25	Norway	133
4	United Kingdom	2,489	26	Finland	126
5	South Korea	1,514	27	Malaysia	124
6	Hong Kong	1,229	28	Mexico	118
7	Germany	1,226	29	Denmark	106
8	Canada	1,208	30	Belgium	103
9	France	1,127	31	Indonesia	92
10	Spain	1,077	32	Israel	67
11	Australia	1,052		Poland	67
12	Brazil	835	34	Austria	47
13	Italy	760		Chile	47
14	Russia	732	36	Philippines	35
15	Taiwan	660	37	Portugal	27
16	Switzerland	641	38	Colombia	26
17	India	622	39	New Zealand	25
18	Saudi Arabia	514	40	Kuwait	23
19	Netherlands	441	41	Iran	22
20	Sweden	376	42	Egypt	20
21	Turkey	349	42	United Arab Emirates	18
22	South Africa	312	44	Qatar	15

Number of listed domestic companies
End 2012

1	India	5,191	25	South Africa	348
2	United States	4,102	26	Sweden	332
3	Canada	3,876	27	Mongolia	329
4	Japan	3,470	28	Vietnam	311
5	Spain	3,167	29	Sri Lanka	287
6	China	2,494	30	Iran	284
7	United Kingdom	2,179	31	Italy	279
8	Australia	1,959	32	Russia	276
9	South Korea	1,767	33	Philippines	268
10	Hong Kong	1,459	34	Greece	267
11	Serbia	1,086	35	Jordan	243
12	Malaysia	921	36	Switzerland	238
13	France	862	37	Egypt	234
14	Poland	844	38	Bangladesh	229
15	Taiwan	783	39	Chile	225
16	Germany	665	40	Nepal	216
17	Pakistan	573	41	Peru	213
18	Israel	532	42	Ukraine	198
19	Thailand	502	43	Nigeria	192
20	Singapore	472	44	Kuwait	189
21	Indonesia	459	45	Croatia	184
22	Turkey	405		Norway	184
23	Bulgaria	387	47	Denmark	174
24	Brazil	353	48	Saudi Arabia	158

Transport: roads and cars

Longest road networks
Km, 2011 or latest

1	United States	6,533,218	21	Saudi Arabia	249,195
2	India	4,242,371	22	Argentina	230,210
3	China	3,985,530	23	Colombia	214,773
4	Brazil	1,581,105	24	Romania	214,458
5	Canada	1,409,016	25	Hungary	198,701
6	Japan	1,211,147	26	Philippines	198,155
7	France	1,054,344	27	Nigeria	196,451
8	Russia	1,012,200	28	Thailand	191,381
9	Australia	819,598	29	Vietnam	189,582
10	South Africa	807,438	30	Iran	183,805
11	Spain	663,494	31	Ukraine	169,509
12	Germany	643,716	32	Belgium	154,317
13	Sweden	627,139	33	Peru	139,674
14	Indonesia	501,521	34	Netherlands	137,660
15	Italy	500,337	35	Czech Republic	130,700
16	United Kingdom	419,677	36	Austria	124,508
17	Poland	409,966	37	Greece	117,037
18	Mexico	369,849	38	Algeria	112,732
19	Turkey	367,249	39	South Korea	105,878
20	Pakistan	257,809	40	Egypt	100,324

Densest road networks
Km of road per km^2 land area, 2011 or latest

1	Monaco	38.1		Italy	1.7
2	Macau	24.3		Switzerland	1.7
3	Malta	9.8		United Kingdom	1.7
4	Bermuda	8.3	25	Austria	1.5
5	Bahrain	6.0	26	Cyprus	1.4
6	Singapore	5.3		Ireland	1.4
7	Belgium	5.1		Sri Lanka	1.4
8	Netherlands	3.3		Sweden	1.4
9	Japan	3.2	30	Estonia	1.3
10	Cayman Islands	3.0		India	1.3
11	Puerto Rico	2.9		Lithuania	1.3
12	Liechtenstein	2.4		Poland	1.3
13	Hungary	2.1		Spain	1.3
14	Luxembourg	2.0	35	Taiwan	1.2
15	France	1.9	36	Latvia	1.1
	Guam	1.9		South Korea	1.1
	Hong Kong	1.9	38	Mauritius	1.0
	Slovenia	1.9	39	Israel	0.9
19	Germany	1.8		Portugal	0.9
20	Czech Republic	1.7		Romania	0.9
	Denmark	1.7		Slovakia	0.9

Most crowded road networks

Number of vehicles per km of road network, 2011 or latest

1	Monaco	413.0	26	Armenia	69.7
2	Hong Kong	297.4	27	Netherlands	68.6
3	Singapore	249.0	28	Bermuda	66.0
4	Kuwait	240.7	29	Tunisia	65.5
5	Macau	229.8	30	Switzerland	63.6
6	South Korea	179.6	31	Brunei	63.5
7	Taiwan	163.5	32	Iran	62.4
8	Israel	139.9	33	Honduras	61.9
9	El Salvador	130.9	34	Croatia	57.0
10	Jordan	118.1	35	Greece	56.6
11	Mauritius	111.7	36	Thailand	56.4
12	Qatar	106.3	37	Poland	51.7
13	Bahrain	101.4	38	Saudi Arabia	51.2
14	Guam	100.2	39	Venezuela	50.3
15	Maldives	100.0	40	Cyprus	48.2
16	Puerto Rico	92.3	41	Indonesia	47.9
17	Malta	91.8	42	Ukraine	47.8
18	Mexico	90.7	43	Moldova	46.8
19	Italy	83.9	44	Slovakia	45.6
20	Liechtenstein	80.9	45	Finland	43.9
21	Bulgaria	76.3	46	Cayman Islands	43.7
22	United Kingdom	74.2	47	Egypt	43.3
23	Luxembourg	73.3	48	Chile	43.1
24	Germany	71.1	49	Russia	42.1
25	Portugal	70.5	50	Spain	41.1

Most car journeys

Average distance travelled per car per year, km, 2011

1	India	23,448	21	Pakistan	14,770
2	Peru	22,804	22	Portugal	14,548
3	Ecuador	21,562	23	China	14,291
4	Chile	19,875	24	Slovenia	14,233
5	Netherlands	19,523	25	Iceland	14,049
6	Tunisia	19,131	26	France	13,561
7	Finland	19,117	27	Estonia	13,553
8	United States	18,964	28	Hong Kong	13,523
9	Ireland	17,364	29	Switzerland	13,256
10	Singapore	17,313	30	Australia	13,160
11	Austria	17,016	31	Germany	13,068
12	Denmark	16,688	32	South Africa	12,901
13	Belgium	16,292	33	Japan	12,831
14	United Kingdom	15,725	34	New Zealand	12,828
15	Morocco	15,713	35	Luxembourg	12,562
16	Greece	15,664	36	Canada	12,423
17	Israel	15,490	37	Italy	10,818
18	Sweden	15,326	38	Croatia	10,795
19	Norway	15,006	39	Spain	10,548
20	Thailand	14,909	40	Romania	10,289

Highest car ownership
Number of cars per 1,000 population, 2011

1	Liechtenstein	766	26	Sweden	467
2	Monaco	758	27	Greece	466
3	Luxembourg	671	28	Brunei	447
4	New Zealand	648	29	Czech Republic	439
5	Iceland	637	30	United States	436
	Ireland	637	31	United Kingdom	434
7	Italy	610	32	Portugal	433
8	Puerto Rico	605	33	Cyprus	429
9	Malta	567	34	Barbados	424
10	Australia	562	35	Estonia	417
11	Finland	548	36	Canada	411
12	Austria	542	37	Guam	402
13	Lithuania	541	38	Denmark	395
14	Switzerland	528	39	Kuwait	380
15	Germany	523	40	Bermuda	374
16	Slovenia	522	41	Lebanon	367
17	France	498	42	Bulgaria	363
18	Netherlands	497	43	Trinidad & Tobago	352
19	Belgium	490	44	Malaysia	344
20	Norway	485	45	Croatia	343
21	Cayman Islands	478	46	Belarus	326
22	Saudi Arabia	476	47	Latvia	321
23	Spain	475	48	Slovakia	313
24	Poland	471	49	Japan	311
25	Aruba	468	50	Bahamas	305

Lowest car ownership
Number of cars per 1,000 population, 2011

1	Central African Rep.	1	22	Burkina Faso	7
	Ethiopia	1		Madagascar	7
	Somalia	1		Niger	7
4	Burundi	2	25	Philippines	8
	Chad	2	26	Mali	9
	Laos	2	27	Mozambique	11
	Liberia	2		Pakistan	11
8	Bangladesh	3	29	Cameroon	13
	Lesotho	3		Sierra Leone	13
	Mauritania	3	31	Kenya	14
	Rwanda	3		Maldives	14
	Uganda	3	33	Côte d'Ivoire	16
13	Congo-Kinshasa	4		India	16
	Nepal	4		Senegal	16
15	Gambia, The	5		Yemen	16
	Malawi	5	37	Ghana	17
	Tanzania	5	38	Nicaragua	18
18	Eritrea	6		Zambia	18
	Guinea	6	40	Afghanistan	19
	Myanmar	6		Vietnam	19
	Papua New Guinea	6			

Car production
Number of cars produced, '000, 2011

1	China	14,485	20	Indonesia	562
2	Japan	7,159	22	Thailand	550
3	Germany	5,872	23	Malaysia	496
4	South Korea	4,222	24	Italy	486
5	India	3,054	25	South Africa	312
6	United States	2,966	26	Romania	310
7	Brazil	2,773	27	Taiwan	289
8	France	1,931	28	Pakistan	203
9	Spain	1,820	29	Hungary	200
10	Russia	1,738	30	Australia	190
11	Mexico	1,657	31	Sweden	189
12	Iran	1,413	32	Slovenia	169
13	United Kingdom	1,344	33	Portugal	142
14	Czech Republic	1,192	34	Austria	130
15	Canada	991		Vietnam	130
16	Poland	740	36	Venezuela	99
17	Slovakia	640	37	Ukraine	98
	Turkey	640	38	Colombia	71
19	Argentina	577	39	Egypt	53
20	Belgium	562	40	Netherlands	41

Cars sold
New car registrations, '000, 2011

1	China	14,356	21	Belgium	572
2	United States	6,125	22	Netherlands	556
3	Japan	3,525	23	Mexico	551
4	Germany	3,174	24	Malaysia	535
5	Russia	2,653	25	Saudi Arabia	485
6	Brazil	2,647	26	South Africa	395
7	France	2,204	27	Austria	356
8	India	1,946	28	Switzerland	319
9	United Kingdom	1,941	29	Sweden	305
10	Italy	1,748	30	Poland	277
11	Iran	1,376	31	Israel	276
12	South Korea	1,313	32	Chile	245
13	Spain	808	33	Taiwan	244
14	Australia	803	34	Colombia	229
15	Canada	701	35	Ukraine	212
16	Argentina	674	36	Czech Republic	173
17	Indonesia	601	37	Denmark	169
18	Turkey	594	38	Portugal	153
19	United Arab Emirates	585	39	Pakistan	139
20	Thailand	582	40	Norway	138

Transport: planes and trains

Most air travel
Million passenger-km[a] per year, 2011

1	United States	1,017,566		16	Japan	92,568
2	China	469,136		17	Ireland	86,001
3	Germany	237,028		18	Spain	79,266
4	United Kingdom	226,596		19	Turkey	60,878
5	France	159,219		20	Thailand	56,211
6	Australia	119,058		21	Qatar	54,515
7	Canada	118,933		22	Italy	46,179
8	Russia	113,452		23	Malaysia	40,618
9	Hong Kong	111,736		24	Indonesia	39,560
10	India	107,494		25	Mexico	32,565
11	United Arab Emirates	106,944		26	South Africa	31,786
12	Brazil	104,616		27	Saudi Arabia	30,610
13	Singapore	103,123		28	New Zealand	27,989
14	Netherlands	98,734		29	Switzerland	26,712
15	South Korea	94,713		30	Portugal	26,542

Busiest airports
Total passengers, m, 2012

1	Atlanta, Hartsfield	95.7
2	Beijing, Capital	81.9
3	London, Heathrow	70.1
4	Tokyo, Haneda	67.8
5	Chicago, O'Hare	67.1
6	Los Angeles, Intl.	63.8
7	Paris, Charles de Gaulle	61.5
8	Dallas, Ft Worth	58.9
9	Dubai Intl.	58.4
10	Jakarta, Soekarno-Hatta	57.8
11	Frankfurt, Main	57.3
12	Hong Kong, Intl.	55.7
13	Denver, Intl.	53.3
14	Bangkok, Suvarnabhumi	52.5
15	Singapore, Changi	51.3

Total cargo, m tonnes, 2012

1	Hong Kong, Intl.	4.12
2	Memphis, Intl.	4.05
3	Shanghai, Pudong Intl.	2.97
4	Anchorage, Intl.	2.47
5	Seoul, Incheon	2.46
6	Dubai, Intl.	2.29
7	Louisville, Standiford Field	2.19
8	Frankfurt, Main	2.07
9	Tokyo, Narita	2.01
10	Miami, Intl.	1.94
	Paris, Charles de Gaulle	1.94
12	Singapore, Changi	1.85
13	Beijing, Capital	1.83
14	Los Angeles, Intl.	1.78
15	Taiwan, Taoyuan Intl.	1.60

Average daily aircraft movements, take-offs and landings, 2011

1	Atlanta, Hartsfield	2,548
2	Chicago, O'Hare	2,406
3	Dallas, Ft Worth	1,788
4	Denver, Intl.	1,675
5	Los Angeles, Intl.	1,656
6	Beijing, Capital	1,528
7	Charlotte/Douglas, Intl.	1,514
8	Las Vegas, McCarran Intl.	1,443
9	Houston, George Bush Intercontinental	1,394
10	Paris, Charles de Gaulle	1,358
11	Frankfurt, Main	1,314
12	London, Heathrow	1,296
13	Phoenix, Skyharbor Intl.	1,230
14	Philadelphia, Intl.	1,213
15	Amsterdam, Schiphol	1,196
16	Toronto, Pearson Intl.	1,190
17	Detroit, Metro	1,169
	Minneapolis, St Paul	1,169
19	San Francisco	1,161
20	Newark	1,135
21	New York, JFK	1,103
22	Munich	1,084
23	Miami	1,073
24	Mexico City, Intl.	1,036
25	Jakarta, Soekarno-Hatta	1,017

a Air passenger–km data refer to the distance travelled by aircraft of national origin.

Longest railway networks
'000 km, 2011

1	United States	228.2	21	Turkey	9.6
2	Russia	85.2	22	Czech Republic	9.5
3	China	66.1	23	Australia	8.6
4	India	64.5	24	Iran	8.4
5	Canada	64.3	25	Hungary	7.9
6	France	34.6	26	Pakistan	7.8
7	United Kingdom	34.1	27	Finland	5.9
8	Germany	33.6	28	Belarus	5.5
9	Brazil	29.8		Chile	5.5
10	Mexico	26.7	30	Thailand	5.3
11	Argentina	25.0	31	Egypt	5.2
12	South Africa	24.8	32	Austria	5.0
13	Ukraine	21.7	33	Algeria	4.7
14	Japan	20.1		Indonesia	4.7
15	Poland	19.7		Sudan	4.7
16	Italy	17.0	36	Uzbekistan	4.3
17	Spain	15.7	37	Norway	4.2
18	Kazakhstan	14.2	38	Bulgaria	3.9
19	Romania	10.8	39	Serbia	3.8
20	Sweden	10.0			

Most rail passengers
Km per person per year, 2011

1	Switzerland	2,310	13	Germany	969
2	Japan	1,912	14	Belarus	836
3	Denmark	1,804	15	India	809
4	France	1,338	16	Taiwan	770
5	Austria	1,225	17	Finland	719
6	Ukraine	1,104	18	Luxembourg	698
7	United Kingdom	1,012	19	Sweden	684
8	Netherlands	1,006	20	Italy	669
9	Belgium	1,004	21	Czech Republic	632
10	Mongolia	1,000	22	China	608
11	Kazakhstan	982	23	Hungary	576
12	Russia	979	24	Norway	543

Most rail freight
Million tonnes-km per year, 2011

1	China	2,562,635	13	Belarus	49,406
2	United States	2,524,585	14	Poland	37,189
3	Russia	2,128,832	15	France	23,242
4	India	625,723	16	Mongolia	22,837
5	Brazil	267,700	17	Uzbekistan	22,482
6	Canada	254,069	18	Iran	21,008
7	Ukraine	243,866	19	Japan	20,255
8	Kazakhstan	223,584	20	United Kingdom	19,230
9	South Africa	113,342	21	Latvia	17,164
10	Germany	111,980	22	Austria	16,899
11	Mexico	69,185	23	Lithuania	15,088
12	Australia	56,649	24	Czech Republic	13,872

Transport: shipping

Merchant fleets
Number of vessels, by country of domicile, January 2012

1	Germany	3,989	11	Denmark	1,043
2	Japan	3,960	12	Indonesia	1,042
3	China	3,629	13	Netherlands	962
4	Greece	3,321	14	Taiwan	853
5	United States	2,055	15	Italy	834
6	Norway	1,992	16	United Kingdom	710
7	Russia	1,787	17	India	560
8	South Korea	1,236	18	Vietnam	556
9	Turkey	1,174	19	Malaysia	539
10	Singapore	1,110	20	France	485

Deadweight tonnage, by country of domicile, m, January 2012

1	Greece	224.1	11	Bermuda	30.0
2	Japan	217.7	12	Italy	25.0
3	Germany	125.6	13	Turkey	23.5
4	China	124.0	14	Canada	21.8
5	South Korea	56.2	15	India	21.4
6	United States	54.6	16	Russia	20.4
7	Taiwan	45.1	17	United Kingdom	18.4
8	Norway	43.1	18	Belgium	14.5
9	Denmark	40.0	19	Malaysia	14.4
10	Singapore	38.6	20	Brazil	13.8

Shipbuilding
Deliveries[a], '000 dwt, 2012

1	China	65,946	11	Turkey	204
2	South Korea	48,536	12	Norway	181
3	Japan	29,580	13	Netherlands	180
4	Philippines	4,998	14	United States	175
5	Vietnam	1,323	15	Russia	144
6	Taiwan	976	16	Singapore	115
7	Romania	581	17	Germany	96
8	Croatia	318	18	Malaysia	78
9	Brazil	300	18	Indonesia	70
10	India	287	20	Bulgaria	56

Order books, % of world total by gross tonnage[b], by country of ownership, Jan. 2013

1	Greece	13.7	11	Denmark	3.1
2	China	12.8		Israel	3.1
3	Japan	9.2	13	Hong Kong	2.7
4	Norway	6.5	14	Italy	2.4
5	Germany	4.8	15	Canada	2.2
6	South Korea	4.7	16	Turkey	1.3
7	Singapore	4.0	17	United Kingdom	1.0
8	Taiwan	3.6	18	India	0.8
9	United States	3.3	19	France	0.7
10	Brazil	3.2		Russia	0.7

a Sea-going propelled merchant ships of 100 gross tons and above.
b Sea-going cargo-carrying vessels.

Tourism

Most tourist arrivals
Number of arrivals, '000, 2011

1	France	79,500	21	Netherlands	11,300
2	United States	62,325	22	Singapore	10,390
3	China	57,581	23	Hungary	10,250
4	Spain	56,694	24	Croatia	9,927
5	Italy	46,119	25	South Korea	9,795
6	Turkey	29,343	26	Egypt	9,497
7	United Kingdom	29,192	27	Morocco	9,342
8	Germany	28,352	28	Czech Republic	8,775
9	Malaysia	24,714	29	Switzerland	8,534
10	Mexico	23,403	30	South Africa	8,339
11	Austria	23,012	31	United Arab Emirates	8,129
12	Russia	22,868	32	Indonesia	7,650
13	Hong Kong	22,316	33	Belgium	7,456
14	Ukraine	21,415	34	Portugal	7,432
15	Thailand	19,098	35	Bulgaria	6,324
16	Saudi Arabia	17,336	36	India	6,290
17	Greece	16,427	37	Japan	6,219
18	Canada	15,976	38	Taiwan	6,087
19	Poland	13,350	39	Vietnam	6,014
20	Macau	12,925	40	Australia	5,875

Biggest tourist spenders
$m, 2011

1	United States	89,118	13	Brazil	19,724
2	Germany	77,922	14	Singapore	19,209
3	United Kingdom	57,847	15	South Korea	17,124
4	China	55,727	16	Hong Kong	17,079
5	France	36,762	17	Spain	17,015
6	Canada	30,578	18	Belgium	16,537
7	Japan	30,032	19	United Arab Emirates	14,699
8	Italy	26,232	20	Sweden	13,821
9	Russia	24,781	21	India	11,766
10	Australia	24,322	22	Switzerland	11,579
11	Saudi Arabia	22,252	23	Taiwan	11,266
12	Netherlands	20,971	24	Austria	10,956

Largest tourist receipts
$m, 2011

1	United States	116,279	13	Malaysia	18,259
2	Spain	59,892	14	Singapore	17,990
3	France	53,845	15	Switzerland	17,553
4	China	48,464	16	India	17,518
5	Italy	42,999	17	Canada	16,936
6	Germany	38,842	18	Greece	14,623
7	United Kingdom	35,928	19	Netherlands	14,445
8	Australia	31,443	20	Sweden	13,886
9	Hong Kong	27,686	21	South Korea	12,304
10	Thailand	26,256	22	Mexico	11,869
11	Turkey	23,020	23	Russia	11,398
12	Austria	19,860	24	Portugal	11,339

Education

Primary enrolment
Number enrolled as % of relevant age group

Highest			Lowest		
1	Gabon	182	1	Somalia	32
2	Burundi	165	2	Eritrea	47
3	Madagascar	148	3	Papua New Guinea	60
4	Rwanda	142	4	Djibouti	61
5	Malawi	141	5	Niger	71
6	Togo	139	6	Sudan	73
7	Benin	129	7	Burkina Faso	79
8	Barbados	126	8	Gambia, The	81
	Cambodia	126	9	Andorra	82
	Laos	126		Mali	82
	Myanmar	126	11	Nigeria	83
12	Sierra Leone	125	12	Armenia	84
13	Angola	124	13	Puerto Rico	86
	Timor-Leste	124		Senegal	86
15	Guinea-Bissau	123	15	Equatorial Guinea	87

Highest secondary enrolment
Number enrolled as % of relevant age group

1	Australia	131		Norway	111
2	Spain	125	13	Greece	109
3	Seychelles	124		Portugal	109
4	Ireland	121	15	Finland	108
	Netherlands	121		Iceland	108
6	Denmark	119	17	Estonia	107
	New Zealand	119	18	Uzbekistan	106
8	France	113	19	Antigua & Barbuda	105
9	Brunei	112		Belarus	105
10	Belgium	111		United Kingdom	105
	Liechtenstein	111			

Highest tertiary enrolment[a]
Number enrolled as % of relevant age group

1	South Korea	103		Cuba	80
2	United States	95	12	Iceland	79
3	Finland	94	13	Spain	78
4	Slovenia	90		Venezuela	78
5	Greece	89	15	Russia	76
6	Puerto Rico	86	16	Argentina	75
7	Belarus	85	17	Denmark	74
8	New Zealand	83		Norway	74
9	Ukraine	82		Sweden	74
10	Australia	80	20	Poland	72

Notes: Latest available year 2007–12. The gross enrolment ratios shown are the actual number enrolled as a percentage of the number of children in the official primary age group. They may exceed 100 when children outside the primary age group are receiving primary education.
a Tertiary education includes all levels of post-secondary education including courses leading to awards not equivalent to a university degree, courses leading to a first university degree and postgraduate courses.

Least literate
% adult population

1	Burkina Faso	28.7		Mozambique	56.1
2	Ethiopia	29.8	16	Côte d'Ivoire	56.2
3	Mali	31.1	17	Bangladesh	56.8
4	Chad	34.5	18	Togo	57.1
5	Guinea	41.0	19	Mauritania	58.0
6	Sierra Leone	42.1	20	Timor-Leste	58.3
7	Benin	42.4	21	Papua New Guinea	60.1
8	Haiti	48.7	22	Nepal	60.3
9	Senegal	49.7	23	Liberia	60.8
10	Gambia, The	50.0	24	Nigeria	61.3
11	Guinea-Bissau	54.2	25	India	62.8
12	Pakistan	54.9	26	Yemen	63.9
13	Central African Rep.	56.0	27	Madagascar	64.5
14	Morocco	56.1	28	Congo-Kinshasa	66.8

Top universities[b]
2012

1	Harvard, US	13	Cornell, US
2	Stanford, US	14	Pennsylvania, US
3	Massachusetts Institute of Technology, US	15	California, San Diego, US
4	California, Berkeley, US	16	Washington, US
5	Cambridge, UK	17	The Johns Hopkins, Baltimore, US
6	California Institute of Technology, US	18	California, San Francisco, US
7	Princeton, US	19	Wisconsin - Madison, US
8	Columbia, US	20	Tokyo, Japan
9	Chicago, US	21	University College London, UK
10	Oxford, UK	22	Michigan - Ann Arbor, US
11	Yale, US	23	Swiss Federal Institute of Technology, Zurich
12	California, Los Angeles, US	24	Imperial College London, UK

Education spending
% of GDP

Highest			Lowest		
1	Lesotho	13.0	1	Myanmar	0.8
2	Cuba	12.9	2	Central African Rep.	1.2
3	Timor-Leste	10.1	3	Zambia	1.3
4	Denmark	8.7	4	Lebanon	1.6
5	Moldova	8.6		Monaco	1.6
6	Djibouti	8.4	6	Liberia	1.9
	Namibia	8.4	7	Sri Lanka	2.0
8	Ghana	8.2	8	Liechtenstein	2.1
9	Botswana	7.8	9	Bangladesh	2.2
	Iceland	7.8		Dominican Republic	2.2
	Swaziland	7.8	11	Pakistan	2.4
12	Bolivia	7.6			
13	Barbados	7.5			

b Based on academic peer review, employer review, faculty/student ratio, research strength and international factors.

Life expectancy

Highest life expectancy
Years, 2010–15

#	Country	Years		#	Country	Years
1	Monaco[a]	89.7		25	South Korea	80.7
2	Japan	83.7		26	Germany	80.6
3	Hong Kong	83.2			Martinique	80.6
4	San Marino[a]	83.1		28	United Kingdom	80.4
5	Andorra[a]	82.5		29	Channel Islands	80.2
	Switzerland	82.5			Finland	80.2
7	Australia	82.1			Luxembourg	80.2
8	Iceland	82.0		32	Greece	80.1
	Israel	82.0		33	Belgium	80.0
	Italy	82.0			Faroe Islands[a]	80.0
11	Spain	81.8			Malta	80.0
12	France	81.7		36	Cyprus	79.9
	Sweden	81.7			Guadeloupe	79.9
14	Liechtenstein[a]	81.5		38	Portugal	79.8
15	Macau	81.3		39	Virgin Islands (US)	79.6
	Norway	81.3		40	Costa Rica	79.5
	Singapore	81.3			Slovenia	79.5
18	Canada	81.2		42	Chile	79.3
19	Austria	81.0			Cuba	79.3
20	Netherlands	80.9			Puerto Rico	79.3
21	Bermuda[a]	80.8		45	Denmark	79.0
	Cayman Islands[a]	80.8		46	United States	78.8
	Ireland	80.8		47	Qatar	78.5
	New Zealand	80.8			Taiwan[a]	78.5

Highest male life expectancy
Years, 2010–15

#	Country	Years		#	Country	Years
1	Monaco[a]	85.7		10	Israel	79.6
2	San Marino[a]	80.6		11	Liechtenstein[a]	79.4
3	Andorra[a]	80.4		12	Italy	79.2
4	Iceland	80.3		13	Macau	79.1
5	Hong Kong	80.2			Norway	79.1
	Switzerland	80.2		15	Canada	78.9
7	Japan	80.1			Netherlands	78.9
8	Australia	79.9			New Zealand	78.9
9	Sweden	79.7			Singapore	78.9

Highest female life expectancy
Years, 2010–15

#	Country	Years		#	Country	Years
1	Monaco[a]	93.8			Switzerland	84.7
2	Denmark	87.4		11	Italy	84.6
3	Japan	87.1		12	Australia	84.3
4	Hong Kong	86.4		13	Israel	84.2
5	San Marino[a]	85.8			Liechtenstein[a]	84.2
6	Canada	85.3		15	Bermuda[a]	84.1
7	France	84.9		16	South Korea	84.0
8	Spain	84.8		17	Iceland	83.8
9	Andorra[a]	84.7			Macau	83.8

a 2012 estimate.

Lowest life expectancy
Years, 2010–15

#	Country		#	Country	
1	Sierra Leone	48.2	27	Côte d'Ivoire	56.4
2	Guinea-Bissau	48.8	28	Benin	56.8
3	Congo-Kinshasa	48.9	29	Liberia	57.5
4	Lesotho	49.1	30	Togo	57.8
5	Swaziland	49.2	31	Congo-Brazzaville	58.0
6	Afghanistan	49.3		Kenya	58.0
7	Central African Rep.	49.5	33	Djibouti	58.5
8	Zambia	49.6	34	Gambia, The	59.0
9	Chad	50.1	35	Mauritania	59.2
10	Mozambique	51.0	36	Tanzania	59.3
11	Burundi	51.1	37	Senegal	59.8
12	Equatorial Guinea	51.5	38	Ethiopia	60.0
13	Angola	51.7	39	Sudan	62.0
	Somalia	51.7	40	Eritrea	62.2
15	Mali	52.1	41	Haiti	62.5
16	Cameroon	52.5	42	Namibia	62.7
	Nigeria	52.5	43	Timor-Leste	63.2
18	Botswana	52.7	44	Gabon	63.3
19	Zimbabwe	53.5		Papua New Guinea	63.3
20	South Africa	53.8	46	Cambodia	63.7
21	Guinea	54.7	47	Ghana	64.7
	Uganda	54.7	48	Turkmenistan	65.2
23	Malawi	55.1	49	Pakistan	65.8
24	Niger	55.3	50	India	66.0
25	Rwanda	55.8		Myanmar	66.0
26	Burkina Faso	56.0	52	Yemen	66.1

Lowest male life expectancy
Years, 2010–15

#	Country		#	Country	
1	Congo-Kinshasa	47.3		Swaziland	49.7
	Guinea-Bissau	47.3	11	Mozambique	50.0
3	Sierra Leone	47.5	12	Somalia	50.1
4	Central African Rep.	47.7	13	Angola	50.2
5	Chad	48.6	14	Equatorial Guinea	50.3
6	Afghanistan	49.2	15	Mali	50.9
	Zambia	49.2	16	Cameroon	51.4
8	Burundi	49.6	17	Nigeria	51.7
9	Lesotho	49.7	18	South Africa	53.1

Lowest female life expectancy
Years, 2010–15

#	Country		#	Country	
1	Lesotho	48.1	10	Chad	51.6
2	Swaziland	48.5	11	Mozambique	51.8
3	Sierra Leone	48.9	12	Burundi	52.6
4	Afghanistan	49.5	13	Zimbabwe	52.7
5	Zambia	50.0	14	Equatorial Guinea	52.9
6	Guinea-Bissau	50.4	15	Mali	53.1
7	Congo-Kinshasa	50.6	16	Angola	53.2
8	Botswana	51.3	17	Nigeria	53.4
	Central African Rep.	51.3		Somalia	53.4

Death rates and infant mortality

Highest death rates
Number of deaths per 1,000 population, 2010–15

#	Country	Rate		#	Country	Rate
1	Ukraine	16.2			Czech Republic	10.3
2	Guinea-Bissau	15.9			Togo	10.3
3	Congo-Kinshasa	15.7		51	Italy	10.2
4	Chad	15.5			Liberia	10.2
5	Central African Rep.	15.3		53	Denmark	10.1
6	Bulgaria	15.2			North Korea	10.1
7	Afghanistan	15.1			Portugal	10.1
8	Lesotho	15.0		56	Djibouti	9.9
9	Sierra Leone	14.9			Kenya	9.9
	Zambia	14.9			Slovakia	9.9
11	Somalia	14.4		59	Finland	9.8
12	South Africa	14.3			Slovenia	9.8
13	Belarus	14.2		61	Japan	9.6
14	Equatorial Guinea	14.1			Kazakhstan	9.6
	Swaziland	14.1			Sweden	9.6
16	Russia	14.0			Tanzania	9.6
17	Botswana	13.8		65	Macedonia	9.5
	Latvia	13.8			Thailand	9.5
	Mozambique	13.8		67	Austria	9.4
20	Nigeria	13.7			United Kingdom	9.4
21	Angola	13.6		69	Channel Islands	9.3
	Burundi	13.6		70	Mauritania	9.2
	Mali	13.6			Uruguay	9.2
24	Lithuania	13.5		72	Armenia	9.1
25	Cameroon	13.4			Ethiopia	9.1
26	Hungary	13.2		74	France	8.9
27	Moldova	13.1		75	Barbados	8.7
28	Estonia	12.7			Faroe Islands[a]	8.7
29	Guinea	12.4			Gambia, The	8.7
30	Croatia	12.2			Haiti	8.7
	Niger	12.2			Spain	8.7
32	Romania	12.1		80	Gabon	8.6
33	Serbia	12.0			Netherlands	8.6
34	Malawi	11.9			Sudan	8.6
35	Uganda	11.7		83	Monaco[a]	8.5
	Zimbabwe	11.7		84	Malta	8.4
37	Georgia	11.6			Norway	8.4
38	Rwanda	11.5			Senegal	8.4
39	Burkina Faso	11.2		87	Myanmar	8.3
	Côte d'Ivoire	11.2			Switzerland	8.3
41	Benin	11.1			United States	8.3
42	Germany	10.9		90	Greenland[a]	8.2
43	Congo-Brazzaville	10.7			Namibia	8.2
44	Greece	10.5			Trinidad & Tobago	8.2
	Poland	10.5		93	San Marino[a]	8.1
46	Montenegro	10.4		94	Luxembourg	8.0
47	Belgium	10.3			Martinique	8.0
	Bosnia	10.3			Virgin Islands (US)	8.0

Note: Both death and, in particular, infant mortality rates can be underestimated in certain countries where not all deaths are officially recorded.

Highest infant mortality
Number of deaths per 1,000 live births, 2010–15

1	Afghanistan	124.5	23	Uganda	72.3
2	Chad	123.9	24	South Sudan[a]	71.8
3	Guinea-Bissau	109.8	25	Burkina Faso	71.0
4	Congo-Kinshasa	109.5	26	Mauritania	69.9
5	Sierra Leone	103.5	27	Côte d'Ivoire	68.8
6	Somalia	100.0	28	Togo	67.3
7	Angola	96.2	29	Congo-Brazzaville	66.7
8	Central African Rep.	95.8	30	Gambia, The	66.4
9	Burundi	94.1	31	Pakistan	65.7
10	Equatorial Guinea	93.3	32	Swaziland	64.6
11	Rwanda	92.9	33	Ethiopia	62.9
12	Mali	92.2	34	Lesotho	62.1
13	Nigeria	87.6	35	Haiti	58.3
14	Malawi	86.1	36	Kenya	58.1
15	Niger	85.8	37	Sudan	57.3
16	Cameroon	84.9	38	Timor-Leste	56.5
17	Guinea	84.2	39	Tanzania	53.7
18	Zambia	81.0	40	Cambodia	52.8
19	Mozambique	77.9	41	Tajikistan	50.9
20	Liberia	76.9	42	Senegal	49.8
21	Benin	76.7	43	Turkmenistan	48.8
22	Djibouti	75.0	44	India	47.9

Lowest death rates
No. deaths per 1,000 pop., 2010–15

1	United Arab Emirates	1.4
2	Qatar	1.5
3	Bahrain	2.8
4	Kuwait	3.0
5	Brunei	3.4
6	West Bank & Gaza	3.5
7	Maldives	3.6
	Syria	3.6
9	French Guiana	3.7
	Saudi Arabia	3.7
11	Belize	3.8
12	Oman	3.9
13	Jordan	4.0
14	Libya	4.1
15	Costa Rica	4.3
	Macau	4.3
17	Nicaragua	4.6
18	Honduras	4.7
	Malaysia	4.7
20	British Virgin Islands[a]	4.8
	Mexico	4.8
22	Algeria	4.9

Lowest infant mortality
No. deaths per 1,000 live births, 2010–15

1	Monaco[a]	1.8
2	Singapore	1.9
3	Hong Kong	2.0
4	Iceland	2.1
5	Luxembourg	2.3
6	Bermuda[a]	2.5
	Japan	2.5
	Sweden	2.5
9	Finland	2.8
10	Norway	2.9
11	Czech Republic	3.0
12	France	3.3
	Israel	3.3
	Slovenia	3.3
15	Italy	3.4
16	Germany	3.5
	Switzerland	3.5
18	South Korea	3.6
	Spain	3.6
20	Austria	3.7
	Belgium	3.7
22	Andorra[a]	3.8

a 2012 estimate.

Death and disease

Diabetes

% of population aged 20–79, 2012 age-standardised estimate[a]

1	Kuwait	23.9
2	Saudi Arabia	23.4
3	Qatar	23.3
4	Bahrain	22.4
5	United Arab Emirates	18.9
6	Lebanon	17.0
7	Egypt	16.6
8	Guyana	16.1
9	Belize	16.0
	Réunion	16.0
11	Mexico	15.6
12	Mauritius	14.8
13	Puerto Rico	13.0
14	British Virgin Islands	12.9
15	Chile	12.8
16	Trinidad & Tobago	12.7
17	Antigua & Barbuda	12.5

Malaria

Deaths per 100,000 population, estimate, 2010

1	Burkina Faso	191
2	Sierra Leone	177
3	Chad	172
4	Central African Rep.	169
5	Guinea	144
6	Mali	138
7	Nigeria	131
8	Mozambique	125
9	Congo-Kinshasa	119
10	Côte d'Ivoire	116
11	Guinea-Bissau	108
12	Benin	104
13	Niger	100
14	Congo-Brazzaville	93
15	Liberia	86
16	Gambia, The	83

Cancer

Deaths per 100,000 population, estimate, 2008

1	Hungary	318
2	Croatia	301
3	Denmark	290
4	Slovenia	282
5	Italy	277
6	Japan	275
7	Latvia	274
8	Estonia	269
9	Czech Republic	267
10	Germany	266
11	Greece	264
12	United Kingdom	262
13	Poland	261
14	Serbia	260
15	France	259
16	Netherlands	255
17	Lithuania	252
18	Portugal	250
19	Uruguay	247
20	Belgium	244
21	Bulgaria	243
22	Sweden	241
23	Austria	237

Tuberculosis

Incidence per 100,000 population, 2011

1	Swaziland	1,317
2	South Africa	993
3	Namibia	723
	Sierra Leone	723
5	Lesotho	632
6	Djibouti	620
7	Zimbabwe	603
8	Mozambique	548
9	Timor-Leste	498
10	Botswana	455
11	Gabon	450
12	Zambia	444
13	Cambodia	424
14	Central African Rep.	400
15	Congo-Brazzaville	387
16	Myanmar	381
17	Papua New Guinea	346
18	North Korea	345
19	Mauritania	344
20	Congo-Kinshasa	327
21	Angola	310
22	Liberia	299
23	Kenya	288

a Assumes that every country and region has the same age profile (the age profile of the world population has been used).
Note: Statistics are not available for all countries. The number of cases diagnosed and reported depends on the quality of medical practice and administration and can be under-reported in a number of countries.

Measles immunisation

Lowest % of children aged 12–23 months, 2011

1	Chad	28
2	Liberia	40
3	Somalia	46
4	Côte d'Ivoire	49
5	Equatorial Guinea	51
6	Gabon	55
7	Mali	56
8	Ethiopia	57
9	Guinea	58
10	Haiti	59
11	Papua New Guinea	60
12	Guinea-Bissau	61
13	Afghanistan	62
	Central African Rep.	62
	Timor-Leste	62
16	Burkina Faso	63
17	South Sudan	64

DPT[a] immunisation

Lowest % of children aged 12–23 months, 2011

1	Chad	22
2	Equatorial Guinea	33
3	Somalia	41
4	Gabon	45
5	South Sudan	46
6	Nigeria	47
7	Liberia	49
8	Ukraine	50
9	Ethiopia	51
10	Central African Rep.	54
11	Guinea	59
	Haiti	59
13	Papua New Guinea	61
14	Côte d'Ivoire	62
15	Indonesia	63
16	Afghanistan	66
	Cameroon	66
18	Timor-Leste	67

HIV/AIDS

Prevalence among population aged 15–49, %, 2011

1	Swaziland	26.0
2	Botswana	23.4
3	Lesotho	23.3
4	South Africa	17.3
5	Zimbabwe	14.9
6	Namibia	13.4
7	Zambia	12.5
8	Mozambique	11.3
9	Malawi	10.0
10	Uganda	7.2
11	Kenya	6.2
12	Tanzania	5.8
13	Gabon	5.0
14	Equatorial Guinea	4.7
15	Cameroon	4.6
	Central African Rep.	4.6
17	Nigeria	3.7
18	Togo	3.4
19	Congo-Brazzaville	3.3
20	Chad	3.1
	South Sudan	3.1
22	Côte d'Ivoire	3.0
23	Rwanda	2.9
24	Bahamas	2.8
25	Guinea-Bissau	2.5
26	Belize	2.3

AIDS

Estimated deaths per 100,000 pop., 2011

1	Lesotho	636.4
2	Swaziland	566.7
3	South Africa	534.6
4	Zimbabwe	453.1
5	Mozambique	309.6
6	Malawi	285.7
7	Zambia	229.6
8	Namibia	226.1
9	Central African Rep.	222.2
10	Botswana	210.0
11	Tanzania	181.8
12	Uganda	179.7
13	Cameroon	170.0
14	Bahamas	166.7
	Belize	166.7
	Gabon	166.7
17	Kenya	149.0
18	Togo	143.5
19	Equatorial Guinea	142.9
20	Nigeria	129.2
21	Côte d'Ivoire	113.9
22	Congo-Brazzaville	112.2
23	Djibouti	111.1
24	South Sudan	108.9
25	Chad	104.4
26	Suriname	100.0

a Diptheria, pertussis and tetanus

Health

Highest health spending
As % of GDP, 2011

1	Liberia	19.5
2	Sierra Leone	18.8
3	United States	17.9
4	Lesotho	12.8
5	Netherlands	12.0
6	France	11.6
7	Moldova	11.4
8	Canada	11.2
	Denmark	11.2
10	Germany	11.1
11	Costa Rica	10.9
	Switzerland	10.9
13	Greece	10.8
	Rwanda	10.8
15	Austria	10.6
	Belgium	10.6
17	Portugal	10.4
	Serbia	10.4
19	Bosnia	10.2
20	Cuba	10.0
	New Zealand	10.0
	Nicaragua	10.0
23	Georgia	9.9
24	Paraguay	9.7
25	Afghanistan	9.6
26	Italy	9.5
	Uganda	9.5

Lowest health spending
As % of GDP, 2011

1	South Sudan	1.6
2	Qatar	1.9
3	Myanmar	2.0
4	Oman	2.3
5	Brunei	2.5
	Congo-Brazzaville	2.5
	Pakistan	2.5
8	Eritrea	2.6
9	Indonesia	2.7
	Kuwait	2.7
	Turkmenistan	2.7
12	Laos	2.8
13	Gabon	3.2
14	United Arab Emirates	3.3
15	Sri Lanka	3.4
16	Angola	3.5
17	Malaysia	3.6
18	Bangladesh	3.7
	Saudi Arabia	3.7
	Syria	3.7
21	Central African Rep.	3.8
	Fiji	3.8
	Seychelles	3.8
24	Algeria	3.9
	India	3.9
	Kazakhstan	3.9
27	Equatorial Guinea	4.0

Highest pop. per doctor
2011 or latest[a]

1	Tanzania	125,000
2	Liberia	71,429
3	Colombia	68,027
4	Niger	52,632
	Malawi	52,632
6	Ethiopia	45,455
	Sierra Leone	45,455
8	Bhutan	43,478
9	Mozambique	38,462
10	Somalia	28,571
11	Gambia, The	26,316
12	Guinea-Bissau	22,222
13	Burkina Faso	21,277
14	Central African Rep.	20,833
15	Papua New Guinea	18,868
	Togo	18,868
17	Rwanda	17,857
18	Benin	16,949

Lowest pop. per doctor
2011 or latest[a]

1	Monaco	142
2	Cuba	149
3	Greece	162
4	San Marino	205
5	Austria	206
6	Russia	232
7	Georgia	236
8	Norway	240
9	Switzerland	245
10	Spain	252
11	Andorra	256
12	Portugal	259
13	Australia	260
	Kazakhstan	260
15	Belgium	264
16	Sweden	265
17	Belarus	266
	Bulgaria	266

a 2008–11   b Fat as a percentage of total daily energy intake is recommended at between 15–30%.   c Defined as body mass index of 30 or more – see page 248.

Most hospital beds
Beds per 1,000 pop., 2011 or latest[a]

1	Monaco	16.5	10	Czech Republic	7.0
2	Japan	13.7	11	Lithuania	6.8
3	Belarus	11.1		Mongolia	6.8
4	South Korea	10.3	13	Barbados	6.6
5	Ukraine	8.7		France	6.6
6	Germany	8.3		Poland	6.6
7	Austria	7.6	16	Belgium	6.5
	Kazakhstan	7.6		Bulgaria	6.5
9	Hungary	7.2	18	Slovakia	6.4

Food supply
Average per person per day, 2011 or latest

Highest calories available			Lowest calories available		
1	Austria	3,836	1	Congo-Kinshasa	1,587
2	United States	3,763	2	Burundi	1,599
3	Belgium	3,727	3	Eritrea	1,659
4	Kuwait	3,685	4	Somalia	1,830
5	Turkey	3,674	5	Zambia	1,873
6	Greece	3,660	6	Haiti	1,970
7	Ireland	3,628	7	Congo-Brazzaville	2,013
8	Italy	3,626	8	Chad	2,076
9	Portugal	3,621	9	North Korea	2,085
10	Luxembourg	3,608	10	Madagascar	2,119
11	France	3,564	11	Mozambique	2,123
12	Israel	3,561	12	Kenya	2,125

Highest fat as % of calories[b]			Lowest fat as % of calories[b]		
1	Australia	41	1	Bangladesh	10
	France	41		Burundi	10
	Spain	41		Rwanda	10
4	Belgium	40	4	Ethiopia	11
	Bermuda	40		Madagascar	11
	Cyprus	40	6	Eritrea	12
	Iceland	40		Lesotho	12
	Italy	40	8	Congo-Kinshasa	14

Obesity[c]
% of total population, 2010

Male			Female		
1	United States	44.2	1	Barbados	57.2
2	Argentina	37.4	2	Kuwait	55.2
3	Greece	30.3	3	Trinidad & Tobago	52.7
4	Mexico	30.1	4	United States	48.3
5	Kuwait	29.6	4	Jamaica	48.3
6	Venezuela	29.5	6	Egypt	48.0
7	New Zealand	28.9	7	United Arab Emirates	42.0
8	Australia	28.4	8	St Lucia	41.7
9	Malta	28.1	9	Nicaragua	41.1
10	Uruguay	25.7	10	Mexico	41.0

Marriage and divorce

Highest marriage rates
Number of marriages per 1,000 population, 2011 or latest available year

1	Antigua & Barbuda	21.7	25	Hong Kong	7.5
2	Seychelles	17.4		Jamaica	7.5
3	Tajikistan	13.5	27	Moldova	7.3
4	Iran	12.2	28	Macedonia	7.2
5	Indonesia	11.2	29	Georgia	6.9
6	Egypt	11.0	30	United States	6.7
7	Bermuda	10.6	31	Israel	6.5
8	Jordan	10.2		South Korea	6.5
9	Barbados	10.1	33	Macau	6.4
10	Azerbaijan	9.7		Tunisia	6.4
	Cayman Islands	9.7	35	Channel Islands[a]	6.3
	Kyrgyzstan	9.7		Kuwait	6.3
13	Algeria	9.6		Turkmenistan	6.3
14	Lebanon	9.5	38	Cyprus	6.2
15	Belarus	9.2	39	Malta	6.1
	Russia	9.2		San Marino	6.1
	West Bank & Gaza	9.2	41	Armenia	6.0
18	Kazakhstan	9.0		Lithuania	6.0
19	Albania	8.9	43	Bahamas	5.8
20	Mauritius	8.2	44	Montenegro	5.7
21	China	8.0	45	Ecuador	5.6
	Turkey	8.0		Philippines	5.6
23	Guam	7.8	47	Japan	5.5
	Ukraine	7.8		Mexico	5.5

Lowest marriage rates
Number of marriages per 1,000 population, 2011 or latest available year

1	United Arab Emirates	1.8	20	Hungary	3.6
2	French Guiana	2.5		Italy	3.6
3	Bulgaria	2.9		New Caledonia	3.6
4	Colombia	3.1		Réunion	3.6
5	Martinique	3.2	24	France	3.7
	Slovenia	3.2		Panama	3.7
	Uruguay	3.2	26	Aruba	3.8
8	Chile	3.3		Guatemala	3.8
	Luxembourg	3.3	28	Belgium	4.1
	Qatar	3.3		Estonia	4.1
	Venezuela	3.3	30	Suriname	4.2
12	Andorra	3.4	31	Austria	4.3
	Argentina	3.4		Czech Republic	4.3
	Mongolia	3.4	33	Dominican Republic	4.4
	Portugal	3.4		Monaco	4.4
	Spain	3.4	35	Faroe Islands	4.5
17	Guadeloupe	3.5		Liechtenstein	4.5
	Peru	3.5		Saudi Arabia	4.5
	South Africa	3.5			

a Jersey only
Note: The data are based on latest available figures (no earlier than 2007) and hence will be affected by the population age structure at the time. Marriage rates refer to registered marriages only and, therefore, reflect the customs surrounding registry and efficiency of administration.

Highest divorce rates
Number of divorces per 1,000 population, 2011 or latest available year

1	Guam	4.7		Estonia	2.3
	Russia	4.7		Germany	2.3
3	Aruba	4.3		Hungary	2.3
4	Belarus	4.1		Liechtenstein	2.3
5	Latvia	4.0		South Korea	2.3
6	Puerto Rico	3.8	32	Canada	2.2
7	United States	3.5		Kuwait	2.2
8	Lithuania	3.2		Spain	2.2
9	Moldova	3.1		Switzerland	2.2
10	Belgium	2.9	36	Austria	2.1
	Cuba	2.9		Luxembourg	2.1
12	Ukraine	2.8		Norway	2.1
13	Bermuda	2.7		Slovakia	2.1
	Czech Republic	2.7	40	China	2.0
15	Denmark	2.6		France	2.0
	Jordan	2.6		Japan	2.0
17	Costa Rica	2.5		Netherlands	2.0
	Finland	2.5		New Zealand	2.0
	Hong Kong	2.5	45	Egypt	1.9
	Portugal	2.5		Israel	1.9
	San Marino	2.5		Seychelles	1.9
	Sweden	2.5	48	Cayman Islands	1.8
	Taiwan	2.5		Dominican Republic	1.8
24	Kazakhstan	2.4		Iceland	1.8
	United Kingdom	2.4		Monaco	1.8
26	Australia	2.3			

Lowest divorce rates
Number of divorces per 1,000 population, 2011 or latest available year

1	Malta	0.1	22	Croatia	1.1
2	Chile	0.2		Mongolia	1.1
	Guatemala	0.2		Qatar	1.1
	Vietnam	0.2		Serbia	1.1
5	Bahamas	0.3		Slovenia	1.1
6	Bosnia	0.4		Thailand	1.1
7	United Arab Emirates	0.5		Tunisia	1.1
8	South Africa	0.6	29	Antigua & Barbuda	1.2
9	Indonesia	0.7		Azerbaijan	1.2
	Ireland	0.7		Ecuador	1.2
	Jamaica	0.7		Greece	1.2
12	Brazil	0.8		New Caledonia	1.2
	Macedonia	0.8		Turkmenistan	1.2
	Mexico	0.8	35	Faroe Islands	1.3
	Montenegro	0.8		Georgia	1.3
	Tajikistan	0.8		Suriname	1.3
	Venezuela	0.8	38	Bulgaria	1.4
18	Italy	0.9		Mauritius	1.4
	Saudi Arabia	0.9	40	Singapore	1.5
20	Armenia	1.0		West Bank & Gaza	1.5
	Panama	1.0			

Households, living costs – and giving

Number of households
Biggest, m, 2011

1	China	427.5	14	France	27.4
2	India	229.4	15	Italy	24.7
3	United States	118.7	16	Iran	21.2
4	Indonesia	61.9	17	Thailand	20.8
5	Brazil	56.5	18	Vietnam	20.5
6	Russia	52.6	19	Egypt	20.1
7	Japan	51.1	20	Philippines	20.0
8	Germany	40.0		Ukraine	20.0
9	Bangladesh	36.3	22	Ethiopia	19.3
10	Nigeria	33.1	23	Turkey	18.9
11	Mexico	29.0	24	South Korea	18.4
12	Pakistan	27.7	25	Spain	17.9
13	United Kingdom	27.6	26	Poland	14.7

Household occupation

Single occupation, % of total, 2011			*With 6+ occupants, % of total, 2011*		
1	Sweden	47.1	1	Kuwait	60.7
2	Norway	40.0	2	Pakistan	58.4
3	Denmark	39.6	3	United Arab Emirates	56.5
4	Finland	39.4	4	Saudi Arabia	47.3
5	Germany	38.7	5	Algeria	45.0
6	Switzerland	37.9	6	Turkmenistan	43.2
7	Slovakia	36.9	7	Jordan	39.6
8	Netherlands	36.4	8	Morocco	39.1
9	Austria	36.3	9	India	37.6
10	Estonia	35.4		Nigeria	37.6
11	France	34.3	11	Tunisia	32.6
12	United Kingdom	34.2	12	Philippines	32.4
13	Czech Republic	33.4	13	Cameroon	30.3
	Ukraine	33.4	14	Azerbaijan	28.0

Average household size, people

Biggest, 2011			*Smallest, 2011*		
1	Senegal	8.9	1	Germany	2.0
2	Angola	8.7	2	Bermuda	2.1
3	Gambia, The	8.2		Finland	2.1
4	Equatorial Guinea	8.1		Nicaragua	2.1
5	Gabon	8.0		Sweden	2.1
6	Chad	7.9	6	Denmark	2.2
7	Iraq	7.6		Monaco	2.2
8	Kuwait	7.0		Norway	2.2
9	Oman	6.7		Switzerland	2.2
10	Congo-Kinshasa	6.6			
11	Guinea	6.5			
	Mali	6.5			

a The cost of living index shown is compiled by the Economist Intelligence Unit for use
   by companies in determining expatriate compensation: it is a comparison of the cost
   of maintaining a typical international lifestyle in the country rather than a
   comparison of the purchasing power of a citizen of the country. The index is based on
   typical urban prices an international executive and family will face abroad. The prices

Cost of living[a]
December 2012, US = 100

Highest				Lowest	
1	Japan	152	1	Pakistan	44
2	Australia	137	2	India	48
3	Norway	136	3	Nepal	50
4	Singapore	135	4	Algeria	54
5	France	128		Romania	54
6	Venezuela	126	6	Sri Lanka	55
7	Switzerland	124	7	Panama	56
8	Hong Kong	116	8	Iran	58
9	Denmark	114	9	Bangladesh	59
10	United Kingdom	112	10	Paraguay	60
11	Finland	111		Saudi Arabia	60
12	New Zealand	108	12	Oman	62
13	Canada	106		Qatar	62
	South Korea	106	14	Syria	62
15	Austria	105	15	Cambodia	64
16	Sweden	104		Kazakhstan	64
17	New Caledonia	103	17	Bahrain	65
18	Spain	100		Ecuador	65
19	Belgium	99		Kuwait	65
20	Ireland	98		Serbia	65
	Israel	98		Uzbekistan	65
22	Italy	97	22	Nigeria	66
23	Germany	94		Philippines	66
24	Turkey	92	24	Bulgaria	67
25	Russia	91		Egypt	67

World Giving Index[b]
Top givers, % of population, 2012

1	Australia	60	16	Finland	45
	Ireland	60		Philippines	45
3	Canada	58		Trinidad & Tobago	45
4	New Zealand	57	19	Cyprus	44
	United States	57		Hong Kong	44
6	Netherlands	53		Malta	44
7	Indonesia	52		Oman	44
8	United Kingdom	51	23	Dominican Republic	43
9	Paraguay	50		Uzbekistan	43
10	Denmark	49	25	Somalia	42
	Liberia	49		Thailand	42
12	Iran	48	27	Austria	41
	Turkmenistan	48		Luxembourg	41
14	Qatar	47	29	Angola	40
	Sri Lanka	47		Honduras	40

are for products of international comparable quality found in a supermarket or department store. Prices found in local markets and bazaars are not used unless the available merchandise is of the specified quality and the shopping area itself is safe for executive and family members. New York City prices are used as the base, so United States = 100.

b Three criteria are used to assess giving: in the previous month those surveyed either gave money to charity, gave time to those in need or helped a stranger.

Telephones, computers and broadband

Telephones
Telephone lines per 100 people, 2011

1	Monaco	125.6	16	Barbados	51.4
2	Taiwan	72.7	17	Japan	51.1
3	Cayman Islands	65.6	18	Greece	50.4
4	France	63.2	19	Sweden	48.7
5	Germany	63.1	20	Australia	46.8
6	Hong Kong	61.0	21	United States	46.6
7	South Korea	60.9	22	Israel	46.3
8	Switzerland	59.9	23	Ireland	45.2
9	Iceland	58.9	24	Denmark	45.1
	San Marino	58.9	25	Netherlands Antilles	44.9
11	Malta	55.6	26	Andorra	44.6
12	Luxembourg	54.1	27	Belarus	44.0
13	Liechtenstein	54.0	28	Netherlands	43.5
14	United Kingdom	53.3	29	Belgium	43.1
15	Canada	53.0	30	Slovenia	42.9

Mobile telephones
Subscribers per 100 people, 2011

1	Macau	243.5	18	Singapore	150.2
2	Hong Kong	214.7	19	United Arab Emirates	148.6
3	Antigua & Barbuda	196.4	20	Luxembourg	148.3
4	Saudi Arabia	191.2	21	Seychelles	145.7
5	Panama	188.6	22	Vietnam	143.4
6	Russia	179.3	23	Botswana	142.8
7	Suriname	178.9	24	Uruguay	140.8
8	Kuwait	175.1	25	Bulgaria	140.7
9	Oman	169.0	26	Guatemala	140.4
10	Cayman Islands	167.7	27	Estonia	139.0
11	Finland	166.0	28	Trinidad & Tobago	135.6
12	Maldives	165.7	29	Argentina	134.9
13	Italy	157.9	30	El Salvador	133.5
14	Kazakhstan	155.7	31	Germany	132.3
14	Libya	155.7	32	Switzerland	131.4
16	Austria	154.8	33	Poland	131.0
17	Lithuania	151.3	34	United Kingdom	130.8

Mobile banking[a]
% of population, 2011

1	Kenya	68	11	Tanzania	23
2	Sudan	52	12	Swaziland	20
3	Gabon	50	13	Liberia	19
4	Algeria	44		Mauritania	19
5	Congo-Brazzaville	37	15	Chad	18
6	Somalia	34		Kosovo	18
7	Albania	31	17	Macedonia	16
8	Tajikistan	29	18	Haiti	15
9	Uganda	27		Philippines	15
10	Angola	26	20	Nigeria	13

a Used a mobile phone to either pay a bill, send or receive money in the previous year.
Excludes high-income economies.

Computers
Computers per 100 people, 2011

1	Canada	129.1	26	Spain	56.0
2	Netherlands	120.7	27	Slovenia	55.7
3	Switzerland	103.4	28	Belgium	52.3
4	United Kingdom	100.4	29	Macau	48.2
5	Sweden	98.9	30	Czech Republic	47.4
6	United States	96.7	31	Latvia	47.3
7	Taiwan	93.6		Macedonia	47.3
8	Germany	86.3	33	Malta	45.3
9	Denmark	85.7	34	Cyprus	43.1
10	Australia	84.6	35	New Caledonia	39.5
	France	84.6	36	Israel	37.4
12	Singapore	83.1	37	Costa Rica	35.7
13	Austria	81.7	38	Malaysia	34.9
14	Norway	77.9	39	Kuwait	33.5
15	Hong Kong	77.3	40	Maldives	32.7
16	Iceland	76.0	41	Croatia	32.5
17	Luxembourg	75.8	42	Bermuda	31.9
18	Slovakia	73.5	43	Estonia	31.5
19	Ireland	70.3	44	Lithuania	30.4
20	Finland	65.7	45	Mongolia	30.3
21	New Zealand	64.5	46	Antigua & Barbuda	29.5
22	Japan	64.2	47	United Arab Emirates	28.9
23	South Korea	63.6	48	Hungary	27.6
24	Bahrain	59.8	49	Seychelles	27.0
25	Italy	59.3	50	Mauritius	26.7

Broadband
Subscribers per 100 people, 2011

1	Liechtenstein	71.6	22	Japan	27.6
2	Bermuda	61.8	23	United States	27.4
3	Monaco	44.3	24	New Zealand	25.8
4	Switzerland	40.0	25	Singapore	25.6
5	Netherlands	38.7	26	Austria	25.4
6	Denmark	37.6	27	Israel	24.9
7	South Korea	36.9	28	Estonia	24.8
8	France	36.0	29	Macau	24.7
9	Norway	35.4	30	Australia	24.3
10	Iceland	33.9		Slovenia	24.3
11	Cayman Islands	33.2	32	Spain	23.8
12	Germany	33.1	33	Taiwan	23.7
13	Belgium	33.0	34	Hungary	22.2
14	Luxembourg	32.9	35	Barbados	22.1
15	United Kingdom	32.7		Italy	22.1
16	Canada	31.8		Lithuania	22.1
	Sweden	31.8	38	Ireland	22.0
18	Hong Kong	31.6	39	Belarus	21.9
19	Malta	31.0	40	Greece	21.6
20	Andorra	29.9	41	Greenland	20.7
21	Finland	29.5	42	San Marino	20.6

The internet and music

Internet hosts

By country, January 2013

1	United States[a]	539,394,988
2	Japan	64,453,007
3	Brazil	26,576,848
4	Italy	25,662,458
5	China	20,602,175
6	Germany	20,042,730
7	France	17,266,304
8	Australia	17,081,052
9	Mexico	16,233,310
10	Russia	14,533,447
11	Netherlands	13,698,582
12	Poland	13,265,387
13	Argentina	11,232,185
14	Canada	8,743,054
15	United Kingdom	8,106,577
16	Turkey	7,093,037
17	India	6,746,392
18	Taiwan	6,271,944
19	Sweden	5,978,228
20	Switzerland	5,301,437
21	Belgium	5,191,904
22	Finland	4,762,553
23	South Africa	4,761,282
24	Colombia	4,409,710
25	Denmark	4,297,161
26	Spain	4,227,727
27	Czech Republic	4,148,325
28	Portugal	3,747,512

Per 1,000 pop., January 2013

1	United States[a]	1,722.8
2	Iceland	1,233.2
3	Finland	882.0
4	Monaco	839.0
5	Netherlands	820.3
6	Denmark	767.4
7	Australia	755.8
8	Norway	732.2
9	Switzerland	688.5
10	New Zealand	687.7
11	Estonia	665.8
12	Sweden	636.0
13	Netherlands Antilles	605.1
14	Japan	509.5
15	Luxembourg	501.8
16	Belgium	480.7
17	Cayman Islands	460.2
18	Italy	422.1
19	Austria	418.1
20	Liechtenstein	396.6
21	Czech Republic	395.1
22	Aruba	382.6
23	Singapore	377.0
24	Lithuania	365.3
25	Portugal	350.2
26	Poland	346.4
27	San Marino	344.2
28	Andorra	333.9

Music sales

Total including downloads, $m, 2012

1	United States	4,482
2	Japan	4,422
3	United Kingdom	1,326
4	Germany	1,298
5	France	908
6	Australia	507
7	Canada	454
8	Brazil	257
9	Italy	218
10	Netherlands	216
11	South Korea	188
12	Sweden	177
13	Spain	167
14	India	147
15	Mexico	145
16	Switzerland	129
17	Belgium	122
18	Norway	118

$ per head, 2012

1	Japan	34.7
2	Norway	23.7
3	Australia	23.1
4	United Kingdom	21.0
5	Sweden	18.6
6	Switzerland	16.3
7	Denmark	16.0
	Germany	16.0
9	United States	14.3
10	France	13.8
11	Canada	13.2
12	New Zealand	13.1
13	Netherlands	13.0
14	Austria	11.7
	Belgium	11.7
16	Ireland	8.9
17	Hong Kong	5.5
18	Finland	5.3

a   Includes all hosts ending ".com", ".net" and ".org", which exaggerates the numbers.

Facebook users

	'000, May 2013			Per 1,000 pop., May 2013	
1	United States	158,923	1	Monaco	984
2	Brazil	71,865	2	Iceland	744
3	India	63,793	3	Faroe Islands	642
4	Indonesia	47,971	4	Cayman Islands	593
5	Mexico	42,571	5	Taiwan	578
6	Turkey	32,775	6	Norway	565
7	United Kingdom	31,130	7	Chile	558
8	Philippines	30,285	8	Bahamas	552
9	France	25,392	9	Malta	551
10	Germany	24,970	10	Hong Kong	547
11	Italy	23,345	11	Denmark	534
12	Argentina	21,298	12	Cyprus	533
13	Thailand	18,550	13	Brunei	523
14	Colombia	18,328	14	Argentina	522
15	Canada	17,809	15	Singapore	520
16	Spain	16,941	16	Canada	519
17	Egypt	13,981	17	New Zealand	517
18	Japan	13,820	18	Uruguay	516
19	Vietnam	13,817	19	Australia	510
20	Taiwan	13,418	20	Montenegro	509
21	Malaysia	13,347	21	United States	508
22	Australia	11,535	22	Aruba	505
23	Poland	10,679	23	Sweden	504
24	Peru	10,455	24	United Kingdom	499
25	Venezuela	9,912	25	Ireland	492

Internet users

	Per 100 population, 2011				
1	Iceland	95.0	23	Australia	79.0
2	Norway	94.0	24	Belgium	78.0
3	Netherlands	92.3	25	United States	77.9
4	Sweden	91.0	26	Bahrain	77.0
5	Luxembourg	90.9	27	Ireland	76.8
6	Denmark	90.0	28	Estonia	76.5
7	Finland	89.4	29	Monaco	75.0
8	Bermuda	88.3	30	Hong Kong	74.5
9	Qatar	86.2	31	Slovakia	74.4
10	New Zealand	86.0	32	Kuwait	74.2
11	Switzerland	85.2	33	Czech Republic	73.0
12	Liechtenstein	85.0	34	Slovenia	72.0
13	South Korea	83.8		Taiwan	72.0
14	Canada	83.0	36	Barbados	71.8
	Germany	83.0	37	Latvia	71.7
16	Antigua & Barbuda	82.0	38	Singapore	71.0
	United Kingdom	82.0	39	Croatia	70.7
18	Andorra	81.0	40	Israel	70.0
19	Faroe Islands	80.7		United Arab Emirates	70.0
20	Austria	79.8	42	Cayman Islands	69.5
21	France	79.6	43	Malta	69.2
22	Japan	79.5	44	Oman	68.0

Movies and museums

Cinema attendances

Total visits, m, 2011

1	India	3,172.3
2	United States	1,373.2
3	China	309.0
4	France	213.0
5	Russia	184.5
6	Mexico	181.9
7	Japan	178.9
8	United Kingdom	173.9
9	South Korea	161.8
10	Germany	129.2
11	Brazil	128.6
12	Italy	124.7
13	Spain	97.0
14	Australia	92.8
15	Philippines	72.9
16	Malaysia	53.8
17	Turkey	44.1
18	Poland	38.0
19	Venezuela	32.0
20	Colombia	31.4
21	Argentina	30.6
22	Netherlands	29.1
23	South Africa	26.5
24	Peru	24.4
25	Belgium	24.0
26	Singapore	21.8
27	Iran	21.3
28	Austria	18.9
29	Ireland	17.4
30	Portugal	17.2

Visits per head, 2011

1	Iceland	5.8
2	United States	4.3
3	Singapore	4.2
4	Australia	4.1
5	Singapore	4.0
6	Ireland	3.9
7	France	3.4
8	South Korea	3.3
9	United Kingdom	2.8
10	India	2.7
11	Denmark	2.4
	Luxembourg	2.4
13	Norway	2.3
14	Austria	2.2
	Belgium	2.2
	Malta	2.2
17	Italy	2.1
	Spain	2.1
19	Malaysia	1.9
	Switzerland	1.9
21	Estonia	1.7
	Netherlands	1.7
	Sweden	1.7
24	Belarus	1.6
	Germany	1.6
	Mexico	1.6
	Portugal	1.6
28	Finland	1.5
	Slovenia	1.5
30	Japan	1.4

Most popular museums and art galleries

Total visits, m, 2012

1	Louvre, Paris	9.72
2	Metropolitan Museum of Art, New York	6.12
3	British Museum, London	5.58
4	Tate Modern, London	5.30
5	National Gallery, London	5.16
6	Vatican Museums, Vatican City	5.06
7	National Palace Museum, Taipei	4.36
8	National Gallery of Art, Washington, DC	4.20
9	Centre Pompidou, Paris	3.80
10	Musée d'Orsay, Paris	3.60
11	Victoria & Albert Museum, London	3.23
12	National Museum of Korea, Seoul	3.13
13	State Hermitage Museum, St Petersburg	2.88
14	Museum of Modern Art, New York	2.81
15	National Folk Museum of Korea, Seoul	2.64
16	Reina Sofía, Madrid	2.57
17	Bank of Brazil Cultural Centre, Rio de Janiero	2.24
18	National Portrait Gallery, London	2.10
19	Shanghai Museum, Shanghai	1.94
20	National Museum of Scotland, Edinburgh	1.89
21	Uffizi Gallery, Florence	1.77
22	Moscow Kremlin Museums, Moscow	1.74

The press

Daily newspapers
Copies per '000 population, 2011

1	Hong Kong	514	16	Malta	242
2	Luxembourg	494	17	Germany	228
3	Japan	393	18	Slovenia	208
4	Kuwait	385	19	Belarus	190
5	Sweden	365	20	Lithuania	186
6	Finland	353	21	Taiwan	173
7	Austria	350	22	Estonia	170
8	Norway	348	23	Canada	157
9	South Korea	333	24	Hungary	156
10	Iceland	321		Ireland	156
11	Singapore	303	26	Belgium	152
12	Switzerland	284	27	Israel	150
13	United Kingdom	278	28	France	149
14	Netherlands	248	29	Bulgaria	147
15	Denmark	244		United States	147

Press freedom[a]
Scores, 2012

Most free			Least free		
1	Finland	6.38	1	Eritrea	84.83
2	Netherlands	6.48	2	North Korea	83.90
3	Norway	6.52	3	Turkmenistan	79.14
4	Luxembourg	6.68	4	Syria	78.53
5	Andorra	6.82	5	Somalia	73.59
6	Denmark	7.08	6	Iran	73.40
7	Liechtenstein	7.35	7	China	73.07
8	New Zealand	8.38	8	Vietnam	71.78
9	Iceland	8.49	9	Cuba	71.64
10	Sweden	9.23	10	Sudan	70.06
11	Estonia	9.26	11	Yemen	69.22
12	Austria	9.40	12	Laos	67.99
13	Jamaica	9.88	13	Djibouti	67.40
14	Switzerland	9.94	14	Guinea	67.20
15	Ireland	10.06	15	Bahrain	62.75
16	Czech Republic	10.17	16	Uzbekistan	60.39
17	Germany	10.24	17	Saudi Arabia	56.88
18	Costa Rica	12.08	18	Sri Lanka	56.59
19	Namibia	12.50	19	Rwanda	55.46
20	Canada	12.69	20	Kazakhstan	55.08
21	Belgium	12.94	21	Pakistan	51.31
22	Poland	13.11	22	Egypt	48.66
23	Slovakia	13.25	23	Belarus	48.35
24	Cyprus	13.83	24	Azerbaijan	47.73
25	Cape Verde	14.33	25	Swaziland	46.76
26	Australia	15.24	26	Turkey	46.56
27	Uruguay	15.92	27	Mexico	45.30
28	Portugal	16.75	28	Gambia, The	45.09

a Based on data for deaths and violence, plus 74 questions on topics such as media
 independence, monopolies, legal status, censorship and pressure, answered by
 journalists and media experts.

Nobel prize winners: 1901–2012

Peace (two or more)

1	United States	19
2	United Kingdom	11
3	France	9
4	Sweden	5
5	Belgium	4
	Germany	4
7	Austria	3
	Norway	3
	South Africa	3
	Switzerland	3
11	Argentina	2
	Egypt	2
	Israel	2
	Russia	2

Economics[a]

1	United States	36
2	United Kingdom	9
3	Norway	2
	Sweden	2
5	Denmark	1
	France	1
	Germany	1
	Israel	1
	Netherlands	1
	Russia	1

Literature (three or more)

1	France	15
2	United States	12
3	United Kingdom	11
4	Germany	8
5	Sweden	7
6	Italy	5
	Spain	5
8	Norway	3
	Poland	3
	Russia	3

Medicine (three or more)

1	United States	54
2	United Kingdom	24
3	Germany	15
4	France	8
5	Sweden	7
6	Switzerland	6
7	Austria	5
	Denmark	5
9	Australia	3
	Belgium	3
	Italy	3

Physics

1	United States	52
2	United Kingdom	20
3	Germany	19
4	France	10
5	Netherlands	6
	Russia	6
7	Japan	5
8	Sweden	4
	Switzerland	4
10	Austria	3
	Italy	3
12	Canada	2
	Denmark	2
14	China	1
	India	1
	Ireland	1
	Pakistan	1
	Poland	1

Chemistry

1	United States	46
2	United Kingdom	23
3	Germany	15
4	France	7
5	Switzerland	6
6	Japan	5
	Sweden	5
8	Canada	4
9	Israel	3
10	Argentina	1
	Austria	1
	Belgium	1
	Czech Republic	1
	Denmark	1
	Finland	1
	Italy	1
	Netherlands	1
	Norway	1
	Russia	1

a Since 1969.
Notes: Prizes by country of residence at time awarded. When prizes have been shared in the same field, one credit given to each country.

Olympics

Summer games, 1896–2012

	Country	Athletes per medal	Total medals	Games attended
1	East Germany (1968–88)	3.3	409	5
2	Soviet Union/Unified team (1952–92)	3.4	1,122	10
3	United States	4.1	2,292	25
4	Russia	5.8	325	7
5	China	6.2	385	11
6	Ethiopia	6.3	38	11
7	British West Indies (Antilles)	6.5	2	1
8	Germany	6.9	647	17
9	Hungary	7.0	458	24
	Romania	7.0	292	19
11	Finland	7.2	299	23
12	Georgia	7.6	18	4
	Kenya	7.6	75	12
14	Sweden	7.9	475	25
15	Bulgaria	8.1	212	17

Summer games, 2012

Olympics

	Country	Athletes per medal	Total medals			Country	Athletes per medal	Total medals
1	Jamaica	3.8	12			Qatar	6.0	2
2	Botswana	4.0	1		14	Trinidad & Tob.	6.3	4
3	China	4.3	88		15	Belarus	7.4	12
	Kenya	4.3	11		16	Japan	7.7	38
5	Iran	4.4	12		17	Cuba	7.8	14
6	Ethiopia	4.7	7		18	Armenia	8.0	3
7	Georgia	4.9	7			Grenada	8.0	1
8	United States	5.1	104		20	Great Britain	8.2	65
9	Azerbaijan	5.2	10		21	Germany	8.7	44
	Russia	5.2	82			Netherlands	8.7	20
11	Mongolia	5.8	5			North Korea	8.7	6
12	Afghanistan	6.0	1		24	Kazakhstan	8.8	13

Paralympics

	Country	Athletes per medal	Total medals			Country	Athletes per medal	Total medals
1	Fiji	1.0	1			Nigeria	2.2	13
2	China	1.3	231			South Africa	2.2	29
3	Tunisia	1.6	19		16	Azerbaijan	2.3	12
4	Algeria	1.7	19			Germany	2.3	66
	Cuba	1.7	17			Hong Kong	2.3	12
6	New Zealand	1.8	17			Netherlands	2.3	39
	Russia	1.8	102			United States	2.3	98
	Ukraine	1.8	84		21	Hungary	2.4	14
9	Switzerland	1.9	13		22	Austria	2.5	13
10	Angola	2.0	2			Great Britain	2.5	120
	Australia	2.0	85			Namibia	2.5	2
	Macedonia	2.0	1			Romania	2.5	2
13	Kenya	2.2	6					

Note: Athletes per medal is the number of medals won divided by number of athletes sent.

Drinking and smoking

Beer drinkers
Retail sales, litres per head of population, 2011

1	Czech Republic	144.8
2	Ireland	110.3
3	Germany	105.2
4	Austria	101.0
5	Estonia	98.3
6	Slovenia	95.0
7	Poland	93.7
8	Lithuania	92.3
9	Luxembourg	87.7
10	Belgium	87.3
11	Finland	81.3
12	Romania	79.4
13	Australia	77.6
14	Latvia	76.3
15	United States	75.4
16	Croatia	73.3
17	Slovakia	72.9
18	South Africa	69.9
19	Russia	69.7
20	Spain	69.1
21	Brazil	69.0
22	United Kingdom	68.8
23	Netherlands	68.4

Wine drinkers
Retail sales, litres per head of population, 2011

1	Luxembourg	62.0
2	Portugal	46.2
3	Italy	41.0
4	France	39.1
5	Switzerland	38.2
6	Slovenia	36.5
7	Liechtenstein	33.9
8	Austria	33.4
9	Denmark	31.8
10	Belgium	28.1
11	Greece	27.8
12	Germany	25.8
13	Belarus	25.2
14	Netherlands	25.0
15	Argentina	24.4
16	Australia	23.9
17	Hungary	23.7
18	Sweden	22.4
	United Kingdom	22.4
20	New Zealand	22.1
21	Spain	21.7
22	Czech Republic	18.7
23	Ireland	18.0

Alcoholic drink
Retail sales, litres per head of population, 2011

1	Czech Republic	173.3
2	Luxembourg	153.3
3	Ireland	149.7
4	Slovenia	145.5
5	Germany	144.9
6	Austria	144.2
7	Estonia	141.1
8	Australia	121.6
9	Belgium	119.9
10	Finland	117.3
11	United Kingdom	113.2
12	Lithuania	112.8
13	Poland	110.2
14	New Zealand	106.3
15	Denmark	105.3
16	Portugal	101.4
17	Latvia	100.6
18	Spain	99.9
19	Switzerland	99.6
20	Netherlands	98.2
21	Slovakia	97.8
22	Belarus	95.4

Cigarettes
Av. ann. consumption of cigarettes per head per day, 2012

1	Serbia	9.1
2	Belarus	8.3
3	Russia	7.1
4	Lebanon	6.5
	Moldova	6.5
6	Slovenia	6.0
7	Bosnia	5.7
8	Czech Republic	5.4
9	Greece	5.2
10	China	5.0
	South Korea	5.0
	Ukraine	5.0
13	Macedonia	4.9
14	Kuwait	4.8
15	Bulgaria	4.6
16	Georgia	4.5
17	Armenia	4.4
	Austria	4.4
	Taiwan	4.4
20	Japan	4.2
21	Azerbaijan	3.9
	Switzerland	3.9

Crime and punishment

Murders

Homicides per 100,000 pop., 2010 or latest

1	Honduras	82.1
2	El Salvador	64.7
3	Côte d'Ivoire	56.9
4	Jamaica	52.2
5	Venezuela	45.1
6	Belize	41.4
	Guatemala	41.4
8	Virgin Islands (US)	39.2
9	Zambia	38.0
10	Uganda	36.3
11	Malawi	36.0
12	Lesotho	35.2
	Trinidad & Tobago	35.2
14	Colombia	33.4
15	South Africa	31.8
16	Congo-Brazzaville	30.8
17	Central African Rep.	29.3
18	Bahamas	27.4
19	Puerto Rico	26.2
20	Ethiopia	25.5

Robberies

Per 100,000 pop., 2010 or latest

1	Belgium	1,714
2	Spain	1,146
3	Argentina	974
4	Mexico	651
5	Dominican Republic	573
6	Costa Rica	529
7	Nicaragua	491
8	Chile	477
9	Trinidad & Tobago	452
10	Nicaragua	443
11	Ecuador	386
12	Uruguay	277
13	Bosnia	275
14	Panama	270
15	Maldives	194
16	Portugal	191
17	France	180
18	Peru	170
19	Belize	153
20	Guyana	145

Prisoners

Total prison pop., latest available year

1	United States	2,239,751
2	China	1,640,000
3	Russia	695,500
4	Brazil	548,003
5	India	372,296
6	Thailand	262,077
7	Mexico	242,754
8	Iran	217,000
9	Indonesia	151,723
10	South Africa	149,959
11	Ukraine	144,491
12	Vietnam	130,180
13	Turkey	129,506
14	Colombia	116,370
15	Ethiopia	112,361
16	Philippines	109,045
17	United Kingdom	93,751
18	Poland	86,049
19	Pakistan	74,944
20	Bangladesh	72,104
21	Morocco	72,000
22	Spain	68,900
23	Japan	68,788
24	France	66,995
25	Taiwan	66,163

Per 100,000 pop., latest available year

1	United States	716
2	Seychelles	641
3	Virgin Islands (US)	539
4	Rwanda	527
5	Cuba	510
6	Russia	486
7	British Virgin Islands	460
8	Belarus	438
9	El Salvador	425
10	Bermuda	417
11	Azerbaijan	413
12	Belize	407
13	Panama	406
14	Antigua & Barbuda	395
15	Cayman Islands	382
16	Barbados	377
17	Thailand	373
18	Bahamas	371
19	Greenland	340
20	Ukraine	320
21	Guam	316
	Kazakhstan	316
23	Costa Rica	314
	Lithuania	314
	Swaziland	314
26	St Lucia	313

War and peace

Defence spending
As % of GDP, 2012

1	Iraq	11.3	14	Armenia	3.7
2	Afghanistan	10.5	15	Angola	3.6
3	Oman	8.4		Singapore	3.6
4	Saudi Arabia	8.0	17	Libya	3.5
5	Israel	7.9		Morocco	3.5
6	Jordan	5.6	19	Russia	3.1
7	Iran	5.0	20	Greece	3.0
8	South Sudan	4.7	21	Lebanon	2.9
9	Yemen	4.6	22	Tunisia	2.7
10	Algeria	4.5	23	Georgia	2.6
11	Myanmar	4.2		Kuwait	2.6
12	United States	4.1		Pakistan	2.6
13	Bahrain	3.9		United Kingdom	2.6

Defence spending

$bn, 2012			*Per head, $, 2012*		
1	United States	645.7	1	Israel	2,551
2	China[a]	102.4	2	Oman	2,178
3	United Kingdom	64.1	3	United States	2,057
4	Russia	59.9	4	Saudi Arabia	1,979
5	Japan	59.4	5	Singapore	1,808
6	Saudi Arabia	52.5	6	Kuwait	1,744
7	France	48.1	7	Norway	1,455
8	Germany	40.4	8	Australia	1,140
8	India	38.5	9	United Kingdom	1,016
10	Brazil	35.3	10	Brunei	990
11	South Korea	29.0	11	Denmark	789
12	Australia	25.1	12	France	733
13	Iran	23.9	13	Greece	707
14	Italy	23.6	14	Finland	683
15	Israel	19.4	15	Sweden	636

Armed forces
'000, 2013[b]

		Regulars	Reserves			Regulars	Reserves
1	China	2,285	510	14	Thailand	361	200
2	United States	1,520	810	15	Brazil	318	1,340
3	India	1,325	1,155	16	Taiwan	290	1,657
4	North Korea	1,190	600	17	Colombia	281	62
5	Russia	845	20,000	18	Iraq	271	0
6	South Korea	655	4,500	19	Mexico	270	87
7	Pakistan	642	0	20	Japan	247	56
8	Iran	523	350	21	Sudan	244	0
9	Turkey	511	379	22	Saudi Arabia	234	0
10	Vietnam	482	5,000	23	France	229	30
11	Egypt	439	479	24	South Sudan	210	0
12	Myanmar	406	0	25	Eritrea	202	120
13	Indonesia	396	400				

a Official budget only at market exchange rates.   b Estimates.

Arms exporters
$m, 2012

1	United States	8,760
2	Russia	8,003
3	China	1,783
4	Ukraine	1,344
5	Germany	1,193
6	France	1,139
7	Italy	1,046
8	United Kingdom	863
9	Netherlands	760
10	Spain	720
11	Israel	533
12	Sweden	496
13	Canada	276
14	Switzerland	210
15	South Korea	183
16	Norway	169
17	South Africa	145
18	Poland	140
19	Romania	108
20	Singapore	76

Arms importers
$m, 2012

1	India	4,764
2	China	1,689
3	United States	1,297
4	Turkey	1,269
5	Pakistan	1,244
6	United Arab Emirates	1,094
7	South Korea	1,078
8	Saudi Arabia	923
9	Australia	889
10	Morocco	790
11	Algeria	650
12	Venezuela	643
13	Singapore	627
14	Myanmar	619
15	United Kingdom	598
16	Afghanistan	576
17	Iraq	455
18	Taiwan	412
19	Brazil	410
20	Israel	387

Global Peace Index[a]

Most peaceful, 2013

1	Iceland	1.162
2	Denmark	1.207
3	New Zealand	1.237
4	Austria	1.250
5	Switzerland	1.272
6	Japan	1.293
7	Finland	1.297
8	Canada	1.306
9	Sweden	1.319
10	Belgium	1.339
11	Norway	1.359
12	Ireland	1.370
13	Slovenia	1.374
14	Czech Republic	1.404
15	Germany	1.431
16	Australia	1.438
	Singapore	1.438
18	Portugal	1.467
19	Qatar	1.480
20	Bhutan	1.487
21	Mauritius	1.497
22	Netherlands	1.508
23	Hungary	1.520
24	Uruguay	1.528

Least peaceful, 2013

1	Afghanistan	3.440
2	Somalia	3.394
3	Syria	3.393
4	Iraq	3.245
5	Sudan	3.242
6	Pakistan	3.106
7	Congo-Kinshasa	3.085
8	Russia	3.060
9	North Korea	3.044
10	Central African Rep.	3.031
11	Yemen	2.747
12	Côte d'Ivoire	2.732
13	Israel	2.730
14	Zimbabwe	2.696
15	Nigeria	2.693
16	Colombia	2.634
17	Ethiopia	2.630
18	Libya	2.604
19	Burundi	2.593
20	South Sudan	2.576
21	Lebanon	2.575
22	India	2.570
23	Myanmar	2.528
24	Georgia	2.511

a Ranks 162 countries using 22 indicators which gauge the level of safety and security in society, the extent of domestic or international conflict and the degree of militarisation.

Environment

Environmental Performance Index[a]
Best performers, scores, 2010

1	Switzerland	76.7	21	Denmark	63.6
2	Latvia	70.4	22	Poland	63.5
3	Norway	69.9	23	Japan	63.4
4	Luxembourg	69.2	24	Belgium	63.0
5	Costa Rica	69.0	25	Brunei	62.5
	France	69.0		Malaysia	62.5
7	Austria	68.9	27	Colombia	62.3
	Italy	68.9		Slovenia	62.3
9	Sweden	68.8	29	Taiwan	62.2
	United Kingdom	68.8	30	Brazil	60.9
11	Germany	66.9	31	Ecuador	60.6
12	Slovakia	66.6	32	Spain	60.3
13	Iceland	66.3	33	Greece	60.0
14	New Zealand	66.0	34	Thailand	59.9
15	Albania	65.9	35	Nicaragua	59.2
16	Netherlands	65.7	36	Ireland	58.7
17	Lithuania	65.5	37	Canada	58.4
18	Czech Republic	64.8	38	Nepal	58.0
19	Finland	64.4	39	Gabon	57.9
20	Croatia	64.2		Panama	57.9

Air quality[b]
Concentration of particulate matter[c], micrograms per cubic metre, 2009

	Urban areas			Cities	
1	Uruguay	142	1	Delhi, India	118
2	Sudan	137	2	Xian, China	115
3	Bangladesh	121	3	Cairo, Egypt	112
4	Iraq	110	4	Tianjin, China	103
5	Mali	106	5	Chongqing, China	101
6	Saudi Arabia	103		Kolkata, India	101
7	Mongolia	101	7	Buenos Aires, Argentina	92
	Pakistan	101	8	Kanpur, India	86
9	Togo	98		Lucknow, India	86
10	Kuwait	95	10	Shenyang, China	83
11	Niger	92	11	Zhenzhou, China	80
12	Egypt	88	12	Jinan, China	77
13	Chad	82	13	Lanzhou, China	75
	Oman	82	14	Beijing, China	73
15	Libya	81	15	Chengdu, China	71
16	Senegal	80	16	Jakarta, Indonesia	70
17	Algeria	75	17	Anshan, China	68
18	Sri Lanka	71	18	Ahmedabad, India	66
	Syria	71	19	Nanchang, China	65
20	Guatemala	68		Wuhan, China	65
	Indonesia	68	21	Harbin, China	63
	Mauritania	68	22	Changchun, China	61
23	Botswana	66		Zibo, China	61

a An overall rank on scores over various indicators that include environmental, public health and ecosystem vitality.   b Data are weighted for the size of a country's urban population.   c Less than 10 microns in diameter.

Biggest emitters of carbon dioxide
Million tonnes, 2009

1	China	7,687.1	26	Malaysia	198.3
2	United States	5,266.6	27	Venezuela	184.8
3	India	1,979.4	28	Argentina	174.7
4	Russia	1,574.4	29	Netherlands	169.7
5	Japan	1,101.1	30	Pakistan	161.2
6	Germany	734.6	31	United Arab Emirates	156.8
7	Iran	602.1	32	Vietnam	142.3
8	Canada	513.9	33	Algeria	121.3
9	South Korea	509.4	34	Uzbekistan	116.5
10	South Africa	499.0	35	Iraq	109.0
11	United Kingdom	474.6	36	Czech Republic	108.1
12	Indonesia	451.8	37	Belgium	103.6
13	Mexico	446.2	38	Greece	94.9
14	Saudi Arabia	432.8	39	Kuwait	80.2
15	Italy	400.8	40	Romania	79.5
16	Australia	400.2	41	North Korea	75.1
17	Brazil	367.1	42	Colombia	71.2
18	France	363.4	43	Qatar	70.3
19	Poland	298.9	44	Nigeria	70.2
20	Spain	288.2	45	Philippines	68.6
21	Turkey	277.8	46	Israel	67.2
22	Ukraine	272.2	47	Chile	66.7
23	Thailand	271.7	48	Syria	65.3
24	Kazakhstan	225.8	49	Libya	62.9
25	Egypt	216.1	50	Austria	62.3

Largest amount of carbon dioxide emitted per person
Tonnes, 2009

1	Qatar	44.0	23	Finland	10.0
2	Trinidad & Tobago	35.8		Libya	10.0
3	Kuwait	30.3	25	Norway	9.7
4	Brunei	23.7		Turkmenistan	9.7
5	United Arab Emirates	22.6	27	Belgium	9.6
6	Aruba	21.5	28	Ireland	9.3
7	Bahrain	20.7	29	Cayman Islands	9.2
8	Luxembourg	20.4	30	Germany	9.0
9	Australia	18.2		Israel	9.0
10	United States	17.3	32	Japan	8.6
11	Saudi Arabia	16.1	33	Greece	8.4
12	Canada	15.2	34	Denmark	8.3
	Oman	15.2	35	Iran	8.2
14	Faroe Islands	14.6	36	Bosnia	8.0
15	Kazakhstan	14.0	37	Poland	7.8
16	Estonia	11.9	38	United Kingdom	7.7
17	Russia	11.1	39	Bahamas	7.6
18	South Korea	10.4	40	Cyprus	7.5
19	Czech Republic	10.3		Slovenia	7.5
	Netherlands	10.3	42	Austria	7.4
21	Greenland	10.2		New Zealand	7.4
22	South Africa	10.1	44	Bermuda	7.2

Sources of carbon dioxide emissions
As % of total emissions in each country, 2009
Electricity, heat, energy industry

1	Estonia	75.9	11	Mongolia	63.5
2	Malta	75.1	12	Australia	61.6
3	Bosnia	70.7	13	Cuba	61.5
4	Kuwait	70.3		South Africa	61.5
5	Serbia	70.2	15	Zimbabwe	59.1
6	Macedonia	70.0	16	Libya	58.7
7	Bulgaria	67.8	17	Oman	58.5
8	Hong Kong	64.8	18	India	58.0
9	Montenegro	64.5	19	Russia	57.8
10	Israel	63.6	20	Brunei	56.5

Manufacturing and construction

1	North Korea	63.1	11	Myanmar	31.3
2	Trinidad & Tobago	60.0	12	Bahrain	30.1
3	Zambia	48.3		Thailand	30.1
4	United Arab Emirates	43.2	14	Qatar	29.2
5	Gabon	38.7	15	Indonesia	28.9
6	Singapore	37.8	16	Brazil	28.5
7	Vietnam	35.6	17	Cuba	28.1
8	Congo-Kinshasa	34.8	18	Brunei	27.2
9	China	33.0	19	Botswana	26.7
10	Pakistan	32.2	20	Kyrgyzstan	26.6

Transport

1	Paraguay	91.3	11	Ghana	53.0
2	Congo-Brazzaville	79.6	12	Tanzania	52.8
3	Togo	78.1	13	Cameroon	52.2
4	Costa Rica	69.6	14	Namibia	51.1
5	Mozambique	67.4	15	Sweden	51.0
6	Benin	67.0	16	Cambodia	50.8
7	Albania	63.3	17	Sudan	50.7
8	Luxembourg	61.1	18	Nepal	50.6
9	Nigeria	55.7	19	Guatemala	50.0
10	Haiti	54.4	20	Ecuador	49.7

Renewable sources[a] of energy
As % of electricity production, 2010

1	Denmark	32.1	11	Philippines	14.8
2	El Salvador	30.2	12	Finland	14.0
3	Guatemala	29.6	13	Germany	13.4
4	Iceland	26.2	14	Ireland	11.0
5	Kenya	23.8	15	Sweden	10.6
6	Nicaragua	23.2	16	Austria	9.9
7	Portugal	22.7	17	Netherlands	9.4
8	Spain	18.4	18	Uruguay	8.8
9	New Zealand	18.1	19	Italy	8.7
10	Costa Rica	17.5	20	Estonia	7.8

a Includes geothermal, solar, municipal waste, biofuels.

Freshwater withdrawals[a]
Billions of cubic metres, 2011

1	India	761.0		17	Canada	46.0
2	China	554.1		18	Italy	45.4
3	United States	478.4		19	Turkey	40.1
4	Pakistan	183.5		20	Ukraine	38.5
5	Indonesia	113.3		21	Sudan	37.1
6	Iran	93.3		22	Bangladesh	35.9
7	Japan	90.0		23	Myanmar	33.2
8	Vietnam	82.0		24	Argentina	32.6
9	Philippines	81.6		25	Spain	32.5
10	Mexico	79.8		26	Germany	32.3
11	Egypt	68.3		27	France	31.6
12	Russia	66.2		28	Turkmenistan	28.0
13	Iraq	66.0		29	South Korea	25.5
14	Brazil	58.1		30	Saudi Arabia	23.7
15	Thailand	57.3		31	Australia	22.6
16	Uzbekistan	56.0		32	Kazakhstan	21.1

% used for industry, 2011

1	Estonia	97		17	Romania	61
2	Lithuania	90		18	Poland	60
3	Belgium	88			Russia	60
4	Netherlands	87		20	Sweden	59
5	Germany	84		21	Switzerland	58
6	Hungary	82		22	Czech Republic	57
	Serbia	82		23	Belarus	54
	Slovenia	82		24	Moldova	52
9	Austria	79		25	Singapore	51
10	Ireland	74		26	Latvia	50
11	Belize	73			Slovakia	50
12	Finland	72		28	United States	46
13	Canada	69		29	Norway	43
	France	69			Papua New Guinea	43
15	Bulgaria	68		31	Lesotho	40
16	Macedonia	67		32	Montenegro	39

% used for agriculture, 2011

1	Afghanistan	99			Mauritania	94
	Somalia	99			Pakistan	94
3	Guyana	98			Turkmenistan	94
	Nepal	98		17	Laos	93
5	Madagascar	97			Senegal	93
	Sudan	97			Suriname	93
	Swaziland	97		20	Ecuador	92
8	Eritrea	95			Iran	92
	Vietnam	95		22	Cape Verde	91
10	Bhutan	94			Tajikistan	91
	Cambodia	94			Timor-Leste	91
	Ethiopia	94			Yemen	91
	Kyrgyzstan	94				

a Extraction of fresh and desalinated water.

Drought, extreme temperatures and floods
% of total population affected, 2009

1	Swaziland	9.2		Somalia	4.6
2	Malawi	8.8	14	India	4.4
3	China	8.0	15	Zambia	4.2
4	Niger	7.5	16	Thailand	3.8
5	Eritrea	7.3	17	Mozambique	3.7
6	Guyana	7.2	18	Lesotho	3.4
7	Djibouti	6.8		Namibia	3.4
8	Cambodia	6.6	20	Ethiopia	3.3
9	Kenya	6.5	21	Iran	3.1
10	Tajikistan	5.4		Mauritania	3.1
11	Albania	5.3	23	Australia	3.0
12	Bangladesh	4.6	24	Sudan	2.8

Number of species under threat
2011

Mammals

1	Indonesia	184		Vietnam	54
2	Mexico	100	12	Colombia	52
3	India	94	13	Laos	45
4	Brazil	81		Myanmar	45
5	China	75	15	Ecuador	43
6	Malaysia	70	16	Papua New Guinea	39
7	Madagascar	65	17	Argentina	38
8	Thailand	57		Cameroon	38
9	Australia	55		Philippines	38
10	Peru	54			

Birds

1	Brazil	122	11	Mexico	56
2	Indonesia	119	12	Australia	52
3	Peru	98	13	Argentina	49
4	Colombia	94		Russia	49
5	China	86	15	Thailand	46
6	India	78	16	Malaysia	45
7	United States	76	17	Myanmar	43
8	Philippines	74		Vietnam	43
9	Ecuador	73	19	Tanzania	42
10	New Zealand	70	20	South Africa	40

Fish

1	India	212	11	South Africa	87
2	United States	183	12	Madagascar	85
3	Tanzania	174	13	Brazil	84
4	Mexico	152	14	Congo-Kinshasa	83
5	Indonesia	140	15	Greece	75
6	China	113	16	Philippines	71
7	Cameroon	112		Spain	71
8	Australia	103	18	Turkey	70
9	Malawi	101	19	Kenya	68
10	Thailand	97		Vietnam	68

Country profiles

ALGERIA

Area	2,381,741 sq km	Capital	Algiers
Arable as % of total land	3.1	Currency	Algerian dinar (AD)

People

Population	36.0m	Life expectancy: men	71.9 yrs
Pop. per sq km	15.1	women	75.0 yrs
Total growth		Adult literacy	72.6%
in pop. 2000–10	16.2%	Fertility rate (per woman)	2.1
Pop. under 15	27.0%	Urban population	73.0%
Pop. over 60	6.9%		per 1,000 pop.
No. of men per 100 women	101.9	Crude birth rate	19.2
Human Development Index	71.3	Crude death rate	4.9

The economy

GDP	AD13,762bn	GDP per head	$5,240
GDP	$189bn	GDP per head in purchasing	
Av. ann. growth in real		power parity (USA=100)	18.0
GDP 2006–11	2.6%	Economic freedom index	49.6

Origins of GDP		Components of GDP	
	% of total		% of total
Agriculture	7	Private consumption	35
Industry, of which:	62	Public consumption	14
manufacturing	6	Investment	41
Services	31	Exports	31
		Imports	-21

Structure of employment

	% of total		% of labour force
Agriculture	12	Unemployed 2010	10.0
Industry	33	Av. ann. rate 2000–10	18.1
Services	55		

Energy

	m TOE		
Total output	150.5	Net energy imports as %	
Total consumption	40.4	of energy use	-273
Consumption per head,			
kg oil equivalent	1,138		

Inflation and finance

		av. ann. increase 2006–11	
Consumer price			
inflation 2012	8.9%	Narrow money (M1)	17.3%
Av. ann. inflation 2007–12	5.6%	Broad money	15.3%
Treasury bill rate, Dec. 2012	0.20%		

Exchange rates

	end 2012		2012
AD per $	78.19	Effective rates	2005 = 100
AD per SDR	120.03	– nominal	90.2
AD per €	102.58	– real	106.5

Trade

Principal exports		Principal imports	
	$bn fob		$bn cif
Hydrocarbons	71.4	Capital goods	16.1
Semi-finished goods	1.5	Semi-finished goods	10.7
Raw materials	0.2	Food	9.9
Total incl. others	**72.9**	Consumer goods	7.3
		Total incl. others	**47.3**

Main export destinations		Main origins of imports	
	% of total		% of total
United States	18.6	France	18.6
Italy	9.7	China	10.4
Canada	7.6	Italy	9.5
France	7.6	Spain	8.0

Balance of payments, reserves and debt, $bn

Visible exports fob	72.8	Change in reserves	20.9
Visible imports fob	-44.8	Level of reserves	
Trade balance	28.0	end Dec.	191.4
Invisibles inflows	8.2	No. months of import cover	35.9
Invisibles outflows	-19.2	Official gold holdings, m oz	5.6
Net transfers	2.3	Foreign debt	3.7
Current account balance	19.4	– as % of GDP	2.4
– as % of GDP	10.3	– as % of total exports	5.6
Capital balance	-2.7	Debt service ratio[a]	1.0
Overall balance	19.9		

Health and education

Health spending, % of GDP	3.9	Education spending, % of GDP	4.3
Doctors per 1,000 pop.	1.2	Enrolment, %: primary	109
Hospital beds per 1,000 pop.	...	secondary	95
Improved-water source access,		tertiary	32
% of pop.	83		

Society

No. of households	6.4m	Cost of living, Dec. 2012	
Av. no. per household	5.6	New York = 100	54
Marriages per 1,000 pop.	9.6	Cars per 1,000 pop.	84
Divorces per 1,000 pop.	...	Colour TV households, % with:	
Religion, % of pop.		cable	0
Muslim	97.9	satellite	93
Non-religious	1.8	Telephone lines per 100 pop.	8.5
Christian	0.2	Mobile telephone subscribers	
Hindu	<0.1	per 100 pop.	99
Jewish	<0.1	Broadband subs per 100 pop.	2.8
Other	<0.1	Internet hosts per 1,000 pop.	0

a 2008

ARGENTINA

Area	2,766,889 sq km	Capital	Buenos Aires
Arable as % of total land	13.9	Currency	Peso (P)

People

Population	40.8m	Life expectancy: men	72.4 yrs
Pop. per sq km	14.7	women	79.9 yrs
Total growth		Adult literacy	97.8%
in pop. 2000–10	9.4%	Fertility rate (per woman)	2.1
Pop. under 15	24.9%	Urban population	92.5%
Pop. over 60	14.7%		per 1,000 pop.
No. of men per 100 women	95.8	Crude birth rate	16.8
Human Development Index	81.1	Crude death rate	7.7

The economy

GDP	P1,842bn	GDP per head	$10,940
GDP	$446bn	GDP per head in purchasing	
Av. ann. growth in real		power parity (USA=100)	33.2
GDP 2006–11	6.8%	Economic freedom index	46.7

Origins of GDP		Components of GDP	
	% of total		% of total
Agriculture	11	Private consumption	60
Industry, of which:	31	Public consumption	15
manufacturing	21	Investment	23
Services	59	Exports	22
		Imports	-20

Structure of employment

	% of total		% of labour force
Agriculture	1	Unemployed 2011	7.2
Industry	24	Av. ann. rate 2000–11	11.9
Services	74		

Energy

	m TOE		
Total output	78.8	Net energy imports as %	
Total consumption	74.6	of energy use	-6
Consumption per head			
kg oil equivalent	1,847		

Inflation and finance

Consumer price		av. ann. increase 2006–11	
inflation 2012	10.0%	Narrow money (M1)	22.4%
Av. ann. inflation 2007–12	9.0%	Broad money	21.4%
Money market rate, Dec. 2012	10.71%		

Exchange rates

	end 2012		2012
P per $	4.86	Effective rates	2005 = 100
P per SDR	7.53	– nominal	...
P per €	6.38	– real	...

Trade

Principal exports		Principal imports	
	$bn fob		*$bn cif*
Manufactures	29.0	Intermediate goods	21.8
Processed agricultural products	28.2	Capital goods	14.0
Primary products	20.2	Fuels	9.4
Fuels	6.6	Consumer goods	8.0
Total incl. others	**84.0**	Total incl. others	**66.7**

Main export destinations		Main origins of imports	
	% of total		*% of total*
Brazil	20.1	Brazil	37.4
China	6.8	United States	16.3
Chile	5.1	China	14.0
United States	5.1	Germany	5.3

Balance of payments, reserves and debt, $bn

Visible exports fob	83.9	Change in reserves	-6.3
Visible imports fob	-70.7	Level of reserves	
Trade balance	13.1	end Dec.	45.9
Invisibles inflows	18.4	No. months of import cover	5.4
Invisibles outflows	-31.4	Official gold holdings, m oz	1.8
Net transfers	-0.5	Foreign debt	114.7
Current account balance	-0.3	– as % of GDP	28.6
– as % of GDP	-0.1	– as % of total exports	122.5
Capital balance	-7.0	Debt service ratio	15
Overall balance	10.9		

Health and education

Health spending, % of GDP	8.1	Education spending, % of GDP	5.8
Doctors per 1,000 pop.	3.2	Enrolment, %: primary	118
Hospital beds per 1,000 pop.	4.5	secondary	90
Improved-water source access,		tertiary	75
% of pop.	97		

Society

No. of households	11.3m	Cost of living, Dec. 2012	
Av. no. per household	3.6	New York = 100	73
Marriages per 1,000 pop.	3.4	Cars per 1,000 pop.	142
Divorces per 1,000 pop.	...	Colour TV households, % with:	
Religion, % of pop.		cable	59.4
Christian	85.2	satellite	13.7
Non-religious	12.2	Telephone lines per 100 pop.	24.9
Other	1.1	Mobile telephone subscribers	
Muslim	1.0	per 100 pop.	134.9
Jewish	0.5	Broadband subs per 100 pop.	10.5
Hindu	<0.1	Internet hosts per 1,000 pop.	275.3

AUSTRALIA

Area	7,682,300 sq km	Capital	Canberra
Arable as % of total land	5.5	Currency	Australian dollar (A$)

People

Population	22.6m	Life expectancy: men	79.9 yrs
Pop. per sq km	2.9	women	84.3 yrs
Total growth		Adult literacy	...
in pop. 2000–10	16.2%	Fertility rate (per woman)	2.0
Pop. under 15	18.9%	Urban population	89.2%
Pop. over 60	19.5%		per 1,000 pop.
No. of men per 100 women	99.3	Crude birth rate	13.5
Human Development Index	93.8	Crude death rate	6.8

The economy

GDP	A$1,399bn	GDP per head	$61,790
GDP	$1,379bn	GDP per head in purchasing	
Av. ann. growth in real		power parity (USA=100)	87.2
GDP 2006–11	2.7%	Economic freedom index	82.6

Origins of GDP		Components of GDP	
	% of total		% of total
Agriculture	2	Private consumption	54
Industry, of which:	20	Public consumption	18
manufacturing	9	Investment	27
Services	78	Exports	21
		Imports	-20

Structure of employment

	% of total		% of labour force
Agriculture	3	Unemployed 2011	5.1
Industry	21	Av. ann. rate 2000–11	5.5
Services	76		

Energy

	m TOE		
Total output	310.6	Net energy imports as %	
Total consumption	124.7	of energy use	-149
Consumption per head,			
kg oil equivalent	5,653		

Inflation and finance

Consumer price		av. ann. increase 2006–11	
inflation 2011	3.4%	Narrow money (M1)	10.2%
Av. ann. inflation 2007–11	3.1%	Broad money	12.0%
Money market rate, Dec. 2012	3.03%	H'hold saving rate, Dec. 2012	10.3%

Exchange rates

	end 2012		2012
A$ per $	0.96	Effective rates	2005 = 100
A$ per SDR	1.48	– nominal	123.7
A$ per €	1.26	– real	128.0

Trade

Principal exports	$bn fob	Principal imports	$bn cif
Coal	48.2	Intermediate & other goods	120.7
Meat & meat products	11.9	Consumption goods	64.1
Wheat	6.3	Capital goods	50.0
Total incl. others	**270.6**	Total	**234.9**

Main export destinations	% of total	Main origins of imports	% of total
China	27.4	China	20.4
Japan	19.3	United States	12.6
South Korea	8.9	Japan	8.7
India	5.8	Singapore	6.9
United States	3.7	Germany	5.1

Balance of payments, reserves and aid, $bn

Visible exports fob	271.6	Overall balance	1.6
Visible imports fob	-242.3	Change in reserves	4.4
Trade balance	29.3	Level of reserves	
Invisibles inflows	93.6	end Dec.	46.7
Invisibles outflows	-156.2	No. months of import cover	1.4
Net transfers	-1.4	Official gold holdings, m oz	2.6
Current account balance	-33.8	Aid given	4.98
– as % of GDP	-2.4	– as % of GDP	0.34
Capital balance	36.8		

Health and education

Health spending, % of GDP	9.0	Education spending, % of GDP	5.1
Doctors per 1,000 pop.	3.9	Enrolment, %: primary	105
Hospital beds per 1,000 pop.	3.9	secondary	131
Improved-water source access,		tertiary	80
% of pop.	100		

Society

No. of households	8.2m	Cost of living, Dec. 2012	
Av. no. per household	2.7	New York = 100	137
Marriages per 1,000 pop.	5.4	Cars per 1,000 pop.	562
Divorces per 1,000 pop.	2.3	Colour TV households, % with:	
Religion, % of pop.		cable	24.8
Christian	67.3	satellite	14.0
Non-religious	24.2	Telephone lines per 100 pop.	46.8
Other	4.2	Mobile telephone subscribers	
Muslim	2.4	per 100 pop.	108.3
Hindu	1.4	Broadband subs per 100 pop.	24.3
Jewish	0.5	Internet hosts per 1,000 pop.	755.8

AUSTRIA

Area	83,855 sq km	Capital	Vienna
Arable as % of total land	16.6	Currency	Euro (€)

People

Population	8.4m	Life expectancy: men	78.4 yrs
Pop. per sq km	100.1	women	83.6 yrs
Total growth		Adult literacy	...
in pop. 2000–10	4.9%	Fertility rate (per woman)	1.4
Pop. under 15	14.7%	Urban population	67.7%
Pop. over 60	23.1%		per 1,000 pop.
No. of men per 100 women	95.3	Crude birth rate	9.0
Human Development Index	89.5	Crude death rate	9.4

The economy

GDP	€301bn	GDP per head	$49,580
GDP	$418bn	GDP per head in purchasing	
Av. ann. growth in real		power parity (USA=100)	87.7
GDP 2006–11	1.2%	Economic freedom index	71.8

Origins of GDP		**Components of GDP**	
	% of total		% of total
Agriculture	2	Private consumption	55
Industry, of which:	29	Public consumption	19
manufacturing	19	Investment	23
Services	69	Exports	57
		Imports	-54

Structure of employment

	% of total		% of labour force
Agriculture	5	Unemployed 2011	4.1
Industry	26	Av. ann. rate 2000–11	4.3
Services	69		

Energy

	m TOE		
Total output	11.8	Net energy imports as %	
Total consumption	33.8	of energy use	65
Consumption per head,			
kg oil equivalent	4,034		

Inflation and finance

Consumer price		av. ann. increase 2006–11	
inflation 2012	2.5%	Euro area:	
Av. ann. inflation 2007–12	2.3%	Narrow money (M1)	5.3%
Deposit rate, h'holds, Dec. 2012	1.15%	Broad money	4.7%
		H'hold saving rate, Dec. 2012	7.7%

Exchange rates

	end 2012		December 2012
€ per $	0.76	Effective rates	2005 = 100
€ per SDR	1.16	– nominal	99.4
		– real	98.7

Trade

Principal exports		Principal imports	
	$bn fob		*$bn cif*
Machinery & transport equip.	65.3	Machinery & transport equip.	60.6
Chemicals & related products	21.4	Chemicals & related products	22.4
Food, drink & tobacco	11.9	Mineral fuels & lubricants	21.3
Raw materials	5.9	Food, drink & tobacco	12.2
Mineral fuels & lubricants	5.8	Raw materials	8.2
Total incl. others	**169.6**	Total incl. others	**182.4**

Main export destinations		Main origins of imports	
	% of total		*% of total*
Germany	32.7	Germany	44.2
Italy	7.9	Italy	7.0
Switzerland	4.5	Switzerland	5.7
France	4.3	Netherlands	4.2
EU27	70.5	EU27	76.9

Balance of payments, reserves and aid, $bn

Visible exports fob	169.9	Overall balance	1.0
Visible imports fob	-175.4	Change in reserves	2.5
Trade balance	-5.5	Level of reserves	
Invisibles inflows	100.4	end Dec.	24.8
Invisibles outflows	-89.9	No. months of import cover	1.1
Net transfers	-2.7	Official gold holdings, m oz	9.0
Current account balance	2.3	Aid given	1.11
– as % of GDP	1.9	– as % of GDP	0.27
Capital balance	-5.0		

Health and education

Health spending, % of GDP	10.6	Education spending, % of GDP	6.0
Doctors per 1,000 pop.	4.9	Enrolment, %: primary	99
Hospital beds per 1,000 pop.	7.6	secondary	99
Improved-water source access,		tertiary	68
% of pop.	100		

Society

No. of households	3.7m	Cost of living, Dec. 2012	
Av. no. per household	2.3	New York = 100	105
Marriages per 1,000 pop.	4.3	Cars per 1,000 pop.	542
Divorces per 1,000 pop.	2.1	Colour TV households, % with:	
Religion, % of pop.		cable	38.7
Christian	80.4	satellite	54.1
Non-religious	13.5	Telephone lines per 100 pop.	40.3
Muslim	5.4	Mobile telephone subscribers	
Other	0.5	per 100 pop.	154.8
Jewish	0.2	Broadband subs per 100 pop.	25.4
Hindu	<0.1	Internet hosts per 1,000 pop.	418.1

BANGLADESH

Area	143,998 sq km	Capital	Dhaka
Arable as % of total land	59.5	Currency	Taka (Tk)

People

Population	150.5m	Life expectancy: men	68.5 yrs
Pop. per sq km	1,045.2	women	70.2 yrs
Total growth		Adult literacy	56.8%
in pop. 2000–10	14.7%	Fertility rate (per woman)	2.2
Pop. under 15	30.9%	Urban population	28.4%
Pop. over 60	6.2%		per 1,000 pop.
No. of men per 100 women	102.6	Crude birth rate	19.5
Human Development Index	51.5	Crude death rate	6.0

The economy

GDP	Tk7,967bn	GDP per head	$740
GDP	$112bn	GDP per head in purchasing	
Av. ann. growth in real		power parity (USA=100)	3.7
GDP 2005–10	6.2%	Economic freedom index	52.6

Origins of GDP		**Components of GDP**	
	% of total		% of total
Agriculture	18	Private consumption	78
Industry, of which:	28	Public consumption	6
manufacturing	18	Investment	25
Services	54	Exports	23
		Imports	-32

Structure of employment

	% of total		% of labour force
Agriculture	...	Unemployed 2009	5.0
Industry	...	Av. ann. rate 2000–09	3.6
Services	...		

Energy

			m TOE
Total output	25.8	Net energy imports as %	
Total consumption	31.1	of energy use	17
Consumption per head,			
kg oil equivalent	209		

Inflation and finance

			av. ann. increase 2006–11
Consumer price			
inflation 2012	8.7%	Narrow money (M1)	16.6%
Av. ann. inflation 2007–12	8.4%	Broad money	17.6%
Deposit rate, July 2012	11.76%		

Exchange rates

	end 2012		2012
		Effective rates	2005 = 100
Tk per $	80.60		
Tk per SDR	122.72	– nominal	...
Tk per €	105.74	– real	...

Trade

Principal exports[a]	$bn fob	Principal imports[a]	$bn cif
Clothing	16.3	Fuels	5.1
Fish & fish products	0.7	Textiles & yarns	3.1
Jute goods	0.7	Capital goods	2.4
Leather	0.5	Cotton	2.4
Total incl. others	**24.1**	Total incl. others	**37.7**

Main export destinations	% of total	Main origins of imports	% of total
United States	19.7	India	18.2
Germany	16.1	China	13.5
United Kingdom	9.5	Kuwait	4.9
France	7.2	Hong Kong	4.0
Italy	4.3	Singapore	4.0

Balance of payments, reserves and debt, $bn

Visible exports fob	24.5	Change in reserves	-2.0
Visible imports fob	-32.6	Level of reserves	
Trade balance	-8.1	end Dec.	9.2
Invisibles inflows	2.6	No. months of import cover	2.8
Invisibles outflows	-6.9	Official gold holdings, m oz	0.4
Net transfers	12.2	Foreign debt	27.0
Current account balance	-0.2	– as % of GDP	15.9
– as % of GDP	0.2	– as % of total exports	78.6
Capital balance	-0.4	Debt service ratio	5
Overall balance	-1.8		

Health and education

Health spending, % of GDP	3.7	Education spending, % of GDP	2.2
Doctors per 1,000 pop.	0.4	Enrolment, %: primary	103
Hospital beds per 1,000 pop.	0.6	secondary	51
Improved-water source access,		tertiary	11
% of pop.	81		

Society

No. of households	36.3m	Cost of living, Dec. 2012	
Av. no. per household	4.2	New York = 100	59
Marriages per 1,000 pop.	...	Cars per 1,000 pop.	3
Divorces per 1,000 pop.	...	Colour TV households, % with:	
Religion, % of pop. of pop.		cable	...
Muslim	89.8	satellite	...
Hindu	9.1	Telephone lines per 100 pop.	0.7
Other	0.9	Mobile telephone subscribers	
Christian	0.2	per 100 pop.	56.1
Jewish	<0.1	Broadband subs per 100 pop.	0.3
Non-religious	<0.1	Internet hosts per 1,000 pop.	0.5

a   Fiscal year ending June 30 2011.

BELGIUM

Area	30,520 sq km	Capital	Brussels
Arable as % of total land	27.6	Currency	Euro (€)

People

Population	10.8m	Life expectancy: men	77.2 yrs
Pop. per sq km	353.9	women	82.8 yrs
Total growth		Adult literacy	...
in pop. 2000–10	5.3%	Fertility rate (per woman)	1.8
Pop. under 15	16.7%	Urban population	97.5%
Pop. over 60	23.4%		per 1,000 pop.
No. of men per 100 women	96	Crude birth rate	11.4
Human Development Index	89.7	Crude death rate	10.3

The economy

GDP	€370bn	GDP per head	$46,610
GDP	$514bn	GDP per head in purchasing	
Av. ann. growth in real		power parity (USA=100)	80.5
GDP 2006–11	1.0%	Economic freedom index	69.2

Origins of GDP		Components of GDP	
	% of total		% of total
Agriculture	1	Private consumption	53
Industry, of which:	22	Public consumption	24
manufacturing	14	Investment	22
Services	78	Exports	84
		Imports	-83

Structure of employment

	% of total		% of labour force
Agriculture	1	Unemployed 2011	7.1
Industry	23	Av. ann. rate 2000–11	7.6
Services	76		

Energy

	m TOE		
Total output	16.0	Net energy imports as %	
Total consumption	60.9	of energy use	74
Consumption per head,			
kg oil equivalent	5,586		

Inflation and finance

Consumer price			av. ann. increase 2006–11
inflation 2012	2.8%	Euro area:	
Av. ann. inflation 2007–12	2.6%	Narrow money (M1)	5.3%
Treasury bill rate, Dec. 2012	-0.01%	Broad money	4.7%
		H'hold saving rate, Dec. 2012	9.7%

Exchange rates

	end 2012		2012
€ per $	0.76	Effective rates	2005 = 100
€ per SDR	1.16	– nominal	101.1
		– real	100.2

Trade

Principal exports		Principal imports	
	$bn fob		*$bn cif*
Chemicals & related products	135.2	Machinery & transport equip.	103.8
Machinery & transport equip.	96.2	Chemicals & related products	103.1
Minerals, fuels & lubricants	50.5	Minerals, fuels & lubricants	74.6
Food, drink & tobacco	38.9	Food, drink & tobacco	33.7
Raw materials	14.4	Raw materials	22.5
Total incl. others	**476.7**	Total incl. others	**466.7**

Main export destinations		Main origins of imports	
	% of total		*% of total*
Germany	18.2	Netherlands	19.6
France	16.4	Germany	14.6
Netherlands	12.2	France	10.5
United Kingdom	7.0	United Kingdom	5.9
EU27	72.0	EU27	67.9

Balance of payments, reserves and aid, $bn

Visible exports fob	324.4	Overall balance	1.5
Visible imports fob	-336.1	Change in reserves	2.3
Trade balance	-11.7	Level of reserves	
Invisibles inflows	172.3	end Dec.	29.1
Invisibles outflows	-158.6	No. months of import cover	0.7
Net transfers	-9.1	Official gold holdings, m oz	7.3
Current account balance	-7.1	Aid given	2.81
– as % of GDP	-1.4	– as % of GDP	0.54
Capital balance	6.5		

Health and education

Health spending, % of GDP	10.6	Education spending, % of GDP	6.6
Doctors per 1,000 pop.	3.8	Enrolment, %: primary	104
Hospital beds per 1,000 pop.	6.5	secondary	111
Improved-water source access,		tertiary	71
% of pop.	100		

Society

No. of households	4.7m	Cost of living, Dec. 2012	
Av. no. per household	2.3	New York = 100	99
Marriages per 1,000 pop.	4.1	Cars per 1,000 pop.	490
Divorces per 1,000 pop.	2.9	Colour TV households, % with:	
Religion, % of pop.		cable	74.3
Christian	64.2	satellite	5.7
Non-religious	29.0	Telephone lines per 100 pop.	43.1
Muslim	5.9	Mobile telephone subscribers	
Other	0.6	per 100 pop.	116.6
Jewish	0.3	Broadband subs per 100 pop.	33.0
Hindu	<0.1	Internet hosts per 1,000 pop.	480.7

BRAZIL

Area	8,511,965 sq km	Capital	Brasilia
Arable as % of total land	8.3	Currency	Real (R)

People

Population	196.7m	Life expectancy: men	70.7 yrs
Pop. per sq km	23.1	women	77.4 yrs
Total growth		Adult literacy	90.3%
in pop. 2000–10	11.8%	Fertility rate (per woman)	1.8
Pop. under 15	25.5%	Urban population	84.6%
Pop. over 60	10.2%		per 1,000 pop.
No. of men per 100 women	96.9	Crude birth rate	15.0
Human Development Index	73.0	Crude death rate	6.4

The economy

GDP	R4,143bn	GDP per head	$12,590
GDP	$2,477bn	GDP per head in purchasing	
Av. ann. growth in real		power parity (USA=100)	24.2
GDP 2006–11	4.2%	Economic freedom index	57.7

Origins of GDP		**Components of GDP**	
	% of total		% of total
Agriculture	5	Private consumption	60
Industry, of which:	28	Public consumption	21
manufacturing	25	Investment	20
Services	67	Exports	12
		Imports	-13

Structure of employment

	% of total		% of labour force
Agriculture	17	Unemployed 2010	8.3
Industry	22	Av. ann. rate 2000–10	8.7
Services	61		

Energy

			m TOE
Total output	246.4	Net energy imports as %	
Total consumption	265.6	of energy use	7
Consumption per head,			
kg oil equivalent	1,363		

Inflation and finance

Consumer price		av. ann. increase 2006–11	
inflation 2012	5.4%	Narrow money (M1)	10.4%
Av. ann. inflation 2007–12	5.5%	Broad money	17.1%
Money market rate, Dec. 2012	6.94%		

Exchange rates

	end 2012		2012
R per $	2.08	Effective rates	2005 = 100
R per sdr	3.14	– nominal	114.3
R per €	2.73	– real	133.0

Trade

Principal exports		Principal imports	
	$bn fob		$bn cif
Primary products	122.5	Intermediate products and raw	
Manufactured products	92.3	materials	102.1
Semi-manufactured products	36.0	Capital goods	47.9
		Consumer goods	40.1
		Fuels and lubricants	36.2
Total incl. others	**256.0**	Total	**236.9**

Main export destinations		Main origins of imports	
	% of total		% of total
China	17.3	United States	15.9
United States	10.1	China	15.2
Argentina	8.9	Argentina	7.8
Netherlands	5.3	Germany	7.1

Balance of payments, reserves and debt, $bn

Visible exports fob	256.0	Change in reserves	63.4
Visible imports fob	-226.2	Level of reserves	
Trade balance	29.8	end Dec.	352.0
Invisibles inflows	49.0	No. months of import cover	11.7
Invisibles outflows	-144.2	Official gold holdings, m oz	1.1
Net transfers	3.0	Foreign debt	404.3
Current account balance	-52.5	– as % of GDP	17.7
– as % of GDP	-2.1	– as % of total exports	147.1
Capital balance	112.4	Debt service ratio	19.0
Overall balance	58.6		

Health and education

Health spending, % of GDP	8.9	Education spending, % of GDP	5.8
Doctors per 1,000 pop.	1.8	Enrolment, %: primary	127
Hospital beds per 1,000 pop.	2.3	secondary	101
Improved-water source access,		tertiary	36
% of pop.	98		

Society

No. of households	56.5m	Cost of living, Dec. 2012	
Av. no. per household	3.4	New York = 100	84
Marriages per 1,000 pop.	5.0	Cars per 1,000 pop.	200
Divorces per 1,000 pop.	0.8	Colour TV households, % with:	
Religion, % of pop.		cable	8.9
Christian	88.9	satellite	4.4
Non-religious	7.9	Telephone lines per 100 pop.	21.9
Other	3.1	Mobile telephone subscribers	
Hindu	<0.1	per 100 pop.	124.3
Jewish	<0.1	Broadband subs per 100 pop.	8.6
Muslim	<0.1	Internet hosts per 1,000 pop.	135.1

BULGARIA

Area	110,994 sq km	Capital	Sofia
Arable as % of total land	29.3	Currency	Lev (BGL)

People

Population	7.4m	Life expectancy: men		70.3 yrs
Pop. per sq km	66.7	women		77.1 yrs
Total growth		Adult literacy		98.4%
in pop. 2000–10	-6.4%	Fertility rate (per woman)		1.6
Pop. under 15	13.5%	Urban population		73.1%
Pop. over 60	24.5%			per 1,000 pop.
No. of men per 100 women	93.6	Crude birth rate		10.0
Human Development Index	78.2	Crude death rate		15.2

The economy

GDP	BGL75.3bn	GDP per head	$7,280
GDP	$53.5bn	GDP per head in purchasing	
Av. ann. growth in real		power parity (USA=100)	31.4
GDP 2007–11	1.8%	Economic freedom index	65.0

Origins of GDP		**Components of GDP**	
	% of total		% of total
Agriculture	6	Private consumption	61
Industry, of which:	31	Public consumption	16
manufacturing	17	Investment	23
Services	63	Exports	67
		Imports	-66

Structure of employment

	% of total		% of labour force
Agriculture	7	Unemployed 2011	11.2
Industry	33	Av. ann. rate 2000–11	11.9
Services	60		

Energy

		m TOE	
Total output	10.6	Net energy imports as %	
Total consumption	17.9	of energy use	41
Consumption per head,			
kg oil equivalent	2,370		

Inflation and finance

Consumer price		av. ann. change 2006–11	
inflation 2012	3.0%	Narrow money (M1)	5.5%
Av. ann. inflation 2007–12	4.9%	Broad money	12.2%
Money market rate, Dec. 2012	0.03%		

Exchange rates

	end 2012		2012
BGL per $	1.49	Effective rates	2005 = 100
BGL per SDR	2.28	– nominal	104.1
BGL per €	1.95	– real	122.7

Trade

Principal exports		Principal imports	
	$bn fob		*$bn cif*
Other metals	3.5	Crude oil & natural gas	5.3
Clothing and footwear	2.1	Chemicals, plastics & rubber	2.2
Chemicals, plastics & rubber	1.2	Machinery & equipment	2.2
Iron & steel	1.2	Textiles	1.5
Total incl. others	**28.1**	Total incl. others	**31.2**

Main export destinations		Main origins of imports	
	% of total		*% of total*
Germany	11.9	Russia	18.3
Romania	9.6	Germany	11.2
Italy	8.3	Italy	7.4
Turkey	8.0	Romania	7.1
EU27	62.2	EU27	59.4

Balance of payments, reserves and debt, $bn

Visible exports fob	28.2	Change in reserves	-0.0
Visible imports fob	-31.2	Level of reserves	
Trade balance	-3.0	end Dec.	17.2
Invisibles inflows	8.4	No. months of import cover	5.3
Invisibles outflows	-7.6	Official gold holdings, m oz	1.3
Net transfers	2.3	Foreign debt	39.9
Current account balance	0.2	– as % of GDP	75.8
– as % of GDP	0.4	– as % of total exports	122.7
Capital balance	-0.5	Debt service ratio	12
Overall balance	0.3	Aid given	0.38
		– as % of GDP	-0.09

Health and education

Health spending, % of GDP	7.3	Education spending, % of GDP	4.1
Doctors per 1,000 pop.	3.8	Enrolment, %: primary	103
Hospital beds per 1,000 pop.	6.5	secondary	89
Improved-water source access,		tertiary	57
% of pop.	100		

Society

No. of households	2.9m	Cost of living, Dec. 2012	
Av. no. per household	2.6	New York = 100	67
Marriages per 1,000 pop.	2.9	Cars per 1,000 pop.	363
Divorces per 1,000 pop.	1.4	Colour TV households, % with:	
Religion, % of pop.		cable	47.3
Christian	82.1	satellite	16.6
Muslim	13.7	Telephone lines per 100 pop.	31.6
Non-religious	4.2	Mobile telephone subscribers	
Hindu	<0.1	per 100 pop.	140.7
Jewish	<0.1	Broadband subs per 100 pop.	16.5
Other	<0.1	Internet hosts per 1,000 pop.	131.9

CAMEROON

Area	475,442 sq km	Capital	Yaoundé
Arable as % of total land	13.1	Currency	CFA franc (CFAfr)

People

Population	20.0m	Life expectancy: men	51.4 yrs
Pop. per sq km	42.0	women	53.6 yrs
Total growth		Adult literacy	70.7%
in pop. 2000–10	25.0%	Fertility rate (per woman)	4.3
Pop. under 15	40.8%	Urban population	52.1%
Pop. over 60	5.4%		per 1,000 pop.
No. of men per 100 women	99.7	Crude birth rate	36.0
Human Development Index	49.5	Crude death rate	13.4

The economy

GDP	CFAfr11,908bn	GDP per head	$1,260
GDP	$25.2bn	GDP per head in purchasing	
Av. ann. growth in real		power parity (USA=100)	4.9
GDP 2006–11	3.1%	Economic freedom index	52.3

Origins of GDP		Components of GDP	
	% of total		% of total
Agriculture	26	Private consumption	69
Industry, of which:	33	Public consumption	15
manufacturing	9	Investment	20
Services	41	Exports	31
		Imports	-35

Structure of employment

	% of total		% of labour force
Agriculture	53	Unemployed 2010	3.8
Industry	13	Av. ann. rate 2000–10	4.7
Services	34		

Energy

	m TOE		
Total output	8.4	Net energy imports as %	
Total consumption	7.1	of energy use	-18
Consumption per head,			
kg oil equivalent	363		

Inflation and finance

Consumer price		av. ann. change 2006–11	
inflation 2011	2.9%	Narrow money (M1)	15.2%
Av. ann. inflation 2007–11	3.1%	Broad money	12.2%
Deposit rate, Dec. 2012	3.25%		

Exchange rates

	end 2012		2012
CFAfr per $	500.00	Effective rates	2005 = 100
CFAfr per SDR	764.10	– nominal	100.5
CFAfr per €	655.95	– real	98.9

Trade

Principal exports[a]		Principal imports[a]	
	$bn fob		*$bn cif*
Oil & petroleum products	2.7	Fuels	1.3
Timber	0.5	Machinery & electrical goods	0.9
Agricultural products	0.4	Grain & cereal products	0.7
Metal products	0.2	Chemicals	0.6
Total incl. others	**4.3**	Total incl. others	**6.2**

Main export destinations		Main origins of imports	
	% of total		*% of total*
Spain	13.3	China	16.9
China	11.4	France	16.8
Netherlands	9.7	Belgium	5.3
Italy	8.8	Italy	4.3

Balance of payments[ab], reserves and debt, $bn

Visible exports fob	4.3	Change in reserves	-0.4
Visible imports fob	-4.6	Level of reserves	
Trade balance	-0.3	end Dec.	3.2
Invisible inflows	1.4	No. months of import cover	4.7
Invisible outflows	-2.0	Official gold holdings, m oz	0
Net transfers	0.1	Foreign debt	3.1
Current account balance	-0.9	– as % of GDP	7
– as % of GDP	-3.8	– as % of total exports	27
Capital balance	-0.4	Debt service ratio	4
Overall balance	0.0		

Health and education

Health spending, % of GDP	5.2	Education spending, % of GDP	3.2
Doctors per 1,000 pop.	0.1	Enrolment, %: primary	119
Hospital beds per 1,000 pop.	1.3	secondary	51
Improved-water source access,		tertiary	12
% of pop.	77		

Society

No. of households	4.1m	Cost of living, Dec. 2012	
Av. no. per household	5.0	New York = 100	...
Marriages per 1,000 pop.	...	Cars per 1,000 pop.	13
Divorces per 1,000 pop.	...	Colour TV households, % with:	
Religion, % of pop.		cable	0.0
Christian	70.3	satellite	2.3
Muslim	18.3	Telephone lines per 100 pop.	3.3
Other	6.0	Mobile telephone subscribers	
Non-religious	5.3	per 100 pop.	52.4
Hindu	<0.1	Broadband subs per 100 pop.	0.0
Jewish	<0.1	Internet hosts per 1,000 pop.	0.5

a 2010
b Estimates.

CANADA

Area[a]	9,970,610 sq km	Capital	Ottawa
Arable as % of total land	4.8	Currency	Canadian dollar (C$)

People

Population	34.3m	Life expectancy: men	78.9 yrs
Pop. per sq km	3.4	women	85.3 yrs
Total growth		Adult literacy	...
in pop. 2000–10	10.9%	Fertility rate (per woman)	1.7
Pop. under 15	16.3%	Urban population	80.7%
Pop. over 60	20.0%		per 1,000 pop.
No. of men per 100 women	98.4	Crude birth rate	11.0
Human Development Index	91.1	Crude death rate	7.7

The economy

GDP	C$1,719bn	GDP per head	$50,340
GDP	$1,736bn	GDP per head in purchasing	
Av. ann. growth in real		power parity (USA=100)	84.0
GDP 2006–11	1.2%	Economic freedom index	79.4

Origins of GDP[b]		Components of GDP	
	% of total		% of total
Agriculture	2	Private consumption	57
Industry, of which:	28	Public consumption	21
manufacturing & mining	...	Investment	23
Services	70	Exports	31
		Imports	-32

Structure of employment

	% of total		% of labour force
Agriculture	2	Unemployed 2011	7.4
Industry	22	Av. ann. rate 2000–11	7.1
Services	76		

Energy

	m TOE		
Total output	397.8	Net energy imports as %	
Total consumption	251.8	of energy use	-58
Consumption per head,			
kg oil equivalent	7,380		

Inflation and finance

Consumer price		av. ann. increase 2006–11	
inflation 2012	1.5%	Narrow money (M1)	10.0%
Av. ann. inflation 2007–12	1.8%	Broad money	7.3%
Money market rate, Dec. 2012	1.00%	H'hold saving rate, Dec. 2012	4.0%

Exchange rates

	end 2012		December 2012
C$ per $	0.99	Effective rates	2005 = 100
C$ per SDR	1.53	– nominal	118.3
C$ per €	1.30	– real	113.7

Trade

Principal exports	$bn fob	Principal imports	$bn cif
Energy products	104.5	Consumer goods	90.3
Motor vehicles & parts	60.2	Motor vehicles & parts	74.8
Metal & mineral products	59.6	Electronic & electrical equip.	55.7
Consumer goods	50.3	Energy products	46.7
Chemicals, plastics & rubber products	36.2	Industrial machinery & equip.	42.7
Total incl. others	**461.4**	Total incl. others	**460.4**

Main export destinations	% of total	Main origins of imports	% of total
United States	73.7	United States	49.5
United Kingdom	4.2	China	10.8
China	3.7	Mexico	5.5
Japan	2.4	Japan	2.9
EU27	8.9	EU 27	11.4

Balance of payments, reserves and aid, $bn

Visible exports fob	461.2	Overall balance	7.9
Visible imports fob	-460.5	Change in reserves	8.7
Trade balance	0.7	Level of reserves	
Invisibles inflows	152.4	end Dec.	65.8
Invisibles outflows	-202.5	No. months of import cover	1.2
Net transfers	-3.5	Official gold holdings, m oz	0.1
Current account balance	-53.0	Aid given	5.46
– as % of GDP	-3.1	– as % of GDP	0.32
Capital balance	65.6		

Health and education

Health spending, % of GDP	11.2	Education spending, % of GDP	5.5
Doctors per 1,000 pop.	2.1	Enrolment, %: primary	100
Hospital beds per 1,000 pop.	3.2	secondary	101
Improved-water source access, % of pop.	100	tertiary	62

Society

No. of households	13.2m	Cost of living, Dec. 2012	
Av. no. per household	2.6	New York = 100	106
Marriages per 1,000 pop.	4.6	Cars per 1,000 pop.	410
Divorces per 1,000 pop.	2.2	Colour TV households, % with:	
Religion, % of pop.		cable	65.7
Christian	69.0	satellite	23.2
Non-religious	23.7	Telephone lines per 100 pop.	53.0
Other	2.8	Mobile telephone subscribers	
Muslim	2.1	per 100 pop.	79.7
Hindu	1.4	Broadband subs per 100 pop.	31.8
Jewish	1.0	Internet hosts per 1,000 pop.	254.9

a Including freshwater. b 2009

CHILE

Area	756,945 sq km	Capital	Santiago
Arable as % of total land	1.7	Currency	Chilean peso (Ps)

People

Population	17.3m	Life expectancy: men		76.2 yrs
Pop. per sq km	22.9	women		82.4 yrs
Total growth		Adult literacy		98.6%
in pop. 2000–10	11.0%	Fertility rate (per woman)		1.8
Pop. under 15	22.3%	Urban population		89.2%
Pop. over 60	13.2%			per 1,000 pop.
No. of men per 100 women	97.8	Crude birth rate		14.0
Human Development Index	81.9	Crude death rate		5.7

The economy

GDP	120.2trn pesos	GDP per head	$14,390
GDP	$249bn	GDP per head in purchasing	
Av. ann. growth in real		power parity (USA=100)	35.9
GDP 2006–11	3.8%	Economic freedom index	79.0

Origins of GDP		Components of GDP	
	% of total		% of total
Agriculture	3	Private consumption	60
Industry, of which:	39	Public consumption	12
manufacturing	12	Investment	25
Services	57	Exports	38
		Imports	-35

Structure of employment

	% of total		% of labour force
Agriculture	11	Unemployed 2011	7.1
Industry	23	Av. ann. rate 2000–11	7.7
Services	66		

Energy

	m TOE		
Total output	9.2	Net energy imports as %	
Total consumption	30.9	of energy use	70
Consumption per head,			
kg oil equivalent	1,867		

Inflation and finance

Consumer price		av. ann. increase 2006–11	
inflation 2012	3.0%	Narrow money (M1)	15.4%
Av. ann. inflation 2007–12	3.6%	Broad money	8.5%
Money market rate, Dec. 2012	4.99%	H'hold saving rate, Dec. 2012	6.5%

Exchange rates

	end 2012		2012
Ps per $	477.22	Effective rates	2005 = 100
Ps per SDR	753.57	– nominal	110.2
Ps per €	626.06	– real	113.6

Trade

Principal exports		Principal imports	
	$bn fob		*$bn cif*
Copper	43.6	Intermediate goods	39.4
Fresh fruit	4.1	Consumer goods	16.0
Paper products	3.7	Capital goods	11.9
Total incl. others	**81.7**	**Total incl. others**	**74.5**

Main export destinations		Main origins of imports	
	% of total		*% of total*
China	21.9	United States	19.9
United States	11.0	China	17.0
Japan	10.8	Brazil	8.4
Brazil	5.4	Argentina	6.4
South Korea	5.3	Japan	4.0

Balance of payments, reserves and debt, $bn

Visible exports fob	81.4	Change in reserves	14.1
Visible imports fob	-70.6	Level of reserves	
Trade balance	10.8	end Dec.	41.9
Invisibles inflows	20.1	No. months of import cover	4.7
Invisibles outflows	-36.5	Official gold holdings, m oz	0.0
Net transfers	2.4	Foreign debt	96.2
Current account balance	-3.2	– as % of GDP	43
– as % of GDP	-1.3	– as % of total exports	99
Capital balance	18.1	Debt service ratio	15
Overall balance	14.2		

Health and education

Health spending, % of GDP	7.5	Education spending, % of GDP	4.1
Doctors per 1,000 pop.	1.0	Enrolment, %: primary	103
Hospital beds per 1,000 pop.	2.0	secondary	89
Improved-water source access,		tertiary	66
% of pop.	96		

Society

No. of households	4.9m	Cost of living, Dec. 2012	
Av. no. per household	3.5	New York = 100	81
Marriages per 1,000 pop.	3.3	Cars per 1,000 pop.	131
Divorces per 1,000 pop.	0.2	Colour TV households, % with:	
Religion, % of pop.		cable	33.6
Christian	89.4	satellite	5.1
Non-religious	8.6	Telephone lines per 100 pop.	19.5
Other	1.9	Mobile telephone subscribers	
Jewish	0.1	per 100 pop.	129.7
Hindu	<0.1	Broadband subs per 100 pop.	11.6
Muslim	<0.1	Internet hosts per 1,000 pop.	124.4

CHINA

Area	9,560,900 sq km	Capital	Beijing
Arable as % of total land	11.9	Currency	Yuan

People

Population	1,347.6m	Life expectancy: men	72.1 yrs
Pop. per sq km	140.9	women	75.6 yrs
Total growth		Adult literacy	94.3%
in pop. 2000–10	5.7%	Fertility rate (per woman)	1.6
Pop. under 15	19.9%	Urban population	50.6%
Pop. over 60	12.3%		per 1,000 pop.
No. of men per 100 women	108.0	Crude birth rate	11.9
Human Development Index	69.9	Crude death rate	7.5

The economy

GDP	Yuan47.2trn	GDP per head	$5,450
GDP	$7,319bn	GDP per head in purchasing	
Av. ann. growth in real		power parity (USA=100)	17.5
GDP 2006–11	10.5%	Economic freedom index	51.9

Origins of GDP		**Components of GDP**	
	% of total		% of total
Agriculture	10	Private consumption	34
Industry, of which:	47	Public consumption	13
manufacturing	30	Investment	48
Services	43	Exports	31
		Imports	-27

Structure of employment

	% of total		% of labour force
Agriculture	37	Unemployed 2011	4.1
Industry	29	Av. ann. rate 2000–11	4.0
Services	34		

Energy

	m TOE		
Total output	2,209.0	Net energy imports as %	
Total consumption	2,417.1	of energy use	9
Consumption per head,			
kg oil equivalent	1,807		

Inflation and finance

		av. ann. increase 2006–11	
Consumer price			
inflation 2012	2.7%	Narrow money (M1)	18.1%
Av. ann. inflation 2007–12	3.3%	Broad money	19.8%
Deposit rate, Dec. 2012	3.00%		

Exchange rates

	end 2012		2012
Yuan per $	6.29	Effective rates	2005 = 100
Yuan per SDR	9.67	– nominal	119.6
Yuan per €	8.25	– real	128.9

Trade

Principal exports		Principal imports	
	$bn fob		$bn cif
Electrical goods	217.9	Electrical machinery	287.3
Telecoms equipment	216.8	Petroleum & products	237.9
Office machinery	210.4	Metal ores & scrap	178.0
Clothing & apparel	153.8	Professional instruments	82.4
Total incl. others	**1,898.5**	Total incl. others	**1,743.0**

Main export destinations		Main origins of imports	
	% of total		% of total
United States	17.1	Japan	11.2
Hong Kong	14.1	South Korea	9.3
Japan	7.8	Taiwan	7.2
South Korea	4.4	United States	6.8
EU27	18.8	EU27	12.1

Balance of payments, reserves and debt, $bn

Visible exports fob	1,812	Change in reserves	341
Visible imports fob	-1,570	Level of reserves	
Trade balance	242	end Dec.	3,255
Invisibles inflows	330	No. months of import cover	19.9
Invisibles outflows	-396	Official gold holdings, m oz	33.9
Net transfers	25	Foreign debt	685.4
Current account balance	202	– as % of GDP	11
– as % of GDP	2.8	– as % of total exports	37
Capital balance	221	Debt service ratio	4
Overall balance	388		

Health and education

Health spending, % of GDP	5.2	Education spending, % of GDP	...
Doctors per 1,000 pop.	1.8	Enrolment, %: primary	113
Hospital beds per 1,000 pop.	3.8	secondary	81
Improved-water source access,		tertiary	27
% of pop.	91		

Society

No. of households	427.5m	Cost of living, Dec. 2012	
Av. no. per household	3.1	New York = 100	88
Marriages per 1,000 pop.	8.0	Cars per 1,000 pop.	58
Divorces per 1,000 pop.	2.0	Colour TV households, % with:	
Religion, % of pop.		cable	43.6
Non-religious	52.2	satellite	0.0
Other	22.7	Telephone lines per 100 pop.	21.2
Buddhist	18.2	Mobile telephone subscribers	
Christian	5.1	per 100 pop.	73.2
Muslim	1.8	Broadband subs per 100 pop.	11.6
Jewish	<0.1	Internet hosts per 1,000 pop.	15.3

Note: Data excludes Special Administrative Regions ie, Hong Kong and Macau.
a 2009

COLOMBIA

Area	1,141,748 sq km	Capital	Bogota
Arable as % of total land	1.6	Currency	Colombian peso (peso)

People

Population	46.9m	Life expectancy: men	70.4 yrs
Pop. per sq km	41.0	women	77.7 yrs
Total growth		Adult literacy	93.4%
in pop. 2000–10	16.4%	Fertility rate (per woman)	2.3
Pop. under 15	28.6%	Urban population	75.3%
Pop. over 60	8.6%		per 1,000 pop.
No. of men per 100 women	96.8	Crude birth rate	18.9
Human Development Index	71.9	Crude death rate	5.5

The economy

GDP	616trn pesos	GDP per head	$7,100
GDP	$333bn	GDP per head in purchasing	
Av. ann. growth in real		power parity (USA=100)	20.9
GDP 2006–11	4.5%	Economic freedom index	69.6

Origins of GDP		Components of GDP	
	% of total		% of total
Agriculture	7	Private consumption	62
Industry, of which:	38	Public consumption	16
manufacturing	14	Investment	23
Services	55	Exports	19
		Imports	-20

Structure of employment

	% of total		% of labour force
Agriculture	18	Unemployed 2010	11.6
Industry	20	Av. ann. rate 2000–10	13.7
Services	62		

Energy

	m TOE		
Total output	105.5	Net energy imports as %	
Total consumption	32.2	of energy use	-227
Consumption per head,			
kg oil equivalent	696		

Inflation and finance

Consumer price		av. ann. increase 2006–11	
inflation 2012	3.2%	Narrow money (M1)	11.1%
Av. ann. inflation 2007–12	4.0%	Broad money	14.8%
Money market rate, Dec. 2012	4.49%		

Exchange rates

	end 2012		2012
Peso per $	1,797	Effective rates	2005 = 100
Peso per SDR	2,723	– nominal	131.3
Peso per €	2,357	– real	127.4

Trade

Principal exports		Principal imports	
	$bn fob		*$bn cif*
Petroleum & products	28.4	Intermediate goods &	
Coal	8.4	raw materials	21.2
Coffee	2.6	Capital goods	19.0
Nickel	0.8	Consumer goods	10.3
Total incl. others	**56.9**	Total	**54.2**

Main export destinations		Main origins of imports	
	% of total		*% of total*
United States	37.9	United States	29.0
Netherlands	4.2	China	11.9
China	3.8	Mexico	8.0
Ecuador	3.6	Brazil	5.2

Balance of payments, reserves and debt, $bn

Visible exports fob	57.6	Change in reserves	2.9
Visible imports fob	-52.0	Level of reserves	
Trade balance	5.5	end Dec.	31.0
Invisibles inflows	7.1	No. months of import cover	4.7
Invisibles outflows	-27.5	Official gold holdings, m oz	0.3
Net transfers	4.9	Foreign debt	76.9
Current account balance	-10.0	– as % of GDP	25
– as % of GDP	-3.0	– as % of total exports	133
Capital balance	13.7	Debt service ratio	16
Overall balance	3.7		

Health and education

Health spending, % of GDP	6.1	Education spending, % of GDP	4.5
Doctors per 1,000 pop.	...	Enrolment, %: primary	112
Hospital beds per 1,000 pop.	1.4	secondary	97
Improved-water source access,		tertiary	43
% of pop.	92		

Society

No. of households	12.7m	Cost of living, Dec. 2012	
Av. no. per household	3.7	New York = 100	89
Marriages per 1,000 pop.	3.1	Cars per 1,000 pop.	43
Divorces per 1,000 pop.	...	Colour TV households, % with:	
Religion, % of pop.		cable	56.4
Christian	92.5	satellite	7.3
Non-religious	6.6	Telephone lines per 100 pop.	15.2
Other	0.8	Mobile telephone subscribers	
Hindu	<0.1	per 100 pop.	98.5
Jewish	<0.1	Broadband subs per 100 pop.	6.9
Muslim	<0.1	Internet hosts per 1,000 pop.	94.0

CÔTE D'IVOIRE

Area	322,463 sq km	Capital	Abidjan/Yamoussoukro
Arable as % of total land	9.1	Currency	CFA franc (CFAfr)

People

Population	20.2m	Life expectancy:	men	55.3 yrs
Pop. per sq km	62.6		women	57.7 yrs
Total growth		Adult literacy		56.2%
in pop. 2000–10	19.0%	Fertility rate (per woman)		4.2
Pop. under 15	40.4%	Urban population		51.3%
Pop. over 60	6.1%			per 1,000 pop.
No. of men per 100 women	103.9	Crude birth rate		34.0
Human Development Index	43.2	Crude death rate		11.2

The economy

GDP	CFAfr11,360bn	GDP per head	$1,200
GDP	$24.1bn	GDP per head in purchasing	
Av. ann. growth in real		power parity (USA=100)	3.7
GDP 2006–11	1.0%	Economic freedom index	54.1

Origins of GDP		Components of GDP	
	% of total		% of total
Agriculture	24	Private consumption	67
Industry, of which:	30	Public consumption	14
manufacturing	21	Investment	2
Services	45	Exports	55
		Imports	-38

Structure of employment

	% of total		% of labour force
Agriculture	...	Unemployed 2011	...
Industry	...	Av. ann. rate 2000–11	...
Services	...		

Energy

	m TOE		
Total output	10.4	Net energy imports as %	
Total consumption	9.6	of energy use	-9
Consumption per head,			
kg oil equivalent	485		

Inflation and finance

Consumer price		av. ann. change 2006–11	
inflation 2012	1.3%	Narrow money (M1)	15.2%
Av. ann. inflation 2007–12	3.0%	Broad money	14.9%
Money market rate, Dec. 2012	3.00%		

Exchange rates

	end 2012		2012
		Effective rates	2005 = 100
CFAfr per $	500.00		
CFAfr per SDR	764.10	– nominal	99.2
CFAfr per €	655.95	– real	100.8

Trade

Principal exports[a]	$bn fob	Principal imports[a]	$bn cif
Petroleum products	3.0	Capital equipment & raw	3.0
Cocoa beans & products	2.7	materials	
Timber	0.3	Fuel & lubricants	1.8
Coffee & products	0.2	Foodstuffs	1.2
Total incl. others	**10.5**	Total incl. others	**7.4**

Main export destinations	% of total	Main origins of imports	% of total
Netherlands	11.6	Nigeria	35.6
United States	11.5	France	9.9
Germany	7.3	China	5.6
Canada	6.0	Thailand	5.4
Nigeria	6.0	Colombia	3.5

Balance of payments[a], reserves and debt, $bn

Visible exports fob	11.4	Change in reserves	0.7
Visible imports fob	-7.8	Level of reserves	
Trade balance	3.6	end Dec.	4.3
Invisibles inflows	1.4	No. months of import cover	4.3
Invisibles outflows	-4.1	Official gold holdings, m oz	0.0
Net transfers	-0.4	Foreign debt	12.0
Current account balance	0.5	– as % of GDP	55
– as % of GDP	2.0	– as % of total exports	99
Capital balance	1.0	Debt service ratio	10
Overall balance	1.4		

Health and education

Health spending, % of GDP	6.8	Education spending, % of GDP	4.6
Doctors per 1,000 pop.	0.1	Enrolment, %: primary	88
Hospital beds per 1,000 pop.	...	secondary	...
Improved-water source access,		tertiary	8
% of pop.	80		

Society

No. of households	3.7m	Cost of living, Dec. 2012	
Av. no. per household	5.5	New York = 100	70
Marriages per 1,000 pop.	...	Cars per 1,000 pop.	16
Divorces per 1,000 pop.	...	Colour TV households, % with:	
Religion, % of pop.		cable	...
Christian	...	satellite	...
Hindu	...	Telephone lines per 100 pop.	1.3
Other	...	Mobile telephone subscribers	
Muslim	...	per 100 pop.	86.1
Jewish	...	Broadband subs per 100 pop.	0.3
Non-religious	...	Internet hosts per 1,000 pop.	0.5

a 2010

CZECH REPUBLIC

Area	78,864 sq km	Capital	Prague
Arable as % of total land	41.1	Currency	Koruna (Kc)

People

Population	10.5m	Life expectancy:	men	74.7 yrs
Pop. per sq km	133.1		women	81.0 yrs
Total growth		Adult literacy		...
in pop. 2000–10	2.4%	Fertility rate (per woman)		1.5
Pop. under 15	14.1%	Urban population		73.4%
Pop. over 60	22.2%			*per 1,000 pop.*
No. of men per 100 women	96.3	Crude birth rate		10.0
Human Development Index	87.3	Crude death rate		10.3

The economy

GDP	Kc3,841bn	GDP per head	$20,680
GDP	$217bn	GDP per head in purchasing	
Av. ann. growth in real		power parity (USA=100)	54.7
GDP 2006–11	1.7%	Economic freedom index	70.9

Origins of GDP		**Components of GDP**	
	% of total		*% of total*
Agriculture	2	Private consumption	51
Industry, of which:	36	Public consumption	21
manufacturing	24	Investment	25
Services	62	Exports	73
		Imports	-69

Structure of employment

	% of total		*% of labour force*
Agriculture	3	Unemployed 2011	6.7
Industry	38	Av. ann. rate 2000–11	7.1
Services	59		

Energy

	m TOE		
Total output	31.6	Net energy imports as %	
Total consumption	44.1	of energy use	28
Consumption per head,			
kg oil equivalent	4,193		

Inflation and finance

Consumer price		*av. ann. increase 2006–11*	
inflation 2012	3.3%	Narrow money (M1)	10.1%
Av. ann. inflation 2007–12	2.8%	Broad money	6.7%
Money market rate, Dec. 2012	0.50%	H'hold saving rate, Dec. 2012	7.9%

Exchange rates

	end 2012		*2012*
Kc per $	19.23	Effective rates	*2005 = 100*
Kc per SDR	29.29	– nominal	117.3
Kc per €	25.23	– real	120.6

Trade

Principal exports		Principal imports	
	$bn fob		$bn cif
Machinery & transport equip.	89.6	Machinery & transport equip.	63.9
Semi-manufactures	29.2	Semi-manufactures	27.5
Chemicals	10.6	Chemicals	17.2
Raw materials & fuels	5.9	Raw materials & fuels	16.4
Total incl. others	**162.9**	Total incl. others	**152.1**

Main export destinations		Main origins of imports	
	% of total		% of total
Germany	32.0	Germany	29.4
Slovakia	8.9	China	7.5
Poland	6.2	Poland	7.1
France	5.4	Slovakia	7.0
EU27	83.1	EU27	74.5

Balance of payments, reserves and debt, $bn

Visible exports fob	131.4	Change in reserves	-2.2
Visible imports fob	-127.0	Level of reserves	
Trade balance	4.4	end Dec.	40.3
Invisibles inflows	30.7	No. months of import cover	2.9
Invisibles outflows	-40.3	Official gold holdings, m oz	0.4
Net transfers	-1.1	Foreign debt	93.9
Current account balance	-6.3	– as % of GDP	43
– as % of GDP	-2.9	– as % of total exports	57
Capital balance	5.9	Debt service ratio	11
Overall balance	-1.0	Aid given	0.02
		– as % of GDP	0.12

Health and education

Health spending, % of GDP	7.4	Education spending, % of GDP	4.2
Doctors per 1,000 pop.	3.7	Enrolment, %: primary	106
Hospital beds per 1,000 pop.	7.0	secondary	90
Improved-water source access,		tertiary	64
% of pop.	100		

Society

No. of households	4.6m	Cost of living, Dec. 2012	
Av. no. per household	2.3	New York = 100	83
Marriages per 1,000 pop.	4.3	Cars per 1,000 pop.	439
Divorces per 1,000 pop.	2.7	Colour TV households, % with:	
Religion, % of pop.		cable	24.3
Non-religious	76.4	satellite	26.5
Christian	23.3	Telephone lines per 100 pop.	21.7
Other	0.2	Mobile telephone subscribers	
Hindu	<0.1	per 100 pop.	123.4
Jewish	<0.1	Broadband subs per 100 pop.	15.8
Muslim	<0.1	Internet hosts per 1,000 pop.	395.1

DENMARK

Area	43,075 sq km	Capital	Copenhagen
Arable as % of total land	57.1	Currency	Danish krone (DKr)

People

Population	5.6m	Life expectancy: men		76.7 yrs
Pop. per sq km	130.0		women	87.4 yrs
Total growth		Adult literacy		...
in pop. 2000–10	3.9%	Fertility rate (per woman)		1.9
Pop. under 15	18.0%	Urban population		86.9%
Pop. over 60	23.4%			per 1,000 pop.
No. of men per 100 women	98.3	Crude birth rate		11.0
Human Development Index	90.1	Crude death rate		10.1

The economy

GDP	DKr1,792bn	GDP per head	$59,890
GDP	$334bn	GDP per head in purchasing	
Av. ann. growth in real		power parity (USA=100)	85.1
GDP 2006–11	-0.5%	Economic freedom index	76.1

Origins of GDP		Components of GDP	
	% of total		% of total
Agriculture	1	Private consumption	49
Industry, of which:	22	Public consumption	28
manufacturing	12	Investment	18
Services	77	Exports	53
		Imports	-48

Structure of employment

	% of total		% of labour force
Agriculture	2	Unemployed 2011	7.6
Industry	20	Av. ann. rate 2000–11	5.2
Services	78		

Energy

	m TOE		
Total output	23.3	Net energy imports as %	
Total consumption	19.3	of energy use	-21
Consumption per head,			
kg oil equivalent	3,470		

Inflation and finance

Consumer price		av. ann. increase 2006–11	
inflation 2012	2.4%	Narrow money (M1)	2.1%
Av. ann. inflation 2007–12	2.4%	Broad money	5.9%
Money market rate, Sep. 2012	-0.19%	H'hold saving rate, Dec. 2012	-2.3%

Exchange rates

	end 2012		2012
DKr per $	5.69	Effective rates	2005 = 100
DKr per SDR	8.70	– nominal	98.7
DKr per €	7.46	– real	98.7

Trade

Principal exports		Principal imports	
	$bn fob		*$bn cif*
Machinery & transport equip.	27.3	Machinery & transport equip.	27.8
Food, drink & tobacco	19.7	Food, drink & tobacco	12.2
Chemicals & related products	17.4	Chemicals & related products	11.0
Minerals, fuels & lubricants	11.0	Minerals, fuels & lubricants	8.8
Total incl. others	**111.3**	Total incl. others	**95.7**

Main export destinations		Main origins of imports	
	% of total		*% of total*
Germany	16.6	Germany	20.9
Sweden	13.0	Sweden	13.7
United Kingdom	9.7	Netherlands	7.2
Norway	5.6	United Kingdom	6.4
United States	5.4	China	6.3
EU27	65.2	EU27	70.5

Balance of payments, reserves and aid, $bn

Visible exports fob	110.6	Overall balance	10.6
Visible imports fob	-100.3	Change in reserves	8.4
Trade balance	10.3	Level of reserves	
Invisibles inflows	96.4	end Dec.	85.0
Invisibles outflows	-81.9	No. months of import cover	5.6
Net transfers	-5.9	Official gold holdings, m oz	2.1
Current account balance	18.9	Aid given	2.93
– as % of GDP	5.7	– as % of GDP	0.85
Capital balance	-4.3		

Health and education

Health spending, % of GDP	11.2	Education spending, % of GDP	8.7
Doctors per 1,000 pop.	3.4	Enrolment, %: primary	99
Hospital beds per 1,000 pop.	3.5	secondary	119
Improved-water source access,		tertiary	74
% of pop.	100		

Society

No. of households	2.6m	Cost of living, Dec. 2012	
Av. no. per household	2.2	New York = 100	114
Marriages per 1,000 pop.	4.9	Cars per 1,000 pop.	395
Divorces per 1,000 pop.	2.6	Colour TV households, % with:	
Religion, % of pop.		cable	58.7
Christian	83.5	satellite	11.4
Non-religious	11.8	Telephone lines per 100 pop.	45.1
Muslim	4.1	Mobile telephone subscribers	
Hindu	0.4	per 100 pop.	128.5
Other	0.2	Broadband subs per 100 pop.	37.6
Jewish	<0.1	Internet hosts per 1,000 pop.	767.4

EGYPT

Area	1,000,250 sq km	Capital	Cairo
Arable as % of total land	2.9	Currency	Egyptian pound (£E)

People

Population	82.5m	Life expectancy: men	71.6 yrs
Pop. per sq km	82.5	women	75.5 yrs
Total growth		Adult literacy	72.0%
in pop. 2000–10	19.9%	Fertility rate (per woman)	2.6
Pop. under 15	32.1%	Urban population	43.5%
Pop. over 60	7.5%		per 1,000 pop.
No. of men per 100 women	100.9	Crude birth rate	22.3
Human Development Index	66.2	Crude death rate	5.1

The economy

GDP	£E1,366bn	GDP per head	$2,780
GDP	$230bn	GDP per head in purchasing	
Av. ann. growth in real		power parity (USA=100)	13.1
GDP 2006–11	5.1%	Economic freedom index	54.8

Origins of GDP		Components of GDP	
	% of total		% of total
Agriculture	14	Private consumption	76
Industry, of which:	37	Public consumption	11
manufacturing	15	Investment	20
Services	49	Exports	23
		Imports	-30

Structure of employment

	% of total		% of labour force
Agriculture	28	Unemployed 2010	9.0
Industry	25	Av. ann. rate 2000–10	9.9
Services	47		

Energy

	m TOE		
Total output	88.4	Net energy imports as %	
Total consumption	73.3	of energy use	-21
Consumption per head,			
kg oil equivalent	903		

Inflation and finance

Consumer price		av. ann. increase 2006–11	
inflation 2012	7.1%	Narrow money (M1)	16.1%
Av. ann. inflation 2007–12	11.6%	Broad money	11.6%
Treasury bill rate, Dec. 2012	12.96%		

Exchange rates

	end 2012		2012
£E per $	6.31	Effective rates	2005 = 100
£E per SDR	9.69	– nominal	...
£E per €	8.28	– real	...

Trade

Principal exports[a]		Principal imports[a]	
	$bn fob		$bn cif
Petroleum & products	13.9	Intermediate goods	16.2
Finished goods incl. textiles	10.6	Consumer goods	12.6
Semi-finished products	2.1	Capital goods	10.5
Iron & steel	0.4	Fuels	6.2
Total incl. others	**27.9**	Total incl. others	**56.1**

Main export destinations		Main origins of imports	
	% of total		% of total
Italy	8.8	China	11.5
Germany	5.5	United States	9.8
United States	5.5	Italy	5.6
India	5.2	Germany	4.9

Balance of payments, reserves and debt, $bn

Visible exports fob	27.9	Change in reserves	-18.4
Visible imports fob	-47.3	Level of reserves	
Trade balance	-19.4	end Dec.	18.6
Invisibles inflows	19.5	No. months of import cover	3.3
Invisibles outflows	-20.8	Official gold holdings, m oz	2.4
Net transfers	15.2	Foreign debt	35.0
Current account balance	-5.5	– as % of GDP	13
– as % of GDP	-2.4	– as % of total exports	58
Capital balance	-11.4	Debt service ratio	7
Overall balance	-19.7		

Health and education

Health spending, % of GDP	4.9	Education spending, % of GDP	3.8
Doctors per 1,000 pop.	2.8	Enrolment, %: primary	106
Hospital beds per 1,000 pop.	1.7	secondary	72
Improved-water source access,		tertiary	32
% of pop.	99		

Society

No. of households	20.1m	Cost of living, Dec. 2012	
Av. no. per household	4.0	New York = 100	67
Marriages per 1,000 pop.	11.0	Cars per 1,000 pop.	42
Divorces per 1,000 pop.	1.9	Colour TV households, % with:	
Religion, % of pop.		cable	0.0
Muslim	94.9	satellite	70.1
Christian	5.1	Telephone lines per 100 pop.	10.6
Hindu	<0.1	Mobile telephone subscribers	
Jewish	<0.1	per 100 pop.	101.1
Non-religious	<0.1	Broadband subs per 100 pop.	2.2
Other	<0.1	Internet hosts per 1,000 pop.	2.4

a Year ending June 30, 2011.

ESTONIA

Area	45,200 sq km	Capital	Tallinn
Arable as % of total land	15.2	Currency	Euro (€)

People

Population	1.3m	Life expectancy: men		69.8 yrs
Pop. per sq km	29.7	women		80.0 yrs
Total growth		Adult literacy		99.8%
in pop. 2000–10	-2.2%	Fertility rate (per woman)		1.7
Pop. under 15	15.4%	Urban population		69.5%
Pop. over 60	22.6%			per 1,000 pop.
No. of men per 100 women	85.5	Crude birth rate		11.0
Human Development Index	84.6	Crude death rate		12.7

The economy

GDP	€16.0bn	GDP per head	$16,530
GDP	$22.2bn	GDP per head in purchasing	
Av. ann. growth in real		power parity (USA=100)	45.7
GDP 2006–11	-0.2%	Economic freedom index	75.3

Origins of GDP		Components of GDP	
	% of total		% of total
Agriculture	4	Private consumption	52
Industry, of which:	29	Public consumption	20
manufacturing	17	Investment	25
Services	68	Exports	92
		Imports	-88

Structure of employment

	% of total		% of labour force
Agriculture	5	Unemployed 2011	12.5
Industry	32	Av. ann. rate 2000–11	10.2
Services	63		

Energy

	m TOE		
Total output	4.9	Net energy imports as %	
Total consumption	5.6	of energy use	11
Consumption per head,			
kg oil equivalent	4,155		

Inflation and finance

Consumer price		av. ann. increase 2006–11	
inflation 2012	3.9%	Euro area:	
Av. ann. inflation 2007–12	4.4%	Narrow money (M1)	5.3%
Deposit rate, h'holds, Dec. 2012	0.46%	Broad money (M2)	4.7%
		H'hold saving rate, Dec. 2012	2.3%

Exchange rates

	end 2012		2012
€ per $	0.76	Effective rates	2005 = 100
€ per SDR	1.16	– nominal	...
		– real	...

Trade

Principal exports		Principal imports	
	$bn fob		$bn cif
Machinery & equipment	4.6	Machinery & equipment	4.8
Mineral products	2.9	Mineral products	3.2
Foodstuffs	1.4	Chemicals	2.2
Non-precious metals & products	1.4	Foodstuffs	1.7
Total incl. others	**16.7**	Total incl. others	**17.7**

Main export destinations		Main origins of imports	
	% of total		% of total
Sweden	15.6	Finland	12.5
Finland	15.0	Latvia	10.8
Russia	11.0	Sweden	10.6
Latvia	8.0	Germany	10.2
Germany	4.5	Russia	8.3
EU27	66.3	EU27	78.5

Balance of payments, reserves and debt, $bn

Visible exports fob	14.5	Change in reserves	-2.4
Visible imports fob	-15.2	Level of reserves	
Trade balance	-0.7	end Dec.	0.2
Invisibles inflows	7.0	No. months of import cover	0.1
Invisibles outflows	-6.2	Official gold holdings, m oz	0.0
Net transfers	0.3	Foreign debt	25.0
Current account balance	0.5	– as % of GDP	112
– as % of GDP	2.2	– as % of total exports	106
Capital balance	-0.4	Debt service ratio	11
Overall balance	0.0	Aid given	0.14
		– as % of GDP	0.11

Health and education

Health spending, % of GDP	6.0	Education spending, % of GDP	5.7
Doctors per 1,000 pop.	3.3	Enrolment, %: primary	99
Hospital beds per 1,000 pop.	5.3	secondary	107
Improved-water source access,		tertiary	64
% of pop.	98		

Society

No. of households	0.6m	Cost of living, Dec. 2012	
Av. no. per household	2.3	New York = 100	...
Marriages per 1,000 pop.	4.1	Cars per 1,000 pop.	417
Divorces per 1,000 pop.	2.3	Colour TV households, % with:	
Religion, % of pop.		cable	46.7
Non-religious	59.6	satellite	16.4
Christian	39.9	Telephone lines per 100 pop.	35.2
Muslim	0.2	Mobile telephone subscribers	
Hindu	<0.1	per 100 pop.	139.0
Jewish	<0.1	Broadband subs per 100 pop.	24.8
Other	<0.1	Internet hosts per 1,000 pop.	665.8

FINLAND

Area	338,145 sq km	Capital	Helsinki
Arable as % of total land	7.4	Currency	Euro (€)

People

Population	5.4m	Life expectancy: men	77.2 yrs
Pop. per sq km	16.0	women	83.3 yrs
Total growth		Adult literacy	...
in pop. 2000–10	3.7%	Fertility rate (per woman)	1.9
Pop. under 15	16.6%	Urban population	83.7%
Pop. over 60	24.7%		per 1,000 pop.
No. of men per 100 women	96.3	Crude birth rate	11.0
Human Development Index	89.2	Crude death rate	9.8

The economy

GDP	€189bn	GDP per head	$48,810
GDP	$263bn	GDP per head in purchasing	
Av. ann. growth in real		power parity (USA=100)	77.9
GDP 2006–11	0.5%	Economic freedom index	74.0

Origins of GDP		Components of GDP	
	% of total		% of total
Agriculture	3	Private consumption	56
Industry, of which:	29	Public consumption	24
manuf., mining & utilities	19	Investment	21
Services	68	Exports	41
		Imports	-41

Structure of employment

	% of total		% of labour force
Agriculture	4	Unemployed 2011	7.7
Industry	23	Av. ann. rate 2000–11	8.3
Services	73		

Energy

	m TOE		
Total output	17.3	Net energy imports as %	
Total consumption	36.4	of energy use	52
Consumption per head,			
kg oil equivalent	6,787		

Inflation and finance

Consumer price		av. ann. increase 2006–11	
inflation 2012	2.8%	Euro area:	
Av. ann. inflation 2007–12	2.3%	Narrow money (M1)	5.3%
Money market rate, Dec. 2012	0.19%	Broad money	4.7%
		H'hold saving rate, Dec. 2012	-0.3%

Exchange rates

	end 2012		2012
€ per $	0.76	Effective rates	2005 = 100
€ per SDR	1.16	– nominal	99.3
		– real	96.0

Trade

Principal exports		Principal imports	
	$bn fob		$bn cif
Machinery & transport equip.	23.1	Machinery & transport equip.	24.6
Chemicals & related products	7.9	Minerals & fuels	18.0
Mineral fuels & lubricants	6.6	Chemicals & related products	8.5
Raw materials	5.5	Raw materials	7.3
Total incl. others	**79.1**	Total incl. others	**80.9**

Main export destinations		Main origins of imports	
	% of total		% of total
Sweden	11.7	Russia	18.5
Germany	9.9	Sweden	14.5
Russia	9.2	Germany	14.3
Netherlands	6.7	Netherlands	8.0
United Kingdom	5.1	China	4.4
United States	4.9	United Kingdom	3.2
EU27	55.7	EU27	61.5

Balance of payments, reserves and aid, $bn

Visible exports fob	82.4	Overall balance	0.4
Visible imports fob	-79.3	Change in reserves	0.7
Trade balance	3.1	Level of reserves	
Invisibles inflows	45.9	end Dec.	10.3
Invisibles outflows	-48.8	No. months of import cover	1.0
Net transfers	-2.2	Official gold holdings, m oz	1.6
Current account balance	-2.0	Aid given	1.41
– as % of GDP	-0.8	– as % of GDP	0.53
Capital balance	14.9		

Health and education

Health spending, % of GDP	8.9	Education spending, % of GDP	6.8
Doctors per 1,000 pop.	2.9	Enrolment, %: primary	99
Hospital beds per 1,000 pop.	5.9	secondary	108
Improved-water source access,		tertiary	94
% of pop.	100		

Society

No. of households	2.6m	Cost of living, Dec. 2012	
Av. no. per household	2.1	New York = 100	111
Marriages per 1,000 pop.	5.3	Cars per 1,000 pop.	548
Divorces per 1,000 pop.	2.5	Colour TV households, % with:	
Religion, % of pop.		cable	53.6
Christian	81.6	satellite	26.8
Non-religious	17.6	Telephone lines per 100 pop.	20.1
Muslim	0.8	Mobile telephone subscribers	
Hindu	<0.1	per 100 pop.	166.0
Jewish	<0.1	Broadband subs per 100 pop.	29.5
Other	<0.1	Internet hosts per 1,000 pop.	882.0

FRANCE

Area	543,965 sq km	Capital	Paris
Arable as % of total land	33.5	Currency	Euro (€)

People

Population	63.1m	Life expectancy: men		78.5 yrs
Pop. per sq km	116.0	women		84.9 yrs
Total growth		Adult literacy		...
in pop. 2000–10	6.3%	Fertility rate (per woman)		2.0
Pop. under 15	18.4%	Urban population		85.8%
Pop. over 60	23.2%			per 1,000 pop.
No. of men per 100 women	94.8	Crude birth rate		12.4
Human Development Index	89.3	Crude death rate		8.9

The economy

GDP	€1,997bn	GDP per head	$42,380
GDP	$2,773bn	GDP per head in purchasing	
Av. ann. growth in real		power parity (USA=100)	73.3
GDP 2006–11	0.5%	Economic freedom index	64.1

Origins of GDP		**Components of GDP**	
	% of total		% of total
Agriculture	2	Private consumption	58
Industry, of which:	19	Public consumption	25
manufacturing	11	Investment	21
Services	79	Exports	27
		Imports	-30

Structure of employment

	% of total		% of labour force
Agriculture	3	Unemployed 2011	9.3
Industry	22	Av. ann. rate 2000–11	9.1
Services	75		

Energy

	m TOE		
Total output	135.6	Net energy imports as %	
Total consumption	262.3	of energy use	48
Consumption per head,			
kg oil equivalent	4,031		

Inflation and finance

Consumer price		av. ann. increase 2006–11	
inflation 2012	2.0%	Euro area:	
Av. ann. inflation 2007–12	1.7%	Narrow money (M1)	5.3%
Treasury bill rate, Dec. 2012	0.07%	Broad money	4.7%
		H'hold saving rate[a], Dec. 2012	15.9%

Exchange rates

	end 2012		2012
€ per $	0.76	Effective rates	2005 = 100
€ per SDR	1.16	– nominal	100.0
		– real	95.5

Trade

Principal exports		Principal imports	
	$bn fob		*$bn cif*
Machinery & transport equip.	216.6	Machinery & transport equip.	231.6
Chemicals & related products	107.3	Chemicals & related products	112.7
Food, drink & tobacco	70.6	Mineral fuels & lubricants	96.7
Mineral fuels & lubricants	28.0	Food, drink & tobacco	54.4
Raw materials	18.4	Raw materials	20.9
Total incl. others	**583.9**	Total incl. others	**709.6**

Main export destinations		Main origins of imports	
	% of total		*% of total*
Germany	16.8	Germany	18.8
Italy	8.3	Belgium	11.1
Spain	7.5	Italy	7.6
Belgium	7.4	Netherlands	7.4
United Kingdom	6.7	Spain	6.5
United States	5.1	United Kingdom	5.1
EU27	60.9	EU27	67.3

Balance of payments, reserves and aid, $bn

Visible exports fob	593.5	Overall balance	-8.4
Visible imports fob	-681.6	Change in reserves	2.6
Trade balance	-88.1	Level of reserves	
Invisibles inflows	449.4	end Dec.	168.5
Invisibles outflows	-364.9	No. months of import cover	1.9
Net transfers	-51.0	Official gold holdings, m oz	78.3
Current account balance	-54.4	Aid given	13.00
– as % of GDP	-2.0	– as % of GDP	0.46
Capital balance	73.7		

Health and education

Health spending, % of GDP	11.6	Education spending, % of GDP	5.9
Doctors per 1,000 pop.	3.4	Enrolment, %: primary	110
Hospital beds per 1,000 pop.	6.6	secondary	113
Improved-water source access,		tertiary	57
% of pop.	100		

Society

No. of households	27.4m	Cost of living, Dec. 2012	
Av. no. per household	2.3	New York = 100	128
Marriages per 1,000 pop.	3.7	Cars per 1,000 pop.	498
Divorces per 1,000 pop.	2.0	Colour TV households, % with:	
Religion, % of pop.		cable	14.0
Christian	63.0	satellite	29.9
Non-religious	28.0	Telephone lines per 100 pop.	63.2
Muslim	7.5	Mobile telephone subscribers	
Other	1.0	per 100 pop.	94.8
Jewish	0.5	Broadband subs per 100 pop.	36.0
Hindu	<0.1	Internet hosts per 1,000 pop.	273.6

a Gross.

GERMANY

Area	357,868 sq km	Capital	Berlin
Arable as % of total land	34.0	Currency	Euro (€)

People

Population	82.2m	Life expectancy: men	78.2 yrs
Pop. per sq km	229.7	women	83.0 yrs
Total growth		Adult literacy	...
in pop. 2000–10	-0.1%	Fertility rate (per woman)	1.5
Pop. under 15	13.4%	Urban population	73.9%
Pop. over 60	26.0%		per 1,000 pop.
No. of men per 100 women	96.1	Crude birth rate	8.0
Human Development Index	92.0	Crude death rate	10.9

The economy

GDP	€2,593bn	GDP per head	$44,020
GDP	$3,601bn	GDP per head in purchasing	
Av. ann. growth in real		power parity (USA=100)	82.0
GDP 2006–11	1.2%	Economic freedom index	72.8

Origins of GDP		**Components of GDP**	
	% of total		% of total
Agriculture	1	Private consumption	57
Industry, of which:	28	Public consumption	19
manufacturing	21	Investment	18
Services	71	Exports	50
		Imports	-45

Structure of employment

	% of total		% of labour force
Agriculture	2	Unemployed 2011	5.9
Industry	28	Av. ann. rate 2000–11	8.5
Services	70		

Energy

	m TOE		
Total output	131.3	Net energy imports as %	
Total consumption	327.4	of energy use	60
Consumption per head,			
kg oil equivalent	4,003		

Inflation and finance

Consumer price		av. ann. increase 2006–11	
inflation 2012	2.0%	Euro area:	
Av. ann. inflation 2007–12	1.6%	Narrow money (M1)	5.3%
Money market rate, 2011	0.81%	Broad money	4.7%
Deposit rate, h'holds, Dec. 2012	1.57%	H'hold saving rate, Dec. 2012	10.3%

Exchange rates

	end 2012		2012
€ per $	0.76	Effective rates	2005 = 100
€ per SDR	1.16	– nominal	99.3
		– real	94.2

Trade

Principal exports		Principal imports	
	$bn fob		*$bn cif*
Machinery & transport equip.	693.4	Machinery & transport equip.	417.6
Chemicals & related products	221.0	Chemicals & related products	167.4
Food, drink & tobacco	74.6	Mineral fuels & lubricants	159.7
Mineral fuels & lubricants	37.0	Food, drink & tobacco	83.2
Raw materials	33.6	Raw materials	59.1
Total incl. others	**1,470.5**	Total incl. others	**1,253.2**

Main export destinations		Main origins of imports	
	% of total		*% of total*
France	9.6	Netherlands	13.8
Netherlands	6.6	France	7.6
United Kingdom	6.2	China	7.0
Italy	5.9	Belgium	6.3
Austria	5.5	Italy	5.4
United States	5.3	United Kingdom	4.8
China	4.9	Austria	4.4
EU27	59.3	EU27	63.4

Balance of payments, reserves and aid, $bn

Visible exports fob	1,494	Overall balance	3.9
Visible imports fob	-1,273	Change in reserves	18.1
Trade balance	220	Level of reserves	
Invisibles inflows	554	end Dec.	234.1
Invisibles outflows	-515	No. months of import cover	1.6
Net transfers	-46	Official gold holdings, m oz	109.2
Current account balance	203	Aid given	14.09
– as % of GDP	5.7	– as % of GDP	0.39
Capital balance	-210		

Health and education

Health spending, % of GDP	11.1	Education spending, % of GDP	5.1
Doctors per 1,000 pop.	3.7	Enrolment, %: primary	102
Hospital beds per 1,000 pop.	8.3	secondary	103
Improved-water source access,		tertiary	46
% of pop.	100		

Society

No. of households	40.0m	Cost of living, Dec. 2012	
Av. no. per household	2.0	New York = 100	94
Marriages per 1,000 pop.	4.6	Cars per 1,000 pop.	523
Divorces per 1,000 pop.	2.3	Colour TV households, % with:	
Religion, % of pop.		cable	48.2
Christian	68.7	satellite	43.8
Non-religious	24.7	Telephone lines per 100 pop.	63.1
Muslim	5.8	Mobile telephone subscribers	
Other	0.5	per 100 pop.	132.3
Jewish	0.3	Broadband subs per 100 pop.	33.1
Hindu	<0.1	Internet hosts per 1,000 pop.	243.8

GREECE

Area	131,957 sq km	Capital	Athens
Arable as % of total land	19.4	Currency	Euro (€)

People

Population	11.4m	Life expectancy: men	77.6 yrs
Pop. per sq km	86.4	women	82.6 yrs
Total growth		Adult literacy	97.2%
in pop. 2000–10	3.4%	Fertility rate (per woman)	1.5
Pop. under 15	14.2%	Urban population	61.4%
Pop. over 60	24.3%		per 1,000 pop.
No. of men per 100 women	97.9	Crude birth rate	9.0
Human Development Index	86.0	Crude death rate	10.5

The economy

GDP	€209bn	GDP per head	$25,630
GDP	$290bn	GDP per head in purchasing	
Av. ann. growth in real		power parity (USA=100)	53.7
GDP 2006–11	-2.4%	Economic freedom index	55.4

Origins of GDP		**Components of GDP**	
	% of total		% of total
Agriculture	3	Private consumption	75
Industry, of which:	16	Public consumption	17
mining & manufacturing	9	Investment	16
Services	81	Exports	25
		Imports	-33

Structure of employment

	% of total		% of labour force
Agriculture	12	Unemployed 2011	17.7
Industry	18	Av. ann. rate 2000–11	10.4
Services	70		

Energy

	m TOE		
Total output	9.4	Net energy imports as %	
Total consumption	27.6	of energy use	66
Consumption per head,			
kg oil equivalent	2,440		

Inflation and finance

Consumer price		av. ann. increase 2006–11	
inflation 2012	1.5%	Euro area:	
Av. ann. inflation 2007–12	3.0%	Narrow money (M1)	5.3%
Treasury bill rate, Dec. 2012	0.55%	Broad money	4.7%

Exchange rates

	end 2012		2012
€ per $	0.76	Effective rates	2005 = 100
€ per SDR	1.16	– nominal	101.0
		– real	104.0

Trade

Principal exports	$bn fob	Principal imports	$bn cif
Mineral fuels & lubricants	9.4	Mineral fuels & lubricants	16.4
Food, drink & tobacco	5.2	Machinery & transport equip.	11.0
Chemicals & related products	3.2	Chemicals & related products	9.4
Machinery & transport equip.	2.9	Food, drink & tobacco	7.7
Raw materials	1.6	Raw materials	2.3
Total incl. others	**33.9**	Total incl. others	**67.4**

Main export destinations	% of total	Main origins of imports	% of total
Italy	9.6	Germany	10.7
Germany	8.0	Italy	9.3
Turkey	7.9	Russia	9.2
Cyprus	6.2	China	5.7
Bulgaria	5.6	Netherlands	5.5
EU27	49.9	EU27	51.9

Balance of payments, reserves and debt, $bn

Visible exports fob	28.0	Overall balance	-5.7
Visible imports fob	-65.8	Change in reserves	0.4
Trade balance	-37.9	Level of reserves	
Invisibles inflows	44.8	end Dec.	6.7
Invisibles outflows	-36.2	No. months of import cover	0.8
Net transfers	0.7	Official gold holdings, m oz	3.6
Current account balance	-28.6	Aid given	0.42
– as % of GDP	-9.9	– as % of GDP	0.15
Capital balance	15.2		

Health and education

Health spending, % of GDP	10.8	Education spending, % of GDP	...
Doctors per 1,000 pop.	6.2	Enrolment, %: primary	101
Hospital beds per 1,000 pop.	4.9	secondary	109
Improved-water source access,		tertiary	89
% of pop.	100		

Society

No. of households	4.1m	Cost of living, Dec. 2012	
Av. no. per household	2.8	New York = 100	78
Marriages per 1,000 pop.	5.3	Cars per 1,000 pop.	466
Divorces per 1,000 pop.	1.2	Colour TV households, % with:	
Religion, % of pop.		cable	0.9
Christian	88.1	satellite	13.0
Non-religious	6.1	Telephone lines per 100 pop.	50.4
Muslim	5.3	Mobile telephone subscribers	
Other	0.3	per 100 pop.	106.5
Hindu	0.1	Broadband subs per 100 pop.	21.6
Jewish	<0.1	Internet hosts per 1,000 pop.	280.8

HONG KONG

Area	1,075 sq km	Capital	Victoria
Arable as % of total land	5	Currency	Hong Kong dollar (HK$)

People

Population	7.1m	Life expectancy: men	80.2 yrs
Pop. per sq km	6,604.7	women	86.4 yrs
Total growth		Adult literacy	...
in pop. 2000–10	4.0%	Fertility rate (per woman)	1.3
Pop. under 15	11.5%	Urban population	100.0%
Pop. over 60	18.4%		per 1,000 pop.
No. of men per 100 women	90	Crude birth rate	9.0
Human Development Index	90.6	Crude death rate	6.3

The economy

GDP	HK$1,935bn	GDP per head	$35,160
GDP	$249bn	GDP per head in purchasing	
Av. ann. growth in real		power parity (USA=100)	105.1
GDP 2006–11	3.5%	Economic freedom index	89.3

Origins of GDP		Components of GDP	
	% of total		% of total
Agriculture	0	Private consumption	64
Industry, of which:	7	Public consumption	9
manufacturing	2	Investment	23
Services	93	Exports	225
		Imports	-222

Structure of employment

	% of total		% of labour force
Agriculture	0	Unemployed 2011	3.4
Industry	12	Av. ann. rate 2000–11	5.2
Services	88		

Energy

	m TOE		
Total output	0.1	Net energy imports as %	
Total consumption	13.8	of energy use	100
Consumption per head,			
kg oil equivalent	1,951		

Inflation and finance

Consumer price		av. ann. increase 2006–11	
inflation 2012	4.1%	Narrow money (M1)	14.8%
Av. ann. inflation 2007–12	3.3%	Broad money	9.0%
Money market rate, Dec. 2012	0.06%		

Exchange rates

	end 2012		2012
HK$ per $	7.75	Effective rates	2005 = 100
HK$ per SDR	11.91	– nominal	...
HK$ per €	10.17	– real	...

Trade

Principal exports[a]		Principal imports[a]	
	$bn fob		$bn cif
Capital goods	158.2	Raw materials &	
Raw materials &		semi-manufactures	167.2
semi-manufactures	143.9	Capital goods	159.1
Consumer goods	113.5	Consumer goods	120.4
Foodstuffs	5.0	Foodstuffs	18.6
Total incl. others	**429.2**	Total incl. others	**484.0**

Main export destinations		Main origins of imports	
	% of total		% of total
China	52.3	China	45.1
United States	9.9	Japan	8.5
Japan	4.0	Singapore	6.8
Germany	2.7	Taiwan	6.4

Balance of payments, reserves and debt, $bn

Visible exports fob	438.2	Change in reserves	16.7
Visible imports fob	-447.4	Level of reserves	
Trade balance	-9.1	end Dec.	285.4
Invisibles inflows	228.8	No. months of import cover	5.3
Invisibles outflows	-203.9	Official gold holdings, m oz	0.1
Net transfers	-2.5	Foreign debt	67.3
Current account balance	14.7	– as % of GDP	27
– as % of GDP	5.7	– as % of total exports	10
Capital balance	-3.4	Debt service ratio	1
Overall balance	11.2		

Health and education

Health spending, % of GDP	...	Education spending, % of GDP	3.4
Doctors per 1,000 pop.	1.8	Enrolment, %: primary	108
Hospital beds per 1,000 pop.	5.0	secondary	80
Improved-water source access,		tertiary	60
% of pop.	...		

Society

No. of households	2.4m	Cost of living, Dec. 2012	
Av. no. per household	3.0	New York = 100	116
Marriages per 1,000 pop.	7.5	Cars per 1,000 pop.	68
Divorces per 1,000 pop.	2.5	Colour TV households, % with:	
Religion, % of pop.		cable	93.6
Non-religious	56.1	satellite	0.1
Christian	14.3	Telephone lines per 100 pop.	61.0
Other	14.2	Mobile telephone subscribers	
Buddhist	13.2	per 100 pop.	214.7
Muslim	1.8	Broadband subs per 100 pop.	31.6
Hindu	0.4	Internet hosts per 1,000 pop.	122.5

a Including re-exports.
Note: Hong Kong became a Special Administrative Region of China on July 1 1997.

HUNGARY

Area	93,030 sq km	Capital	Budapest
Arable as % of total land	48.5	Currency	Forint (Ft)

People

Population	10.0m	Life expectancy: men	70.8 yrs
Pop. per sq km	107.3	women	78.5 yrs
Total growth		Adult literacy	99.0%
in pop. 2000–10	-2.2%	Fertility rate (per woman)	1.5
Pop. under 15	14.7%	Urban population	69.5%
Pop. over 60	22.4%		per 1,000 pop.
No. of men per 100 women	90.4	Crude birth rate	9.0
Human Development Index	83.1	Crude death rate	13.2

The economy

GDP	Ft28,154bn	GDP per head	$14,040
GDP	$140bn	GDP per head in purchasing	
Av. ann. growth in real		power parity (USA=100)	45.0
GDP 2006–11	-0.6%	Economic freedom index	67.3

Origins of GDP		**Components of GDP**	
	% of total		% of total
Agriculture	4	Private consumption	64
Industry, of which:	31	Public consumption	10
manufacturing	23	Investment	19
Services	65	Exports	92
		Imports	-85

Structure of employment

	% of total		% of labour force
Agriculture	5	Unemployed 2011	10.9
Industry	31	Av. ann. rate 2000–11	7.6
Services	64		

Energy

	m TOE		
Total output	11.0	Net energy imports as %	
Total consumption	25.7	of energy use	57
Consumption per head,			
kg oil equivalent	2,567		

Inflation and finance

Consumer price		*av. ann. increase 2006–11*	
inflation 2012	5.7%	Narrow money (M1)	4.7%
Av. ann. inflation 2007–12	5.0%	Broad money	6.4%
Treasury bill rate, Dec. 2012	5.82%	H'hold saving rate, Dec. 2012	4.0%

Exchange rates

	end 2012		2012
Ft per $	217.53	Effective rates	2005 = 100
Ft per SDR	339.55	– nominal	86.9
Ft per €	285.38	– real	105.9

Trade

Principal exports	$bn fob	Principal imports	$bn cif
Machinery & equipment	63.4	Machinery & equipment	47.6
Other manufactures	32.4	Other manufactures	33.8
Food, drink & tobacco	8.0	Fuels	12.5
Raw materials	3.2	Food, drink & tobacco	5.1
Total incl. others	111.3	Total incl. others	101.3

Main export destinations	% of total	Main origins of imports	% of total
Germany	25.3	Germany	25.0
Romania	5.8	Russia	8.8
Austria	5.5	China	8.5
Slovakia	5.5	Austria	6.3
EU27	75.9	EU27	69.4

Balance of payments, reserves and debt, $bn

Visible exports fob	99.0	Change in reserves	3.8
Visible imports fob	-95.2	Level of reserves	
Trade balance	3.8	end Dec.	48.8
Invisibles inflows	36.1	No. months of import cover	4.4
Invisibles outflows	-40.1	Official gold holdings, m oz	0.1
Net transfers	0.6	Foreign debt	184.7
Current account balance	1.3	– as % of GDP	133
– as % of GDP	0.9	– as % of total exports	128
Capital balance	6.6	Debt service ratio	29
Overall balance	5.5	Aid given	0.03
		– as % of GDP	0.11

Health and education

Health spending, % of GDP	7.7	Education spending, % of GDP	4.9
Doctors per 1,000 pop.	3.4	Enrolment, %: primary	102
Hospital beds per 1,000 pop.	7.2	secondary	100
Improved-water source access,		tertiary	61
% of pop.	100		

Society

No. of households	4.2m	Cost of living, Dec. 2012	
Av. no. per household	2.4	New York = 100	70
Marriages per 1,000 pop.	3.6	Cars per 1,000 pop.	299
Divorces per 1,000 pop.	2.3	Colour TV households, % with:	
Religion, % of pop.		cable	56.5
Christian	81.0	satellite	27.3
Non-religious	18.6	Telephone lines per 100 pop.	29.4
Other	0.2	Mobile telephone subscribers	
Jewish	0.1	per 100 pop.	117.3
Hindu	<0.1	Broadband subs per 100 pop.	22.2
Muslim	<0.1	Internet hosts per 1,000 pop.	314.5

INDIA

Area	3,287,263 sq km	Capital	New Delhi
Arable as % of total land	53.0	Currency	Indian rupee (Rs)

People

Population	1,241.5m	Life expectancy: men	64.4 yrs
Pop. per sq km	377.7	women	67.6 yrs
Total growth		Adult literacy	62.8%
in pop. 2000–10	16.2%	Fertility rate (per woman)	2.5
Pop. under 15	30.8%	Urban population	31.3%
Pop. over 60	7.5%		per 1,000 pop.
No. of men per 100 women	106.8	Crude birth rate	21.3
Human Development Index	55.4	Crude death rate	7.9

The economy

GDP	Rs89.7trn	GDP per head	$1,510
GDP	$1,873bn	GDP per head in purchasing	
Av. ann. growth in real		power parity (USA=100)	7.6
GDP 2006–11	8.0%	Economic freedom index	55.2

Origins of GDP		**Components of GDP**	
	% of total		% of total
Agriculture	18	Private consumption	59
Industry, of which:	27	Public consumption	12
manufacturing	14	Investment	35
Services	56	Exports	24
		Imports	-30

Structure of employment

	% of total		% of labour force
Agriculture	51	Unemployed 2010	3.5
Industry	22	Av. ann. rate 2000–10	4.3
Services	27		

Energy

	m TOE		
Total output	518.7	Net energy imports as %	
Total consumption	692.7	of energy use	25
Consumption per head,			
kg oil equivalent	566		

Inflation and finance

Consumer price		av. ann. increase 2006–11	
inflation 2012	9.3%	Narrow money (M1)	13.6%
Av. ann. inflation 2007–12	9.9%	Broad money	18.9%
Lending rate, Dec. 2012	10.50%		

Exchange rates

	end 2012		2012
Rs per $	54.65	Effective rates	2005 = 100
Rs per SDR	84.19	– nominal	...
Rs per €	71.70	– real	...

Trade

Principal exports[a]		Principal imports[a]	
	$bn fob		*$bn cif*
Engineering goods	67.1	Petroleum & products	154.9
Petroleum & products	55.6	Gold & silver	61.3
Gems & jewellery	46.9	Electronic goods	32.6
Agricultural goods	37.4	Gems	30.5
Textiles	28.0	Machinery	30.2
Total incl. others	**304.6**	Total incl. others	**489.4**

Main export destinations		Main origins of imports	
	% of total		*% of total*
United Arab Emirates	12.6	China	11.0
United States	11.0	United Arab Emirates	7.6
China	6.1	Saudi Arabia	5.3
Singapore	5.2	United States	4.6

Balance of payments, reserves and debt, $bn

Visible exports fob	299.4	Change in reserves	-1.7
Visible imports fob	-415.8	Level of reserves	
Trade balance	-116.4	end Dec.	298.7
Invisibles inflows	147.4	No. months of import cover	6.3
Invisibles outflows	-152.6	Official gold holdings, m oz	17.9
Net transfers	61.6	Foreign debt	334.3
Current account balance	-60.0	– as % of GDP	18
– as % of GDP	-3.2	– as % of total exports	79
Capital balance	56.7	Debt service ratio	7
Overall balance	-4.1		

Health and education

Health spending, % of GDP	3.9	Education spending, % of GDP	3.3
Doctors per 1,000 pop.	0.6	Enrolment, %: primary	116
Hospital beds per 1,000 pop.	...	secondary	63
Improved-water source access,		tertiary	18
% of pop.	92		

Society

No. of households	229.4m	Cost of living, Dec. 2012	
Av. no. per household	5.3	New York = 100	48
Marriages per 1,000 pop.	...	Cars per 1,000 pop.	16
Divorces per 1,000 pop.	...	Colour TV households, % with:	
Religion, % of pop.		cable	57.8
Hindu	79.5	satellite	7.4
Muslim	14.4	Telephone lines per 100 pop.	2.6
Other	3.6	Mobile telephone subscribers	
Christian	2.5	per 100 pop.	72.0
Jewish	<0.1	Broadband subs per 100 pop.	1.1
Non-religious	<0.1	Internet hosts per 1,000 pop.	5.4

a Year ending March 31, 2012.

INDONESIA

Area	1,904,443 sq km	Capital	Jakarta
Arable as % of total land	13.0	Currency	Rupiah (Rp)

People

Population	242.3m	Life expectancy: men	68.3 yrs
Pop. per sq km	127.2	women	71.8 yrs
Total growth		Adult literacy	92.6%
in pop. 2000–10	12.4%	Fertility rate (per woman)	2.1
Pop. under 15	26.7%	Urban population	50.7%
Pop. over 60	8.9%		per 1,000 pop.
No. of men per 100 women	99.5	Crude birth rate	17.4
Human Development Index	62.9	Crude death rate	6.8

The economy

GDP	Rp7,427trn	GDP per head	$3,500
GDP	$847bn	GDP per head in purchasing	
Av. ann. growth in real		power parity (USA=100)	9.6
GDP 2006–11	5.9%	Economic freedom index	56.9

Origins of GDP		Components of GDP	
	% of total		% of total
Agriculture	15	Private consumption	57
Industry, of which:	47	Public consumption	9
manufacturing	24	Investment	33
Services	38	Exports	26
		Imports	-25

Structure of employment

	% of total		% of labour force
Agriculture	36	Unemployed 2011	6.6
Industry	21	Av. ann. rate 2000–11	8.5
Services	43		

Energy

	m TOE		
Total output	381.4	Net energy imports as %	
Total consumption	207.8	of energy use	-84
Consumption per head,			
kg oil equivalent	867		

Inflation and finance

Consumer price		av. ann. increase 2006–11	
inflation 2012	4.3%	Narrow money (M1)	15.8%
Av. ann. inflation 2007–12	5.9%	Broad money	15.8%
Money market rate, Dec. 2012	4.17%		

Exchange rates

	end 2012		2012
Rp per $	9,656	Effective rates	2005 = 100
Rp per SDR	14,862	– nominal	...
Rp per €	12,669	– real	...

Trade

Principal exports		Principal imports	
	$bn fob		*$bn cif*
Mineral fuels	68.9	Machinery & transport equip.	56.1
Machinery & transport equip.	25.5	Mineral fuels	40.8
Raw materials	24.3	Manufactured goods	25.9
Animal & vegetable oils	21.9	Chemicals & related products	22.2
Total incl. others	**203.2**	Total incl. others	**177.4**

Main export destinations		Main origins of imports	
	% of total		*% of total*
Japan	16.6	China	14.8
China	11.3	Singapore	14.6
Singapore	9.1	Japan	11.0
United States	8.1	South Korea	7.3

Balance of payments, reserves and debt, $bn

Visible exports fob	191.7	Change in reserves	13.9
Visible imports fob	-156.9	Level of reserves	
Trade balance	34.8	end Dec.	110.1
Invisibles inflows	23.9	No. months of import cover	6.1
Invisibles outflows	-60.9	Official gold holdings, m oz	2.4
Net transfers	4.2	Foreign debt	213.6
Current account balance	2.1	– as % of GDP	27
– as % of GDP	0.2	– as % of total exports	105
Capital balance	14.0	Debt service ratio	15
Overall balance	11.9		

Health and education

Health spending, % of GDP	2.7	Education spending, % of GDP	2.8
Doctors per 1,000 pop.	0.2	Enrolment, %: primary	118
Hospital beds per 1,000 pop.	0.6	secondary	77
Improved-water source access,		tertiary	23
% of pop.	82		

Society

No. of households	61.9m	Cost of living, Dec. 2012	
Av. no. per household	3.8	New York = 100	77
Marriages per 1,000 pop.	11.2	Cars per 1,000 pop.	58
Divorces per 1,000 pop.	0.7	Colour TV households, % with:	
Religion, % of pop.		cable	1.6
Muslim	87.2	satellite	10.7
Christian	9.9	Telephone lines per 100 pop.	15.9
Hindu	1.7	Mobile telephone subscribers	
Other	1.1	per 100 pop.	103.1
Jewish	<0.1	Broadband subs per 100 pop.	1.1
Non-religious	<0.1	Internet hosts per 1,000 pop.	5.5

IRAN

Area	1,648,000 sq km	Capital	Tehran
Arable as % of total land	10.7	Currency	Rial (IR)

People

Population	74.8m	Life expectancy: men	71.5 yrs
Pop. per sq km	45.4	women	75.3 yrs
Total growth		Adult literacy	85.0%
in pop. 2000–10	13.2%	Fertility rate (per woman)	1.5
Pop. under 15	23.8%	Urban population	69.1%
Pop. over 60	7.1%		per 1,000 pop.
No. of men per 100 women	103.0	Crude birth rate	16.2
Human Development Index	74.2	Crude death rate	5.4

The economy

GDP[a]	IR4,399trn	GDP per head[a]	$5,800
GDP[a]	$429bn	GDP per head in purchasing	
Av. ann. growth in real		power parity (USA=100)[c]	24.5
GDP 2006–11[b]	3.9%	Economic freedom index	43.2

Origins of GDP		Components of GDP	
	% of total		% of total
Agriculture	10	Private consumption	41
Industry, of which:	42	Public consumption	11
manufacturing	12	Investment	42
Services	51	Exports	28
		Imports	-21

Structure of employment

	% of total		% of labour force
Agriculture	21	Unemployed 2008	10.5
Industry	32	Av. ann. rate 2000–08	12.3
Services	47		

Energy

	m TOE		
Total output	349.1	Net energy imports as %	
Total consumption	208.4	of energy use	-68
Consumption per head,			
kg oil equivalent	2,817		

Inflation and finance

Consumer price		av. ann. increase 2006–10	
inflation 2012	27.3%	Narrow money (M1)	3.7%
Av. ann. inflation 2007–12	19.2%	Broad money	1.2%
Deposit rate, Dec. 2012	12.07%		

Exchange rates

	end 2012		2012
IR per $	12,260	Effective rates	2005 = 100
IR per SDR	18,843	– nominal	70.6
IR per €	16,084	– real	205.0

Trade

Principal exports[d]		Principal imports[d]	
	$bn fob		*$bn cif*
Oil & gas	86.1	Machinery & transport equip.	20.6
Industrial goods excl. oil & gas products	15.1	Iron & steel	9.2
		Chemicals	7.0
Agricultural & traditional goods	4.9	Foodstuffs & live animals	6.8
Metallic mineral ores	1.3	Mineral products & fuels	1.4
Total incl. others	**108.6**	Total incl. others	**64.4**

Main export destinations		Main origins of imports	
	% of total		*% of total*
China	21.0	United Arab Emirates	30.6
India	9.3	China	17.2
Japan	8.9	South Korea	8.4
Turkey	8.7	Germany	4.8
South Korea	7.9	Turkey	4.2

Balance of payments[d], reserves and debt, $bn

Visible exports fob	108.6	Change in reserves	...
Visible imports fob	-68.4	Level of reserves	
Trade balance	40.2	end Dec.	...
Net invisibles	-15.2	No. months of import cover	...
Net transfers	0.5	Official gold holdings, m oz	...
Current account balance	25.5	Foreign debt	19.1
– as % of GDP	6.6	– as % of GDP	4
Capital balance	-16.5	– as % of total exports	...
Overall balance	-0.9	Debt service ratio[b]	2

Health and education

Health spending, % of GDP	6.0	Education spending, % of GDP	4.7
Doctors per 1,000 pop.	0.9	Enrolment, %: primary	108
Hospital beds per 1,000 pop.	1.7	secondary	86
Improved-water source access, % of pop.	96	tertiary	49

Society

No. of households	21.2m	Cost of living, Dec. 2012	
Av. no. per household	3.6	New York = 100	58
Marriages per 1,000 pop.	12.2	Cars per 1,000 pop.	130
Divorces per 1,000 pop.	1.7	Colour TV households, % with:	
Religion, % of pop.		cable	0.0
Muslim	99.5	satellite	36.8
Christian	0.2	Telephone lines per 100 pop.	37.1
Other	0.2	Mobile telephone subscribers	
Non-religious	0.1	per 100 pop.	74.9
Hindu	<0.1	Broadband subs per 100 pop.	2.4
Jewish	<0.1	Internet hosts per 1,000 pop.	2.6

a 2010 b Estimate. c 2009 d Iranian year ending March 20, 2011.

IRELAND

Area	70,282 sq km	Capital	Dublin
Arable as % of total land	14.7	Currency	Euro (€)

People

Population	4.5m	Life expectancy: men	78.4 yrs
Pop. per sq km	64.0	women	83.2 yrs
Total growth		Adult literacy	...
in pop. 2000–10	17.5%	Fertility rate (per woman)	2.1
Pop. under 15	20.8%	Urban population	62.2%
Pop. over 60	16.1%		per 1,000 pop.
No. of men per 100 women	100.1	Crude birth rate	15.6
Human Development Index	91.6	Crude death rate	6.4

The economy

GDP	€156bn	GDP per head	$47,480
GDP	$217bn	GDP per head in purchasing	
Av. ann. growth in real		power parity (USA=100)	84.9
GDP 2006–11	-0.4%	Economic freedom index	75.7

Origins of GDP		Components of GDP	
	% of total		% of total
Agriculture	1	Private consumption	49
Industry, of which:	32	Public consumption	19
manufacturing	24	Investment	10
Services	67	Exports	107
		Imports	-84

Structure of employment

	% of total		% of labour force
Agriculture	5	Unemployed 2011	14.4
Industry	19	Av. ann. rate 2000–11	6.6
Services	76		

Energy

	m TOE		
Total output	2.0	Net energy imports as %	
Total consumption	14.4	of energy use	86
Consumption per head,			
kg oil equivalent	3,218		

Inflation and finance

Consumer price		av. ann. increase 2006–11	
inflation 2012	1.7%	Euro area:	
Av. ann. inflation 2007–12	0.5%	Narrow money (M1)	5.3%
Money market rate, Dec. 2012	0.11%	Broad money	4.7%
		H'hold saving rate, Dec. 2012	4.8%

Exchange rates

	end 2012		2012
€ per $	0.76	Effective rates	2005 = 100
€ per SDR	1.16	– nominal	100.6
		– real	96.3

Trade

Principal exports		Principal imports	
	$bn fob		$bn cif
Chemicals & related products	76.4	Machinery & transport equip.	16.5
Machinery & transport equip.	13.3	Chemicals	14.2
Food, drink & tobacco	12.0	Mineral fuels & lubricants	9.4
Mineral fuels & lubricants	1.7	Food, drink & tobacco	7.9
Total incl. others	**127.1**	Total incl. others	**67.2**

Main export destinations		Main origins of imports	
	% of total		% of total
United States	21.5	United Kingdom	39.2
United Kingdom	15.6	United States	12.8
Belgium	14.8	Germany	7.7
Germany	6.8	Netherlands	5.7
France	5.5	France	3.8
Switzerland	4.0	China	3.7
EU27	57.7	EU27	69.5

Balance of payments, reserves and aid, $bn

Visible exports fob	126.7	Overall balance	-17.6
Visible imports fob	-67.1	Change in reserves	-0.4
Trade balance	59.6	Level of reserves	
Invisibles inflows	182.4	end Dec.	1.7
Invisibles outflows	-237.8	No. months of import cover	0.1
Net transfers	-1.7	Official gold holdings, m oz	0.2
Current account balance	2.5	Aid given	0.91
– as % of GDP	1.2	– as % of GDP	0.51
Capital balance	-9.5		

Health and education

Health spending, % of GDP	9.4	Education spending, % of GDP	6.5
Doctors per 1,000 pop.	3.2	Enrolment, %: primary	108
Hospital beds per 1,000 pop.	3.2	secondary	121
Improved-water source access,		tertiary	66
% of pop.	100		

Society

No. of households	1.7m	Cost of living, Dec. 2012	
Av. no. per household	2.6	New York = 100	98
Marriages per 1,000 pop.	4.6	Cars per 1,000 pop.	637
Divorces per 1,000 pop.	0.7	Colour TV households, % with:	
Religion, % of pop.		cable	32.6
Christian	92.0	satellite	47.3
Non-religious	6.2	Telephone lines per 100 pop.	45.2
Muslim	1.1	Mobile telephone subscribers	
Other	0.4	per 100 pop.	108.4
Hindu	0.2	Broadband subs per 100 pop.	22.0
Jewish	<0.1	Internet hosts per 1,000 pop.	308.2

ISRAEL

Area	20,770 sq km	Capital	Jerusalem[a]
Arable as % of total land	14.0	Currency	New Shekel (NIS)

People

Population	7.6m	Life expectancy: men		79.6 yrs
Pop. per sq km	365.9	women		84.2 yrs
Total growth		Adult literacy		...
in pop. 2000–10	23.3%	Fertility rate (per woman)		2.9
Pop. under 15	27.6%	Urban population		91.9%
Pop. over 60	14.6%			per 1,000 pop.
No. of men per 100 women	97.4	Crude birth rate		20.5
Human Development Index	90.0	Crude death rate		5.4

The economy

GDP	NIS869bn	GDP per head	$31,280
GDP	$243bn	GDP per head in purchasing	
Av. ann. growth in real		power parity (USA=100)	59.9
GDP 2006–11	4.1%	Economic freedom index	66.9

Origins of GDP[b]		**Components of GDP**	
	% of total		% of total
Agriculture	2	Private consumption	62
Industry, of which:	22	Public consumption	24
manufacturing	14	Investment	15
Services	76	Exports	37
		Imports	-38

Structure of employment

	% of total		% of labour force
Agriculture	2	Unemployed 2011	5.6
Industry	20	Av. ann. rate 2000–11	8.2
Services	78		

Energy

	m TOE		
Total output	3.9	Net energy imports as %	
Total consumption	22.9	of energy use	83
Consumption per head,			
kg oil equivalent	3,005		

Inflation and finance

Consumer price		av. ann. increase 2006–09	
inflation 2012	1.7%	Narrow money (M1)	24.9%
Av. ann. inflation 2007–12	3.2%	Broad money	8.8%
Treasury bill rate, Nov. 2012	1.88%		

Exchange rates

	end 2012		2012
NIS per $	3.78	Effective rates	2005 = 100
NIS per SDR	5.74	– nominal	113.0
NIS per €	4.96	– real	111.5

Trade

Principal exports		Principal imports	
	$bn fob		*$bn cif*
Chemicals & chemical products	16.6	Fuel	13.6
Polished diamonds	11.0	Diamonds	10.3
Communications, medical &		Machinery & equipment	7.3
scientific equipment	7.9	Chemicals	5.1
Electronics	4.4		
Total incl. others	**58.1**	Total incl. others	**72.7**

Main export destinations		Main origins of imports	
	% of total		*% of total*
United States	33.3	United States	12.0
Hong Kong	9.2	China	7.5
Belgium	6.5	Germany	6.3
United Kingdom	5.8	Belgium	6.1
India	5.2	Switzerland	5.5

Balance of payments, reserves and debt, $bn

Visible exports fob	64.2	Change in reserves	4.0
Visible imports fob	-72.0	Level of reserves	
Trade balance	-7.8	end Dec.	74.9
Invisibles inflows	34.1	No. months of import cover	8.5
Invisibles outflows	-33.1	Official gold holdings, m oz	0.0
Net transfers	8.7	Foreign debt	103.9
Current account balance	1.9	– as % of GDP	43
– as % of GDP	0.8	– as % of total exports	101
Capital balance	0.9	Debt service ratio	17
Overall balance	2.6	Aid given	0.42
		– as % of GDP	0.09

Health and education

Health spending, % of GDP	7.7	Education spending, % of GDP	6.0
Doctors per 1,000 pop.	3.1	Enrolment, %: primary	104
Hospital beds per 1,000 pop.	3.4	secondary	102
Improved-water source access,		tertiary	62
% of pop.	100		

Society

No. of households	2.2m	Cost of living, Dec. 2012	
Av. no. per household	3.5	New York = 100	98
Marriages per 1,000 pop.	6.5	Cars per 1,000 pop.	285
Divorces per 1,000 pop.	1.9	Colour TV households, % with:	
Religion, % of pop.		cable	87.4
Jewish	75.6	satellite	45.7
Muslim	18.6	Telephone lines per 100 pop.	46.3
Non-religious	3.1	Mobile telephone subscribers	
Christian	2.0	per 100 pop.	121.7
Other	0.6	Broadband subs per 100 pop.	24.9
Hindu	<0.1	Internet hosts per 1,000 pop.	326.7

a Sovereignty over the city is disputed.   b 2006

ITALY

Area	301,245 sq km	Capital	Rome
Arable as % of total land	23.9	Currency	Euro (€)

People

Population	60.8m	Life expectancy: men		79.2 yrs
Pop. per sq km	201.8	women		84.6 yrs
Total growth		Adult literacy		98.9%
in pop. 2000–10	6.3%	Fertility rate (per woman)		1.3
Pop. under 15	14.2%	Urban population		68.4%
Pop. over 60	26.7%			per 1,000 pop.
No. of men per 100 women	95.7	Crude birth rate		9.0
Human Development Index	88.1	Crude death rate		10.2

The economy

GDP	€1,580bn	GDP per head	$36,130
GDP	$2,194bn	GDP per head in purchasing	
Av. ann. growth in real		power parity (USA=100)	67.9
GDP 2006–11	-0.6%	Economic freedom index	60.6

Origins of GDP		Components of GDP	
	% of total		% of total
Agriculture	2	Private consumption	61
Industry, of which:	25	Public consumption	20
manufacturing	17	Investment	20
Services	73	Exports	29
		Imports	-30

Structure of employment

	% of total		% of labour force
Agriculture	4	Unemployed 2011	8.4
Industry	28	Av. ann. rate 2000–11	8.1
Services	68		

Energy

	m TOE		
Total output	29.8	Net energy imports as %	
Total consumption	170.2	of energy use	82
Consumption per head,			
kg oil equivalent	2,815		

Inflation and finance

Consumer price		av. ann. increase 2006–11	
inflation 2012	3.0%	Euro area:	
Av. ann. inflation 2007–12	2.3%	Narrow money (M1)	5.3%
Money market rate, Dec. 2012	2.60%	Broad money	4.7%
		H'hold saving rate, Dec. 2012	3.4%

Exchange rates

	end 2012		2012
€ per $	0.76	Effective rates	2005 = 100
€ per SDR	1.16	– nominal	100.0
		– real	98.2

Trade

Principal exports	
	$bn fob
Machinery & transport equip.	180.9
Chemicals & related products	58.3
Food, drink & tobacco	36.8
Mineral fuels & lubricants	26.3
Total incl. others	**523.3**

Principal imports	
	$bn cif
Machinery & transport equip.	138.6
Mineral fuels & lubricants	107.8
Chemicals & related products	76.7
Food, drink & tobacco	45.7
Total incl. others	**558.8**

Main export destinations	
	% of total
Germany	13.1
France	11.6
United States	6.1
United Kingdom	4.7
EU27	56.0

Main origins of imports	
	% of total
Germany	15.6
France	8.3
Netherlands	5.2
United Kingdom	2.7
EU27	53.7

Balance of payments, reserves and aid, $bn

Visible exports fob	503.0	Overall balance	1.2
Visible imports fob	-523.1	Change in reserves	11.4
Trade balance	-20.1	Level of reserves	
Invisibles inflows	190.0	end Dec.	169.9
Invisibles outflows	-215.1	No. months of import cover	2.8
Net transfers	-22.1	Official gold holdings, m oz	78.8
Current account balance	-67.4	Aid given	4.33
– as % of GDP	-3.1	– as % of GDP	0.20
Capital balance	103.4		

Health and education

Health spending, % of GDP	9.5	Education spending, % of GDP	4.5
Doctors per 1,000 pop.	3.5	Enrolment, %: primary	102
Hospital beds per 1,000 pop.	3.5	secondary	100
Improved-water source access,		tertiary	65
% of pop.	100		

Society

No. of households	24.7m	Cost of living, Dec. 2012	
Av. no. per household	2.5	New York = 100	97
Marriages per 1,000 pop.	3.6	Cars per 1,000 pop.	610
Divorces per 1,000 pop.	0.9	Colour TV households, % with:	
Religion, % of pop.		cable	1.0
Christian	83.3	satellite	32.0
Non-religious	12.4	Telephone lines per 100 pop.	36.4
Muslim	3.7	Mobile telephone subscribers	
Other	0.4	per 100 pop.	157.9
Hindu	0.1	Broadband subs per 100 pop.	22.1
Jewish	<0.1	Internet hosts per 1,000 pop.	422.1

JAPAN

Area	377,727 sq km	Capital	Tokyo
Arable as % of total land	11.7	Currency	Yen (¥)

People

Population	126.5m	Life expectancy:	men	80.1 yrs
Pop. per sq km	334.9		women	87.1 yrs
Total growth		Adult literacy		...
in pop. 2000–10	0.6%	Fertility rate (per woman)		1.4
Pop. under 15	13.2%	Urban population		91.3%
Pop. over 60	30.5%			per 1,000 pop.
No. of men per 100 women	95.0	Crude birth rate		8.0
Human Development Index	91.2	Crude death rate		9.6

The economy

GDP	¥468trn	GDP per head	$45,900
GDP	$5,867bn	GDP per head in purchasing	
Av. ann. growth in real		power parity (USA=100)	70.0
GDP 2006–11	-0.1%	Economic freedom index	71.8

Origins of GDP		**Components of GDP**	
	% of total		% of total
Agriculture	1	Private consumption	60
Industry, of which:	27	Public consumption	21
manufacturing	19	Investment	20
Services	71	Exports	15
		Imports	-16

Structure of employment

	% of total		% of labour force
Agriculture	4	Unemployed 2011	4.5
Industry	25	Av. ann. rate 2000–11	4.7
Services	71		

Energy

	m TOE		
Total output	96.8	Net energy imports as %	
Total consumption	496.8	of energy use	81
Consumption per head,			
kg oil equivalent	3,898		

Inflation and finance

Consumer price		av. ann. increase 2006–11	
inflation 2012	0.0%	Narrow money (M1)	2.2%
Av. ann. inflation 2007–12	-0.2%	Broad money	1.8%
Money market rate, Dec. 2012	0.08%	H'hold saving rate, Dec. 2012	0.8%

Exchange rates

	end 2012		2012
¥ per $	83.58	Effective rates	2005 = 100
¥ per SDR	133.02	– nominal	118.2
¥ per €	109.65	– real	96.2

Trade

Principal exports		Principal imports	
	$bn fob		*$bn cif*
Capital equipment	437.7	Industrial supplies	477.1
Industrial supplies	210.6	Capital equipment	179.0
Consumer durable goods	113.1	Food & direct consumer goods	71.2
Consumer non-durable goods	5.4	Consumer durable goods	52.9
Total incl. others	**823.5**	Total incl. others	**856.0**

Main export destinations		Main origins of imports	
	% of total		*% of total*
China	19.7	China	21.5
United States	15.5	United States	8.9
South Korea	8.0	Australia	6.6
Hong Kong	5.2	Saudi Arabia	5.9
Thailand	4.6	United Arab Emirates	5.0

Balance of payments, reserves and aid, $bn

Visible exports fob	790.0	Overall balance	176.6
Visible imports fob	-794.4	Change in reserves	199.8
Trade balance	-4.5	Level of reserves	
Invisibles inflows	364.7	end Dec.	1,295.8
Invisibles outflows	-227.3	No. months of import cover	15.2
Net transfers	-13.8	Official gold holdings, m oz	24.6
Current account balance	119.1	Aid given	10.83
– as % of GDP	2.0	– as % of GDP	0.18
Capital balance	82.9		

Health and education

Health spending, % of GDP	9.3	Education spending, % of GDP	3.8
Doctors per 1,000 pop.	2.1	Enrolment, %: primary	103
Hospital beds per 1,000 pop.	13.7	secondary	102
Improved-water source access,		tertiary	60
% of pop.	100		

Society

No. of households	51.1m	Cost of living, Dec. 2012	
Av. no. per household	2.5	New York = 100	152
Marriages per 1,000 pop.	5.5	Cars per 1,000 pop.	311
Divorces per 1,000 pop.	2.0	Colour TV households, % with:	
Religion, % of pop.		cable	66.3
Non-religious	57.0	satellite	40.8
Buddhist	36.2	Telephone lines per 100 pop.	51.1
Other	5.0	Mobile telephone subscribers	
Christian	1.6	per 100 pop.	105.0
Muslim	0.2	Broadband subs per 100 pop.	27.6
Jewish	<0.1	Internet hosts per 1,000 pop.	509.5

KENYA

Area	582,646 sq km	Capital	Nairobi
Arable as % of total land	9.7	Currency	Kenyan shilling (KSh)

People

Population	41.6m	Life expectancy: men	56.7 yrs
Pop. per sq km	71.4	women	59.2 yrs
Total growth		Adult literacy	87.4%
in pop. 2000–10	29.6%	Fertility rate (per woman)	4.6
Pop. under 15	42.8%	Urban population	24.0%
Pop. over 60	4.1%		per 1,000 pop.
No. of men per 100 women	99.8	Crude birth rate	37.0
Human Development Index	51.9	Crude death rate	9.9

The economy

GDP	KSh2,986bn	GDP per head	$810
GDP	$33.6bn	GDP per head in purchasing	
Av. ann. growth in real		power parity (USA=100)	3.6
GDP 2006–11	4.3%	Economic freedom index	55.9

Origins of GDP		Components of GDP	
	% of total		% of total
Agriculture	28	Private consumption	78
Industry, of which:	18	Public consumption	18
manufacturing	11	Investment	21
Other	54	Exports	29
		Imports	-46

Structure of employment

	% of total		% of labour force
Agriculture	...	Unemployed 2011	...
Industry	...	Av. ann. rate 2000–11	...
Services	...		

Energy

	m TOE		
Total output	15.8	Net energy imports as %	
Total consumption	19.6	of energy use	19
Consumption per head,			
kg oil equivalent	483		

Inflation and finance

		av. ann. increase 2006–11	
Consumer price			
inflation 2012	9.4%	Narrow money (M1)	16.4%
Av. ann. inflation 2007–12	12.3%	Broad money	18.4%
Treasury bill rate, Dec. 2012	8.30%		

Exchange rates

	end 2012		2012
KSh per $	86.01	Effective rates	2005 = 100
KSh per SDR	132.18	– nominal	...
KSh per €	112.84	– real	...

Trade

Principal exports		Principal imports	
	$bn fob		*$bn cif*
Tea	1.2	Industrial supplies	4.6
Horticultural products	0.9	Machinery & other capital equip.	2.4
Coffee	0.2	Transport equipment	1.5
Fish products	0.1	Food & drink	1.2
Total incl. others	**5.8**	Total incl. others	**13.7**

Main export destinations		Main origins of imports	
	% of total		*% of total*
Uganda	9.7	China	14.7
Tanzania	9.5	India	14.0
Netherlands	8.3	United Arab Emirates	10.1
United Kingdom	8.0	South Africa	7.7

Balance of payments, reserves and debt, $bn

Visible exports fob	5.8	Change in reserves	-0.1
Visible imports fob	-14.2	Level of reserves	
Trade balance	-8.4	end Dec.	4.3
Invisibles inflows	4.4	No. months of import cover	3.1
Invisibles outflows	-2.5	Official gold holdings, m oz	0.0
Net transfers	3.1	Foreign debt	10.3
Current account balance	-3.3	– as % of GDP	22
– as % of GDP	-9.9	– as % of total exports	79
Capital balance	2.1	Debt service ratio	4
Overall balance	-1.2		

Health and education

Health spending, % of GDP	4.5	Education spending, % of GDP	6.7
Doctors per 1,000 pop.	0.2	Enrolment, %: primary	113
Hospital beds per 1,000 pop.	1.4	secondary	60
Improved-water source access,		tertiary	4
% of pop.	59		

Society

No. of households	9.6m	Cost of living, Dec. 2012	
Av. no. per household	4.4	New York = 100	78
Marriages per 1,000 pop.	...	Cars per 1,000 pop.	14
Divorces per 1,000 pop.	...	Colour TV households, % with:	
Religion, % of pop.		cable	2.4
Christian	84.8	satellite	3.3
Muslim	9.7	Telephone lines per 100 pop.	0.7
Other	3.0	Mobile telephone subscribers	
Non-religious	2.5	per 100 pop.	67.5
Hindu	0.1	Broadband subs per 100 pop.	0.1
Jewish	<0.1	Internet hosts per 1,000 pop.	1.7

LATVIA

Area	63,700 sq km	Capital	Riga
Arable as % of total land	18.8	Currency	Lats (LVL)

People

Population	2.2m	Life expectancy: men	68.8 yrs
Pop. per sq km	34.9	women	78.5 yrs
Total growth		Adult literacy	99.8%
in pop. 2000–10	-5.6%	Fertility rate (per woman)	1.5
Pop. under 15	13.8%	Urban population	67.7%
Pop. over 60	22.5%		per 1,000 pop.
No. of men per 100 women	85.2	Crude birth rate	9.0
Human Development Index	81.4	Crude death rate	13.8

The economy

GDP	LVL14.2bn	GDP per head	$13,730
GDP	$28.3bn	GDP per head in purchasing	
Av. ann. growth in real		power parity (USA=100)	39.4
GDP 2006–11	-1.8%	Economic freedom index	66.5

Origins of GDP		**Components of GDP**	
	% of total		% of total
Agriculture	4	Private consumption	62
Industry, of which:	22	Public consumption	16
manufacturing	12	Investment	26
Services	74	Exports	59
		Imports	-63

Structure of employment

	% of total		% of labour force
Agriculture	10	Unemployed 2011	15.4
Industry	23	Av. ann. rate 2000–11	11.7
Services	67		

Energy

			m TOE
Total output	2.1	Net energy imports as %	
Total consumption	4.4	of energy use	52
Consumption per head,			
kg oil equivalent	1,971		

Inflation and finance

Consumer price		av. ann. increase 2006–11	
inflation 2012	2.3%	Narrow money (M1)	1.4%
Av. ann. inflation 2007–12	4.8%	Broad money	5.6%
Money market rate, Dec. 2012	0.10%		

Exchange rates

	end 2012		2012
LVL per $	0.54	Effective rates	2005 = 100
LVL per SDR	0.82	– nominal	...
LVL per €	0.71	– real	...

Trade

Principal exports		Principal imports	
	$bn fob		*$bn cif*
Wood & wood products	2.0	Machinery & equipment	2.7
Metals	1.7	Mineral products	2.7
Machinery & equipment	1.5	Metals	1.7
Chemicals	0.9	Chemicals	1.5
Total incl. others	**12.0**	Total incl. others	**15.4**

Main export destinations		Main origins of imports	
	% of total		*% of total*
Lithuania	18.1	Finland	18.8
Estonia	13.6	Germany	12.1
Russia	10.6	Lithuania	8.5
Germany	8.3	Sweden	7.4
Sweden	6.3	Russia	4.6
EU27	66.0	EU27	77.6

Balance of payments, reserves and debt, $bn

Visible exports fob	11.5	Change in reserves	-1.2
Visible imports fob	-14.7	Level of reserves	
Trade balance	-3.2	end Dec.	6.4
Invisibles inflows	5.9	No. months of import cover	4.1
Invisibles outflows	-4.1	Official gold holdings, m oz	0.2
Net transfers	0.9	Foreign debt	38.3
Current account balance	-0.6	– as % of GDP	132
– as % of GDP	-2.2	– as % of total exports	247
Capital balance	-0.5	Debt service ratio	47
Overall balance	-1.2	Aid given	0.03
		– as % of GDP	0.07

Health and education

Health spending, % of GDP	6.2	Education spending, % of GDP	5.0
Doctors per 1,000 pop.	2.9	Enrolment, %: primary	100
Hospital beds per 1,000 pop.	5.3	secondary	96
Improved-water source access,		tertiary	57
% of pop.	99		

Society

No. of households	0.8m	Cost of living, Dec. 2012	
Av. no. per household	2.8	New York = 100	...
Marriages per 1,000 pop.	5.2	Cars per 1,000 pop.	321
Divorces per 1,000 pop.	4.0	Colour TV households, % with:	
Religion, % of pop.		cable	41.5
Christian	55.8	satellite	12.6
Non-religious	43.8	Telephone lines per 100 pop.	23.0
Other	0.2	Mobile telephone subscribers	
Muslim	0.1	per 100 pop.	102.9
Hindu	<0.1	Broadband subs per 100 pop.	20.4
Jewish	<0.1	Internet hosts per 1,000 pop.	163.5

LITHUANIA

Area	65,200 sq km	Capital	Vilnius
Arable as % of total land	32.9	Currency	Litas (LTL)

People

Population	3.3m	Life expectancy: men	67.2 yrs
Pop. per sq km	50.9	women	78.3 yrs
Total growth		Adult literacy	99.7%
in pop. 2000–10	-5.0%	Fertility rate (per woman)	1.5
Pop. under 15	14.6%	Urban population	67.1%
Pop. over 60	21.5%		per 1,000 pop.
No. of men per 100 women	86.8	Crude birth rate	11.0
Human Development Index	81.8	Crude death rate	13.5

The economy

GDP	LTL106bn	GDP per head	$14,100
GDP	$42.7bn	GDP per head in purchasing	
Av. ann. growth in real		power parity (USA=100)	44.6
GDP 2006–11	0.7%	Economic freedom index	72.1

Origins of GDP		**Components of GDP**	
	% of total		% of total
Agriculture	4	Private consumption	64
Industry, of which:	28	Public consumption	19
manufacturing	16	Investment	19
Services	68	Exports	78
		Imports	-79

Structure of employment

	% of total		% of labour force
Agriculture	9	Unemployed 2011	15.4
Industry	24	Av. ann. rate 2000–11	12.0
Services	67		

Energy

		m TOE	
Total output	1.5	Net energy imports as %	
Total consumption	6.9	of energy use	78
Consumption per head,			
kg oil equivalent	2,107		

Inflation and finance

Consumer price		av. ann. increase 2006–11	
inflation 2012	3.1%	Narrow money (M1)	4.7%
Av. ann. inflation 2007–12	4.7%	Broad money	6.8%
Money market rate, Dec. 2012	0.06%		

Exchange rates

	end 2012		2012
LTL per $	2.63	Effective rates	2005 = 100
LTL per SDR	4.01	– nominal	...
LTL per €	3.45	– real	...

Trade

Principal exports		**Principal imports**	
	$bn fob		*$bn cif*
Mineral products	6.7	Mineral products	7.3
Machinery & equipment	3.1	Machinery & equipment	5.6
Transport equipment	2.5	Transport equipment	4.5
Chemicals	2.0	Chemicals	2.9
Total incl. others	**28.0**	Total incl. others	**31.8**

Main export destinations		**Main origins of imports**	
	% of total		*% of total*
Russia	16.6	Russia	32.5
Latvia	10.2	Germany	9.7
Germany	9.3	Poland	9.1
Poland	7.0	Latvia	6.6
Estonia	6.6	Netherlands	4.9
EU27	61.3	EU25	56.7

Balance of payments, reserves and debt, $bn

Visible exports fob	27.0	Change in reserves	2.6
Visible imports fob	-29.5	Level of reserves	
Trade balance	-2.5	end Dec.	8.2
Invisibles inflows	6.5	No. months of import cover	2.8
Invisibles outflows	-6.2	Official gold holdings, m oz	0.2
Net transfers	1.5	Foreign debt	30.0
Current account balance	-0.6	– as % of GDP	73
– as % of GDP	-1.4	– as % of total exports	105
Capital balance	2.4	Debt service ratio	20
Overall balance	1.9	Aid given	0.02
		– as % of GDP	0.13

Health and education

Health spending, % of GDP	6.6	Education spending, % of GDP	5.4
Doctors per 1,000 pop.	3.6	Enrolment, %: primary	94
Hospital beds per 1,000 pop.	6.8	secondary	99
Improved-water source access,		tertiary	69
% of pop.	...		

Society

No. of households	1.4m	Cost of living, Dec. 2012	
Av. no. per household	2.3	New York = 100	...
Marriages per 1,000 pop.	6.0	Cars per 1,000 pop.	541
Divorces per 1,000 pop.	3.2	Colour TV households, % with:	
Religion, % of pop.		cable	51.6
Christian	89.8	satellite	11.7
Non-religious	10.0	Telephone lines per 100 pop.	21.9
Hindu	<0.1	Mobile telephone subscribers	
Jewish	<0.1	per 100 pop.	151.3
Muslim	<0.1	Broadband subs per 100 pop.	22.1
Other	<0.1	Internet hosts per 1,000 pop.	365.3

MALAYSIA

Area	332,665 sq km	Capital	Kuala Lumpur
Arable as % of total land	5.5	Currency	Malaysian dollar/ringgit (M$)

People

Population	28.9m	Life expectancy: men	72.5 yrs
Pop. per sq km	86.9	women	76.9 yrs
Total growth		Adult literacy	93.1%
in pop. 2000–10	21.3%	Fertility rate (per woman)	2.6
Pop. under 15	29.1%	Urban population	72.8%
Pop. over 60	7.8%		per 1,000 pop.
No. of men per 100 women	103.0	Crude birth rate	19.8
Human Development Index	76.9	Crude death rate	4.7

The economy

GDP	M$881bn	GDP per head	$9,980
GDP	$288bn	GDP per head in purchasing	
Av. ann. growth in real		power parity (USA=100)	33.4
GDP 2006–11	4.3%	Economic freedom index	66.1

Origins of GDP		Components of GDP	
	% of total		% of total
Agriculture	12	Private consumption	47
Industry, of which:	40	Public consumption	13
manufacturing	24	Investment	24
Services	48	Exports	92
		Imports	-76

Structure of employment

	% of total		% of labour force
Agriculture	13	Unemployed 2010	3.4
Industry	28	Av. ann. rate 2000–10	3.5
Services	59		

Energy

	m TOE		
Total output	85.9	Net energy imports as %	
Total consumption	72.6	of energy use	-18
Consumption per head,			
kg oil equivalent	2,558		

Inflation and finance

Consumer price		av. ann. increase 2006–11	
inflation 2012	1.7%	Narrow money (M1)	12.8%
Av. ann. inflation 2007–12	2.5%	Broad money	9.6%
Money market rate, Dec. 2012	2.99%		

Exchange rates

	end 2012		2012
M$ per $	3.06	Effective rates	2005 = 100
M$ per SDR	4.70	– nominal	109.1
M$ per €	4.01	– real	109.2

Trade

Principal exports		Principal imports	
	$bn fob		$bn cif
Machinery & transport equip.	88.0	Machinery & transport equip.	83.7
Mineral fuels	40.3	Manufactured goods	24.4
Manufactured goods	21.3	Mineral fuels	22.1
Chemicals	15.1	Chemicals	17.7
Total incl. others	**228.1**	Total incl. others	**187.5**

Main export destinations		Main origins of imports	
	% of total		% of total
China	20.2	China	23.0
Singapore	14.4	Singapore	15.3
Japan	12.0	Japan	11.2
United States	9.6	United States	8.8
Thailand	5.0	Thailand	6.7

Balance of payments, reserves and debt, $bn

Visible exports fob	227.6	Change in reserves	27.1
Visible imports fob	-179.2	Level of reserves	
Trade balance	48.4	end Dec.	133.6
Invisibles inflows	53.1	No. months of import cover	6.6
Invisibles outflows	-62.9	Official gold holdings, m oz	1.2
Net transfers	-6.9	Foreign debt	94.5
Current account balance	31.8	– as % of GDP	37
– as % of GDP	11.0	– as % of total exports	35
Capital balance	7.3	Debt service ratio	4
Overall balance	31.2		

Health and education

Health spending, % of GDP	3.6	Education spending, % of GDP	5.1
Doctors per 1,000 pop.	1.2	Enrolment, %: primary	...
Hospital beds per 1,000 pop.	1.8	secondary	69
Improved-water source access,		tertiary	42
% of pop.	100		

Society

No. of households	6.7m	Cost of living, Dec. 2012	
Av. no. per household	4.3	New York = 100	76
Marriages per 1,000 pop.	5.3	Cars per 1,000 pop.	344
Divorces per 1,000 pop.	...	Colour TV households, % with:	
Religion, % of pop.		cable	12.5
Muslim	63.7	satellite	55.3
Buddhist	17.7	Telephone lines per 100 pop.	14.7
Christian	9.4	Mobile telephone subscribers	
Hindu	6.0	per 100 pop.	127.0
Other	2.5	Broadband subs per 100 pop.	7.4
Non-religious	0.7	Internet hosts per 1,000 pop.	14.6

MEXICO

Area	1,972,545 sq km	Capital	Mexico city
Arable as % of total land	13.0	Currency	Mexican peso (PS)

People

Population	114.8m	Life expectancy:	men	74.8 yrs
Pop. per sq km	58.2		women	79.6 yrs
Total growth		Adult literacy		93.1%
in pop. 2000–10	13.5%	Fertility rate (per woman)		2.2
Pop. under 15	27.9%	Urban population		78.1%
Pop. over 60	9.4%			per 1,000 pop.
No. of men per 100 women	97.3	Crude birth rate		18.5
Human Development Index	77.5	Crude death rate		4.8

The economy

GDP	PS14,342bn	GDP per head	$10,050
GDP	$1,153bn	GDP per head in purchasing	
Av. ann. growth in real		power parity (USA=100)	34.5
GDP 2006–11	1.5%	Economic freedom index	67.0

Origins of GDP		**Components of GDP**	
	% of total		% of total
Agriculture	4	Private consumption	64
Industry, of which:	37	Public consumption	12
manufacturing & mining	18	Investment	25
Services	60	Exports	32
		Imports	-33

Structure of employment

	% of total		% of labour force
Agriculture	13	Unemployed 2011	5.3
Industry	26	Av. ann. rate 2000–11	3.5
Services	61		

Energy

	m TOE		
Total output	226.4	Net energy imports as %	
Total consumption	178.1	of energy use	-27
Consumption per head,			
kg oil equivalent	1,570		

Inflation and finance

Consumer price		av. ann. increase 2006–11	
inflation 2012	4.1%	Narrow money (M1)	11.3%
Av. ann. inflation 2007–12	4.4%	Broad money	11.0%
Money market rate, Dec. 2012	4.84%		

Exchange rates

	end 2012		2012
			2005 = 100
PS per $	12.87	Effective rates	
PS per SDR	20.00	– nominal	80.8
PS per €	16.88	– real	92.9

Trade

Principal exports		Principal imports	
	$bn fob		$bn cif
Manufactured products	278.6	Intermediate goods	264.0
Crude oil & products	56.4	Consumer goods	51.8
Agricultural products	10.6	Capital goods	35.0
Mining products	4.9		
Total	349.4	Total	350.8

Main export destinations		Main origins of imports	
	% of total		% of total
United States	78.5	United States	49.7
Canada	3.1	China	14.9
China	1.7	Japan	4.7
Colombia	1.6	South Korea	3.9

Balance of payments, reserves and debt, $bn

Visible exports fob	349.9	Change in reserves	28.6
Visible imports fob	-351.1	Level of reserves	
Trade balance	-1.2	end Dec.	149.2
Invisibles inflows	25.9	No. months of import cover	4.4
Invisibles outflows	-56.9	Official gold holdings, m oz	3.4
Net transfers	23.0	Foreign debt	287.0
Current account balance	-9.2	– as % of GDP	20
– as % of GDP	-0.8	– as % of total exports	65
Capital balance	44.0	Debt service ratio	11
Overall balance	29.6		

Health and education

Health spending, % of GDP	6.2	Education spending, % of GDP	5.3
Doctors per 1,000 pop.	2.0	Enrolment, %: primary	113
Hospital beds per 1,000 pop.	1.7	secondary	91
Improved-water source access,		tertiary	28
% of pop.	96		

Society

No. of households	29.0m	Cost of living, Dec. 2012	
Av. no. per household	3.8	New York = 100	86
Marriages per 1,000 pop.	5.5	Cars per 1,000 pop.	213
Divorces per 1,000 pop.	0.8	Colour TV households, % with:	
Religion, % of pop.		cable	23.2
Christian	95.1	satellite	7.2
Non-religious	4.7	Telephone lines per 100 pop.	17.2
Hindu	<0.1	Mobile telephone subscribers	
Jewish	<0.1	per 100 pop.	82.4
Muslim	<0.1	Broadband subs per 100 pop.	10.2
Other	<0.1	Internet hosts per 1,000 pop.	141.4

MOROCCO

Area	446,550 sq km	Capital	Rabat
Arable as % of total land	17.5	Currency	Dirham (Dh)

People

Population	32.3m	Life expectancy: men	70.3 yrs
Pop. per sq km	72.3	women	74.9 yrs
Total growth		Adult literacy	56.1%
in pop. 2000–10	11.0%	Fertility rate (per woman)	2.2
Pop. under 15	28.0%	Urban population	57.0%
Pop. over 60	8.1%		per 1,000 pop.
No. of men per 100 women	96.2	Crude birth rate	18.7
Human Development Index	59.1	Crude death rate	5.8

The economy

GDP	Dh811bn	GDP per head	$3,050
GDP	$100bn	GDP per head in purchasing	
Av. ann. growth in real		power parity (USA=100)	10.3
GDP 2006–11	4.3%	Economic freedom index	59.6

Origins of GDP		**Components of GDP**	
	% of total		% of total
Agriculture	15	Private consumption	63
Industry, of which:	30	Public consumption	15
manufacturing	15	Investment	35
Services	55	Exports	35
		Imports	-48

Structure of employment

	% of total		% of labour force
Agriculture	40	Unemployed 2011	8.9
Industry	22	Av. ann. rate 2000–11	10.7
Services	38		

Energy

	m TOE		
Total output	0.9	Net energy imports as %	
Total consumption	16.5	of energy use	95
Consumption per head,			
kg oil equivalent	517		

Inflation and finance

Consumer price		av. ann. increase 2006–11	
inflation 2012	1.3%	Narrow money (M1)	8.6%
Av. ann. inflation 2007–12	1.6%	Broad money	9.6%
Money market rate, Dec. 2012	3.13%		

Exchange rates

	end 2012		2012
Dh per $	8.48	Effective rates	2005 = 100
Dh per SDR	12.96	– nominal	99.5
Dh per €	11.12	– real	94.5

Trade

Principal exports		Principal imports	
	$bn fob		*$bn cif*
Clothing & textiles	2.3	Fuel & lubricants	11.2
Fertilisers	2.3	Semi-finished goods	9.5
Electrical cables & wires	2.0	Capital goods	8.4
Phosphoric acid	2.0	Consumer goods	7.6
Phosphate rock	1.6	Food, drink & tobacco	4.8
Total incl. others	**21.5**	Total incl. others	**44.3**

Main export destinations		Main origins of imports	
	% of total		*% of total*
Spain	18.6	France	15.4
France	16.9	Spain	14.4
Brazil	6.0	China	7.7
United States	4.8	United States	7.3

Balance of payments, reserves and debt, $bn

Visible exports fob	15.9	Change in reserves	-3.0
Visible imports fob	-37.3	Level of reserves	
Trade balance	-21.4	end Dec.	20.6
Invisibles inflows	16.7	No. months of import cover	5.1
Invisibles outflows	-11.4	Official gold holdings, m oz	0.7
Net transfers	7.8	Foreign debt	29.0
Current account balance	-8.3	– as % of GDP	26
– as % of GDP	-8.3	– as % of total exports	82
Capital balance	2.3	Debt service ratio	10
Overall balance	-6.4		

Health and education

Health spending, % of GDP	6.0	Education spending, % of GDP	5.4
Doctors per 1,000 pop.	0.6	Enrolment, %: primary	115
Hospital beds per 1,000 pop.	1.1	secondary	70
Improved-water source access,		tertiary	13
% of pop.	83		

Society

No. of households	6.6m	Cost of living, Dec. 2012	
Av. no. per household	5.0	New York = 100	70
Marriages per 1,000 pop.	...	Cars per 1,000 pop.	55
Divorces per 1,000 pop.	...	Colour TV households, % with:	
Religion, % of pop.		cable	0.0
Muslim	99.9	satellite	90.7
Christian	<0.1	Telephone lines per 100 pop.	11.1
Hindu	<0.1	Mobile telephone subscribers	
Jewish	<0.1	per 100 pop.	113.3
Non-religious	<0.1	Broadband subs per 100 pop.	1.8
Other	<0.1	Internet hosts per 1,000 pop.	8.6

NETHERLANDS

Area[a]	41,526 sq km	Capital	Amsterdam
Arable as % of total land	31.4	Currency	Euro (€)

People

Population	16.7m	Life expectancy:	men	78.9 yrs
Pop. per sq km	402.1		women	82.8 yrs
Total growth		Adult literacy		...
in pop. 2000–10	4.7%	Fertility rate (per woman)		1.8
Pop. under 15	17.6%	Urban population		83.2%
Pop. over 60	21.9%			per 1,000 pop.
No. of men per 100 women	98.5	Crude birth rate		11.0
Human Development Index	92.1	Crude death rate		8.6

The economy

GDP	€602bn	GDP per head	$50,090
GDP	$836bn	GDP per head in purchasing	
Av. ann. growth in real		power parity (USA=100)	88.9
GDP 2006–11	0.9%	Economic freedom index	73.5

Origins of GDP		Components of GDP	
	% of total		% of total
Agriculture	2	Private consumption	45
Industry, of which:	24	Public consumption	28
manufacturing	13	Investment	18
Services	74	Exports	83
		Imports	-74

Structure of employment

	% of total		% of labour force
Agriculture	3	Unemployed 2011	4.4
Industry	15	Av. ann. rate 2000–11	3.7
Services	82		

Energy

	m TOE		
Total output	69.8	Net energy imports as %	
Total consumption	83.4	of energy use	16
Consumption per head,			
kg oil equivalent	5,021		

Inflation and finance

Consumer price		av. ann. increase 2006–11	
inflation 2012	2.4%	Euro area:	
Av. ann. inflation 2007–12	1.9%	Narrow money (M1)	5.3%
Deposit rate, h'holds, Dec. 2012	2.88%	Broad money	4.7%
		H'hold saving rate, Dec. 2012	3.7%

Exchange rates

	end 2012		2012
€ per $	0.76	Effective rates	2005 = 100
€ per SDR	1.16	– nominal	97.1
		– real	97.7

Trade

Principal exports		Principal imports	
	$bn fob		*$bn cif*
Machinery & transport equip.	191.5	Machinery & transport equip.	175.6
Mineral fuels & lubricants	113.9	Mineral fuels & lubricants	130.9
Chemicals & related products	102.2	Chemicals & related products	66.6
Food, drink & tobacco	78.2	Food, drink & tobacco	51.8
Total incl. others	**569.8**	Total incl. others	**508.0**

Main export destinations		Main origins of imports	
	% of total		*% of total*
Germany	29.9	Germany	17.0
Belgium	16.1	China	13.8
France	10.6	Belgium	10.1
United Kingdom	8.7	United Kingdom	7.1
EU27	77.0	EU27	46.3

Balance of payments, reserves and aid, $bn

Visible exports fob	544.2	Overall balance	3.3
Visible imports fob	-480.6	Change in reserves	4.3
Trade balance	63.6	Level of reserves	
Invisibles inflows	224.9	end Dec.	50.4
Invisibles outflows	-192.1	No. months of import cover	0.9
Net transfers	-15.1	Official gold holdings, m oz	19.7
Current account balance	81.3	Aid given	6.34
– as % of GDP	9.7	– as % of GDP	0.75
Capital balance	-70.3		

Health and education

Health spending, % of GDP	12.0	Education spending, % of GDP	6.0
Doctors per 1,000 pop.	2.9	Enrolment, %: primary	108
Hospital beds per 1,000 pop.	4.7	secondary	121
Improved-water source access,		tertiary	65
% of pop.	100		

Society

No. of households	7.4m	Cost of living, Dec. 2012	
Av. no. per household	2.3	New York = 100	89
Marriages per 1,000 pop.	4.9	Cars per 1,000 pop.	497
Divorces per 1,000 pop.	2.0	Colour TV households, % with:	
Religion, % of pop.		cable	71.0
Christian	50.6	satellite	9.7
Non-religious	42.1	Telephone lines per 100 pop.	43.5
Muslim	6.0	Mobile telephone subscribers	
Other	0.6	per 100 pop.	115.5
Hindu	0.5	Broadband subs per 100 pop.	38.7
Jewish	0.2	Internet hosts per 1,000 pop.	820.3

a Includes water.

NEW ZEALAND

Area	270,534 sq km	Capital	Wellington
Arable as % of total land	1.9	Currency	New Zealand dollar (NZ$)

People

Population	4.4m	Life expectancy: men	78.9 yrs
Pop. per sq km	16.3	women	82.8 yrs
Total growth		Adult literacy	...
in pop. 2000–10	13.2%	Fertility rate (per woman)	2.1
Pop. under 15	20.2%	Urban population	86.2%
Pop. over 60	18.2%		per 1,000 pop.
No. of men per 100 women	96.5	Crude birth rate	14.3
Human Development Index	91.9	Crude death rate	7.1

The economy

GDP	NZ$203bn	GDP per head	$36,250
GDP	$160bn	GDP per head in purchasing	
Av. ann. growth in real		power parity (USA=100)	64.6
GDP 2006–11	0.8%	Economic freedom index	81.4

Origins of GDP		Components of GDP	
	% of total		% of total
Agriculture & mining	5	Private consumption	59
Industry	24	Public consumption	20
Services	71	Investment	19
		Exports	30
		Imports	-29

Structure of employment

	% of total		% of labour force
Agriculture	...	Unemployed 2011	6.5
Industry	...	Av. ann. rate 2000–11	4.9
Services	...		

Energy

	m TOE		
Total output	16.9	Net energy imports as %	
Total consumption	18.2	of energy use	7
Consumption per head,			
kg oil equivalent	4,166		

Inflation and finance

Consumer price		av. ann. increase 2006–11	
inflation 2012	0.7%	Narrow money (M1)	5.9%
Av. ann. inflation 2007–12	2.7%	Broad money	5.2%
Money market rate, Dec. 2012	2.51%	H'hold saving rate, Dec. 2012	0.3%

Exchange rates

	end 2012		2012
NZ$ per $	1.20	Effective rates	2005 = 100
NZ$ per SDR	1.87	– nominal	101.4
NZ$ per €	1.57	– real	103.5

Trade

Principal exports		Principal imports	
	$bn fob		$bn cif
Dairy produce	9.4	Machinery & equipment	7.6
Meat	4.4	Mineral fuels	6.2
Forestry products	3.5	Transport equipment	4.7
Wool	0.6		
Total incl. others	**37.7**	Total incl. others	**37.1**

Main export destinations		Main origins of imports	
	% of total		% of total
Australia	22.7	China	15.9
China	12.3	Australia	15.7
United States	8.4	United States	10.7
Japan	7.2	Japan	6.2

Balance of payments, reserves and aid, $bn

Visible exports fob	38.4	Overall balance	0.4
Visible imports fob	-35.6	Change in reserves	0.3
Trade balance	2.8	Level of reserves	
Invisibles inflows	15.1	end Dec.	17.0
Invisibles outflows	-24.4	No. months of import cover	3.5
Net transfers	-0.2	Official gold holdings, m oz	0.0
Current account balance	-6.7	Aid given	0.42
– as % of GDP	-4.2	– as % of GDP	0.28
Capital balance	34.1		

Health and education

Health spending, % of GDP	10.0	Education spending, % of GDP	7.2
Doctors per 1,000 pop.	2.7	Enrolment, %: primary	101
Hospital beds per 1,000 pop.	2.3	secondary	119
Improved-water source access,		tertiary	83
% of pop.	100		

Society

No. of households	1.5m	Cost of living, Dec. 2012	
Av. no. per household	2.9	New York = 100	108
Marriages per 1,000 pop.	4.7	Cars per 1,000 pop.	648
Divorces per 1,000 pop.	2.0	Colour TV households, % with:	
Religion, % of pop.		cable	5.7
Christian	57.0	satellite	40.4
Non-religious	36.6	Telephone lines per 100 pop.	42.6
Other	2.8	Mobile telephone subscribers	
Hindu	2.1	per 100 pop.	109.2
Muslim	1.2	Broadband subs per 100 pop.	25.8
Jewish	0.2	Internet hosts per 1,000 pop.	687.7

NIGERIA

Area	923,768 sq km	Capital	Abuja
Arable as % of total land	39.5	Currency	Naira (N)

People

Population	162.5m	Life expectancy: men		51.7 yrs
Pop. per sq km	175.9		women	53.4 yrs
Total growth		Adult literacy		61.3%
in pop. 2000–10	28.1%	Fertility rate (per woman)		5.2
Pop. under 15	42.4%	Urban population		49.6%
Pop. over 60	4.9%			per 1,000 pop.
No. of men per 100 women	102.5	Crude birth rate		40.0
Human Development Index	47.1	Crude death rate		13.7

The economy

GDP	N37,754bn	GDP per head	$1,500
GDP	$244bn	GDP per head in purchasing	
Av. ann. growth in real		power parity (USA=100)	5.3
GDP 2006–11	7.0%	Economic freedom index	55.1

Origins of GDP[a]		Components of GDP	
	% of total		% of total
Agriculture	31	Private consumption	60
Industry, of which:	44	Public consumption	13
manufacturing	2	Investment	10
Services	25	Exports	53
		Imports	-36

Structure of employment

	% of total		% of labour force
Agriculture	...	Unemployed 2001	3.9
Industry	...	Av. ann. rate 2000–01	4.0
Services	...		

Energy

	m TOE		
Total output	258.4	Net energy imports as %	
Total consumption	113.1	of energy use	-129
Consumption per head,			
kg oil equivalent	714		

Inflation and finance

Consumer price		av. ann. increase 2006–11	
inflation 2012	12.2%	Narrow money (M1)	26.0%
Av. ann. inflation 2007–12	12.0%	Broad money (M2)	26.9%
Treasury bill rate, Dec. 2012	11.77%		

Exchange rates

	end 2012		2012
N per $	155.27	Effective rates	2005 = 100
N per SDR	238.64	– nominal	81.6
N per €	203.70	– real	142.0

Trade

Principal exports[b]		**Principal imports**[b]	
	$bn fob		*$bn cif*
Mineral products, incl oil & gas	76.0	Industrial goods	13.8
Raw hides & skins	3.1	Capital goods	13.4
Prepared foodstuffs, beverages		Transport equipment & parts	10.7
& tobacco	1.6	Food & beverages	4.2
Vegetable products	1.2		
Total incl. others	**86.6**	Total incl. others	**44.2**

Main export destinations		**Main origins of imports**	
	% of total		*% of total*
United States	26.2	China	17.5
India	10.9	United States	9.1
Brazil	7.0	Netherlands	4.9
Spain	6.4	India	4.7

Balance of payments, reserves and debt, $bn

Visible exports fob	92.5	Change in reserves	0.4
Visible imports fob	-61.7	Level of reserves	
Trade balance	30.9	end Dec.	36.3
Invisibles inflows	4.3	No. months of import cover	4.0
Invisibles outflows	-48.3	Official gold holdings, m oz	0.7
Net transfers	21.8	Foreign debt	13.1
Current account balance	8.7	– as % of GDP	4
– as % of GDP	3.6	– as % of total exports	10
Capital balance	-5.1	Debt service ratio	1
Overall balance	0.3		

Health and education

Health spending, % of GDP	5.3	Education spending, % of GDP	...
Doctors per 1,000 pop.	0.4	Enrolment, %: primary	83
Hospital beds per 1,000 pop.	...	secondary	44
Improved-water source access,		tertiary	10
% of pop.	58		

Society

No. of households	33.1m	Cost of living, Dec. 2012	
Av. no. per household	4.9	New York = 100	66
Marriages per 1,000 pop.	...	Cars per 1,000 pop.	...
Divorces per 1,000 pop.	...	Colour TV households, % with:	
Religion, % of pop.		cable	1.9
Christian	49.3	satellite	2.6
Muslim	48.8	Telephone lines per 100 pop.	0.4
Other	1.4	Mobile telephone subscribers	
Non-religious	0.4	per 100 pop.	58.6
Hindu	<0.1	Broadband subs per 100 pop.	0.1
Jewish	<0.1	Internet hosts per 1,000 pop.	0.0

a 2009   b 2010

NORWAY

Area	323,878 sq km	Capital	Oslo
Arable as % of total land	2.7	Currency	Norwegian krone (Nkr)

People

Population	4.9m	Life expectancy: men		79.1 yrs
Pop. per sq km	15.1	women		83.5 yrs
Total growth		Adult literacy		...
in pop. 2000–10	8.7%	Fertility rate (per woman)		2.0
Pop. under 15	18.8%	Urban population		79.4%
Pop. over 60	21.1%			per 1,000 pop.
No. of men per 100 women	100.1	Crude birth rate		12.3
Human Development Index	95.5	Crude death rate		8.4

The economy

GDP	Nkr2,721bn	GDP per head	$98,080
GDP	$486bn	GDP per head in purchasing	
Av. ann. growth in real		power parity (USA=100)	125.5
GDP 2006–11	0.6%	Economic freedom index	70.5

Origins of GDP		**Components of GDP**	
	% of total		% of total
Agriculture	2	Private consumption	41
Industry, of which:	40	Public consumption	22
manufacturing	9	Investment	23
Services	58	Exports	42
		Imports	-28

Structure of employment

	% of total		% of labour force
Agriculture	2	Unemployed 2011	3.3
Industry	20	Av. ann. rate 2000–11	3.6
Services	78		

Energy

	m TOE		
Total output	205.5	Net energy imports as %	
Total consumption	32.5	of energy use	-533
Consumption per head,			
kg oil equivalent	6,637		

Inflation and finance

Consumer price		av. ann. increase 2006–11	
inflation 2012	0.7%	Narrow money (M1)	...
Av. ann. inflation 2007–12	2.1%	Broad money	...
Interbank rate, Dec. 2012	1.87%	H'hold saving rate, Dec. 2012	9.4%

Exchange rates

	end 2012		2012
Nkr per $	5.60	Effective rates	2005 = 100
Nkr per SDR	8.56	– nominal	106.9
Nkr per €	7.35	– real	105.1

Trade

Principal exports	$bn fob	Principal imports	$bn cif
Mineral fuels & lubricants	108.1	Machinery & transport equip.	34.8
Manufactured goods	13.6	Manufactured goods	13.4
Machinery & transport equip.	12.5	Miscellaneous manufactured	
Food & beverages	9.9	articles	13.1
		Chemicals & mineral products	8.9
Total incl. others	**159.2**	Total incl. others	**90.8**

Main export destinations	% of total	Main origins of imports	% of total
United Kingdom	27.1	Sweden	13.4
Netherlands	11.5	Germany	12.0
Germany	11.0	China	9.0
France	7.1	Denmark	6.3
Sweden	6.5	United Kingdom	5.6
United States	5.6	United States	5.4
EU27	81.2	EU27	62.8

Balance of payments, reserves and aid, $bn

Visible exports fob	159.2	Overall balance	-3.0
Visible imports fob	-89.1	Change in reserves	-3.6
Trade balance	70.1	Level of reserves	
Invisibles inflows	83.4	end Dec.	49.3
Invisibles outflows	-81.7	No. months of import cover	3.5
Net transfers	-5.1	Official gold holdings, m oz	0.0
Current account balance	66.7	Aid given	4.93
– as % of GDP	13.7	– as % of GDP	1.00
Capital balance	-89.5		

Health and education

Health spending, % of GDP	9.0	Education spending, % of GDP	6.9
Doctors per 1,000 pop.	4.2	Enrolment, %: primary	99
Hospital beds per 1,000 pop.	3.3	secondary	111
Improved-water source access,		tertiary	74
% of pop.	100		

Society

No. of households	2.2m	Cost of living, Dec. 2012	
Av. no. per household	2.2	New York = 100	136
Marriages per 1,000 pop.	4.7	Cars per 1,000 pop.	485
Divorces per 1,000 pop.	2.1	Colour TV households, % with:	
Religion, % of pop.		cable	44.0
Christian	84.7	satellite	34.4
Non-religious	10.1	Telephone lines per 100 pop.	31.1
Muslim	3.7	Mobile telephone subscribers	
Other	0.9	per 100 pop.	115.6
Hindu	0.5	Broadband subs per 100 pop.	35.4
Jewish	<0.1	Internet hosts per 1,000 pop.	732.2

PAKISTAN

Area	803,940 sq km	Capital	Islamabad
Arable as % of total land	26.7	Currency	Pakistan rupee (PRs)

People

Population	176.7m	Life expectancy: men		64.9 yrs
Pop. per sq km	219.8	women		66.9 yrs
Total growth		Adult literacy		54.9%
in pop. 2000–10	20.1%	Fertility rate (per woman)		3.2
Pop. under 15	36.6%	Urban population		36.2%
Pop. over 60	6.2%			per 1,000 pop.
No. of men per 100 women	103.4	Crude birth rate		26.3
Human Development Index	51.5	Crude death rate		7.3

The economy

GDP	PRs18,033bn	GDP per head	$1,190
GDP	$210bn	GDP per head in purchasing	
Av. ann. growth in real		power parity (USA=100)	5.7
GDP 2006–11	3.7%	Economic freedom index	55.1

Origins of GDP		**Components of GDP**	
	% of total		% of total
Agriculture	22	Private consumption	84
Industry, of which:	25	Public consumption	8
manufacturing	19	Investment	13
Services	53	Exports	14
		Imports	-19

Structure of employment

	% of total		% of labour force
Agriculture	45	Unemployed 2008	5.0
Industry	20	Av. ann. rate 2000–08	6.7
Services	35		

Energy

	m TOE		
Total output	64.3	Net energy imports as %	
Total consumption	84.6	of energy use	24
Consumption per head,			
kg oil equivalent	487		

Inflation and finance

Consumer price		av. ann. increase 2006–11	
inflation 2012	9.7%	Narrow money (M1)	11.8%
Av. ann. inflation 2007–12	13.8%	Broad money (M2)	13.7%
Money market rate, Dec. 2012	9.14%		

Exchange rates

	end 2012		2012
PRs per $	97.29	Effective rates	2005 = 100
PRs per SDR	149.29	– nominal	56.2
PRs per €	127.63	– real	104.5

Trade[a]

Principal exports		Principal imports	
	$bn fob		*$bn cif*
Cotton fabrics	2.6	Petroleum products	10.5
Knitwear	2.6	Crude oil	5.5
Rice	2.0	Palm oil	2.5
Cotton yarn & thread	1.9	Telecommunications equipment	0.9
Total incl. others	**25.2**	Total incl. others	**44.0**

Main export destinations		Main origins of imports	
	% of total		*% of total*
United States	14.5	China	21.1
United Arab Emirates	7.8	Saudi Arabia	13.2
Afghanistan	7.7	United Arab Emirates	13.1
China	7.7	Kuwait	6.8
Germany	5.1	Malaysia	6.7

Balance of payments, reserves and debt, $bn

Visible exports fob	26.3	Change in reserves	0.4
Visible imports fob	-38.9	Level of reserves	
Trade balance	-12.5	end Dec.	17.7
Invisibles inflows	5.9	No. months of import cover	4.2
Invisibles outflows	-12.0	Official gold holdings, m oz	2.1
Net transfers	16.4	Foreign debt	60.2
Current account balance	-2.2	– as % of GDP	23
– as % of GDP	-1.1	– as % of total exports	156
Capital balance	1.8	Debt service ratio	9
Overall balance	-0.3		

Health and education

Health spending, % of GDP	2.5	Education spending, % of GDP	2.4
Doctors per 1,000 pop.	0.8	Enrolment, %: primary	92
Hospital beds per 1,000 pop.	0.6	secondary	35
Improved-water source access,		tertiary	8
% of pop.	92		

Society

No. of households	27.7m	Cost of living, Dec. 2012	
Av. no. per household	6.4	New York = 100	44
Marriages per 1,000 pop.	...	Cars per 1,000 pop.	11
Divorces per 1,000 pop.	...	Colour TV households, % with:	
Religion, % of pop.		cable	1.2
Muslim	96.4	satellite	15.3
Hindu	1.9	Telephone lines per 100 pop.	3.2
Christian	1.6	Mobile telephone subscribers	
Jewish	<0.1	per 100 pop.	61.6
Non-religious	<0.1	Broadband subs per 100 pop.	0.4
Other	<0.1	Internet hosts per 1,000 pop.	2.1

a Fiscal year ending June 30, 2011.

PERU

Area	1,285,216 sq km	Capital	Lima
Arable as % of total land	2.9	Currency	Nuevo Sol (New Sol)

People

Population	29.4m	Life expectancy: men		71.7 yrs
Pop. per sq km	22.9		women	76.9 yrs
Total growth		Adult literacy		89.6%
in pop. 2000–10	12.4%	Fertility rate (per woman)		2.4
Pop. under 15	29.9%	Urban population		77.3%
Pop. over 60	8.7%			per 1,000 pop.
No. of men per 100 women	100.4	Crude birth rate		19.6
Human Development Index	74.1	Crude death rate		5.5

The economy

GDP	New Soles 487bn	GDP per head	$6,020
GDP	$177bn	GDP per head in purchasing	
Av. ann. growth in real		power parity (USA=100)	21.3
GDP 2006–11	7.0%	Economic freedom index	68.2

Origins of GDP		**Components of GDP**	
	% of total		% of total
Agriculture	6	Private consumption	61
Industry, of which:	36	Public consumption	10
manufacturing	14	Investment	25
Services	57	Exports	29
		Imports	-25

Structure of employment

	% of total		% of labour force
Agriculture	1	Unemployed 2011	7.8
Industry	24	Av. ann. rate 2000–11	8.5
Services	75		

Energy

	m TOE		
Total output	19.4	Net energy imports as %	
Total consumption	19.4	of energy use	0
Consumption per head,			
kg oil equivalent	667		

Inflation and finance

Consumer price		av. ann. increase 2006–11	
inflation 2012	3.7%	Narrow money (M1)	16.0%
Av. ann. inflation 2007–12	3.4%	Broad money	15.9%
Money market rate, Dec. 2012	4.24%		

Exchange rates

	end 2012		2012
New Soles per $	2.57	Effective rates	2005 = 100
New Soles per SDR	3.92	– nominal	...
New Soles per €	3.37	– real	...

Trade

Principal exports	$bn fob	Principal imports	$bn cif
Copper	10.7	Intermediate goods	18.3
Gold	10.1	Capital goods	11.7
Fishmeal	2.1	Consumer goods	6.7
Zinc	1.5	Other goods	0.4
Total incl. others	**46.3**	Total	**37.0**

Main export destinations	% of total	Main origins of imports	% of total
China	15.5	United States	24.8
United States	12.8	China	13.9
Canada	9.6	Brazil	6.7
Japan	4.7	Chile	6.0

Balance of payments, reserves and debt, $bn

Visible exports fob	46.3	Change in reserves	4.7
Visible imports fob	-36.3	Level of reserves	
Trade balance	10.0	end Dec.	48.9
Invisibles inflows	4.8	No. months of import cover	10.2
Invisibles outflows	-21.3	Official gold holdings, m oz	1.1
Net transfers	3.2	Foreign debt	44.9
Current account balance	-3.3	– as % of GDP	27
– as % of GDP	-1.9	– as % of total exports	97
Capital balance	9.0	Debt service ratio	6
Overall balance	4.7		

Health and education

Health spending, % of GDP	4.8	Education spending, % of GDP	2.6
Doctors per 1,000 pop.	0.9	Enrolment, %: primary	106
Hospital beds per 1,000 pop.	1.5	secondary	91
Improved-water source access,		tertiary	43
% of pop.	85		

Society

No. of households	7.5m	Cost of living, Dec. 2012	
Av. no. per household	4.0	New York = 100	73
Marriages per 1,000 pop.	3.5	Cars per 1,000 pop.	38
Divorces per 1,000 pop.	...	Colour TV households, % with:	
Religion, % of pop.		cable	32.2
Christian	95.5	satellite	0.2
Non-religious	3.0	Telephone lines per 100 pop.	12.6
Other	1.5	Mobile telephone subscribers	
Hindu	<0.1	per 100 pop.	110.4
Jewish	<0.1	Broadband subs per 100 pop.	4.1
Muslim	<0.1	Internet hosts per 1,000 pop.	8.0

PHILIPPINES

Area	300,000 sq km	Capital	Manila
Arable as % of total land	18.1	Currency	Philippine peso (P)

People

Population	94.9m	Life expectancy: men		66.0 yrs
Pop. per sq km	316.3	women		72.6 yrs
Total growth		Adult literacy		95.4%
in pop. 2000–10	20.6%	Fertility rate (per woman)		3.3
Pop. under 15	33.5%	Urban population		48.8%
Pop. over 60	6.7%			per 1,000 pop.
No. of men per 100 women	100.7	Crude birth rate		24.5
Human Development Index	65.4	Crude death rate		5.7

The economy

GDP	P9,736bn	GDP per head	$2,370
GDP	$225bn	GDP per head in purchasing	
Av. ann. growth in real		power parity (USA=100)	8.6
GDP 2006–11	4.7%	Economic freedom index	58.2

Origins of GDP		**Components of GDP**	
	% of total		% of total
Agriculture	13	Private consumption	74
Industry, of which:	31	Public consumption	10
manufacturing	21	Investment	22
Services	56	Exports	31
		Imports	-36

Structure of employment

	% of total		% of labour force
Agriculture	33	Unemployed 2011	7.0
Industry	15	Av. ann. rate 2000–11	8.5
Services	52		

Energy

	m TOE		
Total output	23.4	Net energy imports as %	
Total consumption	40.5	of energy use	42
Consumption per head,			
kg oil equivalent	434		

Inflation and finance

Consumer price		av. ann. increase 2006–11	
inflation 2012	3.2%	Narrow money (M1)	14.7%
Av. ann. inflation 2007–12	4.8%	Broad money	12.9%
Money market rate, Dec. 2012	3.62%		

Exchange rates

	end 2012		2012
P per $	41.00	Effective rates	2005 = 100
P per SDR	63.31	– nominal	115.4
P per €	53.79	– real	137.0

Trade

Principal exports	$bn fob	Principal imports	$bn cif
Electrical & electronic equip.	23.8	Capital goods	15.3
Clothing	1.9	Mineral fuels	12.5
Coconut oil	1.4	Chemicals	6.4
Petroleum products	0.6	Manufactured goods	5.4
Total incl. others	**48.3**	Total incl. others	**64.1**

Main export destinations	% of total	Main origins of imports	% of total
China	26.4	China	19.0
Japan	17.5	Japan	16.0
United States	17.2	United States	12.3
Singapore	11.0	South Korea	11.0
Hong Kong	9.3	Singapore	10.4

Balance of payments, reserves and debt, $bn

Visible exports fob	38.9	Change in reserves	12.8
Visible imports fob	55.4	Level of reserves	
Trade balance	-16.5	end Dec.	78.1
Invisibles inflows	23.5	No. months of import cover	12.4
Invisibles outflows	-17.6	Official gold holdings, m oz	5.1
Net transfers	17.6	Foreign debt	76.0
Current account balance	7.0	– as % of GDP	33
– as % of GDP	3.1	– as % of total exports	115
Capital balance	5.2	Debt service ratio	18
Overall balance	10.2		

Health and education

Health spending, % of GDP	4.1	Education spending, % of GDP	2.7
Doctors per 1,000 pop.	...	Enrolment, %: primary	106
Hospital beds per 1,000 pop.	1.0	secondary	85
Improved-water source access,		tertiary	28
% of pop.	92		

Society

No. of households	20.0m	Cost of living, Dec. 2012	
Av. no. per household	4.8	New York = 100	66
Marriages per 1,000 pop.	5.6	Cars per 1,000 pop.	8
Divorces per 1,000 pop.	...	Colour TV households, % with:	
Religion, % of pop.		cable	52.1
Christian	92.6	satellite	0.6
Muslim	5.5	Telephone lines per 100 pop.	3.8
Other	1.7	Mobile telephone subscribers	
Non-religious	0.1	per 100 pop.	99.3
Hindu	<0.1	Broadband subs per 100 pop.	1.9
Jewish	<0.1	Internet hosts per 1,000 pop.	4.5

POLAND

Area	312,683 sq km	Capital	Warsaw
Arable as % of total land	35.9	Currency	Zloty (Zl)

People

Population	38.3m	Life expectancy: men	72.2 yrs
Pop. per sq km	122.5	women	80.6 yrs
Total growth		Adult literacy	99.5
in pop. 2000–10	-0.1%	Fertility rate (per woman)	1.5
Pop. under 15	14.8%	Urban population	60.9%
Pop. over 60	19.4%		per 1,000 pop.
No. of men per 100 women	93.2	Crude birth rate	10.0
Human Development Index	82.1	Crude death rate	10.5

The economy

GDP	Zl1,525bn	GDP per head	$13,350
GDP	$515bn	GDP per head in purchasing	
Av. ann. growth in real		power parity (USA=100)	43.8
GDP 2006–11	4.3%	Economic freedom index	66.0

Origins of GDP		Components of GDP	
	% of total		% of total
Agriculture	4	Private consumption	61
Industry, of which:	32	Public consumption	19
manufacturing	18	Investment	21
Services	65	Exports	42
		Imports	-43

Structure of employment

	% of total		% of labour force
Agriculture	13	Unemployed 2011	9.6
Industry	30	Av. ann. rate 2000–11	14.0
Services	57		

Energy

	m TOE		
Total output	67.4	Net energy imports as %	
Total consumption	101.5	of energy use	34
Consumption per head,			
kg oil equivalent	2,657		

Inflation and finance

Consumer price		av. ann. increase 2006–11	
inflation 2012	3.7%	Narrow money (M1)	11.2%
Av. ann. inflation 2007–12	3.8%	Broad money	12.2%
Money market rate, Dec. 2012	4.37%	H'hold saving rate, Dec. 2012	-0.2%

Exchange rates

	end 2012		2012
Zl per $	3.12	Effective rates	2005 = 100
Zl per SDR	4.76	– nominal	98.4
Zl per €	4.09	– real	102.3

Trade

Principal exports		Principal imports	
	$bn fob		*$bn cif*
Machinery & tranport equip.	48.5	Machinery & transport equip.	44.0
Foodstuffs & live animals	19.9	Manufactured goods	24.7
Manufactured goods	6.9	Chemicals & products	13.4
Total incl. others	**188.9**	Total incl. others	**209.4**

Main export destinations		Main origins of imports	
	% of total		*% of total*
Germany	25.9	Germany	27.4
United Kingdom	6.4	Russia	9.8
Czech Republic	6.2	Netherlands	5.6
France	6.1	Italy	5.1
EU27	78.0	EU27	70.0

Balance of payments, reserves and debt, $bn

Visible exports fob	195.2	Change in reserves	4.2
Visible imports fob	-209.2	Level of reserves	
Trade balance	-14.0	end Dec.	97.7
Invisibles inflows	46.1	No. months of import cover	4.3
Invisibles outflows	-63.3	Official gold holdings, m oz	3.3
Net transfers	6.2	Foreign debt	320.6
Current account balance	-25.0	– as % of GDP	62.5
– as % of GDP	-4.9	– as % of total exports	130
Capital balance	40.4	Debt service ratio	27
Overall balance	6.1	Aid given	0.09
		– as % of GDP	0.08

Health and education

Health spending, % of GDP	6.7	Education spending, % of GDP	5.2
Doctors per 1,000 pop.	2.1	Enrolment, %: primary	99
Hospital beds per 1,000 pop.	6.6	secondary	97
Improved-water source access,		tertiary	72
% of pop.	100		

Society

No. of households	14.7m	Cost of living, Dec. 2012	
Av. no. per household	2.6	New York = 100	71
Marriages per 1,000 pop.	5.4	Cars per 1,000 pop.	471
Divorces per 1,000 pop.	1.7	Colour TV households, % with:	
Religion, % of pop.		cable	34.7
Christian	94.3	satellite	69.2
Non-religious	5.6	Telephone lines per 100 pop.	17.9
Hindu	<0.1	Mobile telephone subscribers	
Jewish	<0.1	per 100 pop.	131.0
Muslim	<0.1	Broadband subs per 100 pop.	14.7
Other	<0.1	Internet hosts per 1,000 pop.	346.4

PORTUGAL

Area	88,940 sq km	Capital	Lisbon
Arable as % of total land	12.5	Currency	Euro (€)

People

Population	10.7m	Life expectancy: men	76.8 yrs
Pop. per sq km	116.1	women	82.8 yrs
Total growth		Adult literacy	95.2%
in pop. 2000–10	3.3%	Fertility rate (per woman)	1.3
Pop. under 15	15.2%	Urban population	61.1%
Pop. over 60	23.6%		per 1,000 pop.
No. of men per 100 women	94.0	Crude birth rate	9.0
Human Development Index	81.6	Crude death rate	10.1

The economy

GDP	€171bn	GDP per head	$22,490
GDP	$237bn	GDP per head in purchasing	
Av. ann. growth in real		power parity (USA=100)	53.1
GDP 2006–11	-0.1%	Economic freedom index	63.1

Origins of GDP		Components of GDP	
	% of total		% of total
Agriculture	2	Private consumption	66
Industry, of which:	23	Public consumption	20
manufacturing	13	Investment	17
Services	74	Exports	36
		Imports	-39

Structure of employment

	% of total		% of labour force
Agriculture	11	Unemployed 2011	12.7
Industry	28	Av. ann. rate 2000–11	7.5
Services	61		

Energy

	m TOE		
Total output	5.6	Net energy imports as %	
Total consumption	23.5	of energy use	76
Consumption per head,			
kg oil equivalent	2,213		

Inflation and finance

Consumer price		av. ann. increase 2006–11	
inflation 2012	2.8%	Euro area:	
Av. ann. inflation 2007–12	1.9%	Narrow money (M1)	5.3%
Deposit rate, h'holds, Dec. 2012	2.34%	Broad money	4.7%
		H'hold saving rate[a], Dec. 2012	11.6%

Exchange rates

	end 2012		2012
€ per $	0.76	Effective rates	2005 = 100
€ per SDR	1.16	– nominal	100.5
		– real	99.6

Trade

Principal exports		Principal imports	
	$bn fob		*$bn cif*
Machinery & transport equip.	16.0	Machinery & transport equip.	20.7
Food, drink & tobacco	5.9	Mineral fuels & lubricants	14.2
Chemicals & related products	5.2	Chemicals & related products	10.7
Mineral fuels & lubricants	4.2	Food, drink & tobacco	10.4
Total incl. others	**59.7**	Total incl. others	**82.4**

Main export destinations		Main origins of imports	
	% of total		*% of total*
Spain	24.6	Spain	30.7
Germany	13.4	Germany	12.0
France	11.9	France	6.7
Angola	5.4	Italy	5.2
United Kingdom	5.1	Netherlands	4.7
EU27	74.4	EU27	73.6

Balance of payments, reserves and debt, $bn

Visible exports fob	60.0	Overall balance	-19.9
Visible imports fob	-79.7	Change in reserves	-0.1
Trade balance	-19.7	Level of reserves	
Invisibles inflows	39.2	end Dec.	20.8
Invisibles outflows	-40.5	No. months of import cover	2.1
Net transfers	4.1	Official gold holdings, m oz	12.3
Current account balance	-16.8	Aid given	0.71
– as % of GDP	-7.1	– as % of GDP	0.31
Capital balance	15.0		

Health and education

Health spending, % of GDP	10.4	Education spending, % of GDP	5.8
Doctors per 1,000 pop.	3.9	Enrolment, %: primary	112
Hospital beds per 1,000 pop.	3.4	secondary[b]	109
Improved-water source access,		tertiary	65
% of pop.	99		

Society

No. of households	4.2m	Cost of living, Dec. 2012	
Av. no. per household	2.5	New York = 100	78
Marriages per 1,000 pop.	3.4	Cars per 1,000 pop.	433
Divorces per 1,000 pop.	2.5	Colour TV households, % with:	
Religion, % of pop.		cable	54.5
Christian	93.8	satellite	20.0
Non-religious	4.4	Telephone lines per 100 pop.	42.4
Other	1.0	Mobile telephone subscribers	
Muslim	0.6	per 100 pop.	115.4
Hindu	0.1	Broadband subs per 100 pop.	21.0
Jewish	<0.1	Internet hosts per 1,000 pop.	350.2

a Gross.
b Includes training for unemployed.

ROMANIA

Area	237,500 sq km	Capital	Bucharest
Arable as % of total land	39.8	Currency	Leu (RON)

People

Population	21.4m	Life expectancy: men		70.6 yrs
Pop. per sq km	90.1	women		78.0 yrs
Total growth		Adult literacy		97.7%
in pop. 2000–10	-3.2%	Fertility rate (per woman)		1.4
Pop. under 15	15.2%	Urban population		52.8%
Pop. over 60	20.3%			per 1,000 pop.
No. of men per 100 women	94.3	Crude birth rate		9.0
Human Development Index	78.6	Crude death rate		12.1

The economy

GDP	RON579bn	GDP per head	$8,870
GDP	$190bn	GDP per head in purchasing	
Av. ann. growth in real		power parity (USA=100)	33.2
GDP 2006–11	1.5%	Economic freedom index	65.1

Origins of GDP		Components of GDP	
	% of total		% of total
Agriculture	7	Private consumption	61
Industry, of which:	41	Public consumption	14
manufacturing	21	Investment	29
Services	52	Exports	38
		Imports	-43

Structure of employment

	% of total		% of labour force
Agriculture	30	Unemployed 2011	7.4
Industry	29	Av. ann. rate 2000–11	7.1
Services	41		

Energy

	m TOE		
Total output	27.4	Net energy imports as %	
Total consumption	35.0	of energy use	22
Consumption per head,			
kg oil equivalent	1,632		

Inflation and finance

Consumer price		av. ann. increase 2006–11	
inflation 2012	3.3%	Narrow money (M1)	19.4%
Av. ann. inflation 2007–12	5.7%	Broad money	14.3%
Money market rate, Dec. 2012	5.78%		

Exchange rates

	end 2012		2012
			2005 = 100
RON per $	3.42	Effective rates	
RON per SDR	5.16	– nominal	81.6
RON per €	4.49	– real	101.0

Trade

Principal exports		Principal imports	
	$bn fob		*$bn cif*
Machinery & equipment		Machinery & equipment	
(incl. transport)	16.9	(incl. transport)	20.8
Basic metals & products	7.6	Minerals, fuels & lubricants	9.3
Textiles & apparel	5.0	Chemical products	7.6
Minerals, fuels & lubricants	3.6	Textiles & products	4.9
Total incl. others	**62.7**	Total incl. others	**76.3**

Main export destinations		Main origins of imports	
	% of total		*% of total*
Germany	18.6	Germany	17.1
Italy	12.9	Italy	11.4
France	7.5	Hungary	8.7
Turkey	6.1	France	5.8
EU27	71.0	EU27	72.7

Balance of payments, reserves and debt, $bn

Visible exports fob	55.8	Change in reserves	-0.0
Visible imports fob	-68.4	Level of reserves	
Trade balance	-12.6	end Dec.	48.0
Invisibles inflows	13.9	No. months of import cover	7.0
Invisibles outflows	-14.3	Official gold holdings, m oz	3.3
Net transfers	4.6	Foreign debt	129.8
Current account balance	-8.3	– as % of GDP	66
– as % of GDP	-4.4	– as % of total exports	192
Capital balance	7.7	Debt service ratio	28
Overall balance	-0.1	Aid	0.48
		– as % of GDP	0.09

Health and education

Health spending, % of GDP	5.8	Education spending, % of GDP	4.2
Doctors per 1,000 pop.	2.4	Enrolment, %: primary	96
Hospital beds per 1,000 pop.	6.3	secondary	97
Improved-water source access,		tertiary	59
% of pop.	...		

Society

No. of households	7.5m	Cost of living, Dec. 2012	
Av. no. per household	2.9	New York = 100	54
Marriages per 1,000 pop.	4.9	Cars per 1,000 pop.	207
Divorces per 1,000 pop.	1.7	Colour TV households, % with:	
Religion, % of pop.		cable	46.0
Christian	99.5	satellite	36.9
Muslim	0.3	Telephone lines per 100 pop.	21.8
Non-religious	0.1	Mobile telephone subscribers	
Hindu	<0.1	per 100 pop.	109.2
Jewish	<0.1	Broadband subs per 100 pop.	15.2
Other	<0.1	Internet hosts per 1,000 pop.	124.6

RUSSIA

Area	17,075,400 sq km	Capital	Moscow
Arable as % of total land	7.3	Currency	Rouble (Rb)

People

Population	142.8m	Life expectancy: men	63.3 yrs
Pop. per sq km	8.4	women	75.0 yrs
Total growth		Adult literacy	99.6%
in pop. 2000–10	-2.6%	Fertility rate (per woman)	1.5
Pop. under 15	15.0%	Urban population	73.8%
Pop. over 60	18.1%		per 1,000 pop.
No. of men per 100 women	86.1	Crude birth rate	11.8
Human Development Index	78.8	Crude death rate	14.0

The economy

GDP	Rb54,586bn	GDP per head	$13,000
GDP	$1,858bn	GDP per head in purchasing	
Av. ann. growth in real		power parity (USA=100)	45.6
GDP 2006–11	2.8%	Economic freedom index	51.1

Origins of GDP		Components of GDP	
	% of total		% of total
Agriculture	4	Private consumption	48
Industry, of which:	37	Public consumption	18
manufacturing	16	Investment	25
Services	59	Exports	31
		Imports	-22

Structure of employment

	% of total		% of labour force
Agriculture	10	Unemployed 2011	6.6
Industry	28	Av. ann. rate 2000–11	7.7
Services	62		

Energy

	m TOE		
Total output	1,293.0	Net energy imports as %	
Total consumption	701.5	of energy use	-84
Consumption per head,			
kg oil equivalent	4,927		

Inflation and finance

Consumer price		av. ann. increase 2006–11	
inflation 2012	5.1%	Narrow money (M0)	16.3%
Av. ann. inflation 2007–12	9.2%	Broad money	23.3%
Money market rate, Dec. 2012	6.20%		

Exchange rates

	end 2012		2012
Rb per $	30.74	Effective rates	2005 = 100
Rb per SDR	46.68	– nominal	94.2
Rb per 7	40.33	– real	135.9

Trade

Principal exports		Principal imports	
	$bn fob		*$bn cif*
Fuels	363.0	Machinery & equipment	147.0
Metals	57.4	Chemicals	45.4
Chemicals	31.0	Food & agricultural products	42.5
Machinery & equipment	23.2	Metals	21.8
Total incl. others	**516.7**	**Total incl. others**	**305.8**

Main export destinations		Main origins of imports	
	% of total		*% of total*
Netherlands	12.1	China	15.8
China	6.8	Germany	12.3
Germany	6.6	Ukraine	6.6
Italy	6.3	Italy	4.4

Balance of payments, reserves and debt, $bn

Visible exports fob	512.9	Change in reserves	18.2
Visible imports fob	-315.8	Level of reserves	
Trade balance	197.1	end Dec.	497.4
Invisibles inflows	100.5	No. months of import cover	11.7
Invisibles outflows	-195.6	Official gold holdings, m oz	28.4
Net transfers	-3.2	Foreign debt	543.0
Current account balance	98.8	– as % of GDP	34
– as % of GDP	5.3	– as % of total exports	100
Capital balance	-76.2	Debt service ratio	10
Overall balance	12.6	Aid	5.10
		– as % of GDP	0.03

Health and education

Health spending, % of GDP	6.2	Education spending, % of GDP	4.1
Doctors per 1,000 pop.	4.3	Enrolment, %: primary	99
Hospital beds per 1,000 pop.	...	secondary	89
Improved-water source access,		tertiary	76
% of pop.	97		

Society

No. of households	52.6m	Cost of living, Dec. 2012	
Av. no. per household	2.7	New York = 100	91
Marriages per 1,000 pop.	9.2	Cars per 1,000 pop.	259
Divorces per 1,000 pop.	4.7	Colour TV households, % with:	
Religion, % of pop.		cable	37.5
Christian	73.3	satellite	8.0
Non-religious	16.2	Telephone lines per 100 pop.	30.9
Muslim	10.0	Mobile telephone subscribers	
Jewish	0.2	per 100 pop.	179.3
Hindu	<0.1	Broadband subs per 100 pop.	13.1
Other	<0.1	Internet hosts per 1,000 pop.	101.8

SAUDI ARABIA

Area	2,200,000 sq km	Capital	Riyadh
Arable as % of total land	1.4	Currency	Riyal (SR)

People

Population	28.1m	Life expectancy: men	73.2 yrs
Pop. per sq km	12.8	women	75.6 yrs
Total growth		Adult literacy	86.6%
in pop. 2000–10	36.9%	Fertility rate (per woman)	2.6
Pop. under 15	31.9%	Urban population	82.3%
Pop. over 60	4.6%		per 1,000 pop.
No. of men per 100 women	124.0	Crude birth rate	21.4
Human Development Index	78.2	Crude death rate	3.7

The economy

GDP	SR2,163bn	GDP per head	$20,540
GDP	$577bn	GDP per head in purchasing	
Av. ann. growth in real		power parity (USA=100)	50.4
GDP 2006–11	6.4%	Economic freedom index	60.6

Origins of GDP		Components of GDP	
	% of total		% of total
Agriculture	2	Private consumption	30
Industry, of which:	60	Public consumption	20
manufacturing	10	Investment	19
Services	38	Exports	62
		Imports	-31

Structure of employment

	% of total		% of labour force
Agriculture	4	Unemployed 2009	5.4
Industry	20	Av. ann. rate 2000–09	5.2
Services	76		

Energy

	m TOE		
Total output	1,293.0	Net energy imports as %	
Total consumption	701.5	of energy use	-84
Consumption per head,			
kg oil equivalent	4,927		

Inflation and finance

Consumer price		av. ann. increase 2006–11	
inflation 2012	4.5%	Narrow money (M1)	19.5%
Av. ann. inflation 2007–12	5.9%	Broad money	13.3%
Money market rate, Dec. 2012	0.99%		

Exchange rates

	end 2012		2012
SR per $	3.75	Effective rates	2005 = 100
SR per SDR	5.76	– nominal	92.3
SRE per €	4.92	– real	106.6

Trade

Principal exports		**Principal imports**	
	$bn fob		*$bn cif*
Crude oil	283.4	Machinery & transport equip.	50.2
Refined petroleum products	39.4	Foodstuffs	18.5
		Chemicals & metal products	9.9
Total incl. others	**364.7**	Total incl. others	**130.6**

Main export destinations		**Main origins of imports**	
	% of total		*% of total*
Japan	13.9	China	12.8
China	13.7	United States	11.9
United States	13.4	Germany	7.1
South Korea	10.2	South Korea	6.0

Balance of payments, reserves and aid, $bn

Visible exports fob	364.7	Overall balance	96.1
Visible imports fob	-120.0	Change in reserves	97.3
Trade balance	244.8	Level of reserves	
Invisibles inflows	31.3	end Dec.	556.6
Invisibles outflows	-88.1	No. months of import cover	32.1
Net transfers	-29.4	Official gold holdings, m oz	10.4
Current account balance	158.5	Aid given	0.03
– as % of GDP	27.5	– as % of GDP	0.01
Capital balance	-14.4		

Health and education

Health spending, % of GDP	3.7	Education spending, % of GDP	5.6
Doctors per 1,000 pop.	0.9	Enrolment, %: primary	106
Hospital beds per 1,000 pop.	2.2	secondary	97
Improved-water source access,		tertiary	41
% of pop.	...		

Society

No. of households	5.0m	Cost of living, Dec. 2012	
Av. no. per household	5.3	New York = 100	60
Marriages per 1,000 pop.	4.5	Cars per 1,000 pop.	476
Divorces per 1,000 pop.	0.9	Colour TV households, % with:	
Religion, % of pop.		cable	0.3
Muslim	93.0	satellite	99.5
Christian	4.4	Telephone lines per 100 pop.	16.5
Jewish	1.1	Mobile telephone subscribers	
Other	0.9	per 100 pop.	191.2
Non-religious	0.7	Broadband subs per 100 pop.	5.6
Hindu	<0.1	Internet hosts per 1,000 pop.	5.2

SINGAPORE

Area	639 sq km	Capital	Singapore
Arable as % of total land	0.9	Currency	Singapore dollar (S$)

People

Population	5.2m	Life expectancy:	men	78.9 yrs
Pop. per sq km	8,137.7		women	83.7 yrs
Total growth		Adult literacy		95.5%
in pop. 2000–10	29.8%	Fertility rate (per woman)		1.5
Pop. under 15	15.6%	Urban population		100.0%
Pop. over 60	16.0%			per 1,000 pop.
No. of men per 100 women	101.7	Crude birth rate		10.0
Human Development Index	89.5	Crude death rate		5.1

The economy

GDP	S$327bn	GDP per head	$46,240
GDP	$240bn	GDP per head in purchasing	
Av. ann. growth in real		power parity (USA=100)	126.1
GDP 2006–11	5.8%	Economic freedom index	88.0

Origins of GDP		Components of GDP	
	% of total		% of total
Agriculture	0	Private consumption	41
Industry, of which:	27	Public consumption	10
manufacturing	21	Investment	22
Services	73	Exports	209
		Imports	-182

Structure of employment

	% of total		% of labour force
Agriculture	1	Unemployed 2011	2.9
Industry	22	Av. ann. rate 2000–11	4.3
Services	77		

Energy

	m TOE		
Total output	0.4	Net energy imports as %	
Total consumption	32.8	of energy use	99
Consumption per head,			
kg oil equivalent	6,456		

Inflation and finance

Consumer price		av. ann. increase 2006–11	
inflation 2012	4.5%	Narrow money (M1)	19.8%
Av. ann. inflation 2007–12	3.9%	Broad money	11.1%
Money market rate, Dec. 2012	0.38%		

Exchange rates

	end 2012		2012
S$ per $	1.22	Effective rates	2005 = 100
S$ per SDR	1.88	– nominal	121.4
S$ per 7	1.60	– real	126.9

Trade

Principal exports		Principal imports	
	$bn fob		*$bn cif*
Mineral fuels	108.7	Machinery & transport equip.	149.7
Electronic components & parts	84.6	Mineral fuels	119.2
Chemicals & products	51.5	Misc. manufactured articles	25.5
Manufactured products	28.8	Manufactured products	24.6
Total incl. others	**409.6**	Total incl. others	**365.8**

Main export destinations		Main origins of imports	
	% of total		*% of total*
Malaysia	12.2	Malaysia	10.7
Hong Kong	11.0	United States	10.7
China	10.4	China	10.4
United States	5.4	Japan	7.2
Japan	4.5	Taiwan	5.9
Australia	3.9	Saudi Arabia	4.8
Taiwan	3.6	Thailand	3.1

Balance of payments, reserves and debt, $bn

Visible exports fob	429.4	Change in reserves	12.4
Visible imports fob	-361.9	Level of reserves	
Trade balance	67.5	end Dec.	243.8
Invisibles inflows	181.6	No. months of import cover	5.3
Invisibles outflows	-185.3	Official gold holdings, m oz	4.0
Net transfers	-6.7	Foreign debt	23.6
Current account balance	57.0	– as % of GDP	9
– as % of GDP	23.8	– as % of total exports	4
Capital balance	-40.0	Debt service ratio	1
Overall balance	17.2		

Health and education

Health spending, % of GDP	4.6	Education spending, % of GDP	3.3
Doctors per 1,000 pop.	1.9	Enrolment, %: primary	...
Hospital beds per 1,000 pop.	2.7	secondary	...
Improved-water source access,		tertiary	...
% of pop.	100		

Society

No. of households	1.5m	Cost of living, Dec. 2012	
Av. no. per household	3.5	New York = 100	135
Marriages per 1,000 pop.	5.3	Cars per 1,000 pop.	129
Divorces per 1,000 pop.	1.5	Colour TV households, % with:	
Religion, % of pop.		cable	55.3
Buddhist	33.9	satellite	0.0
Christian	18.2	Telephone lines per 100 pop.	38.9
Non-religious	16.4	Mobile telephone subscribers	
Muslim	14.3	per 100 pop.	150.2
Other	12.0	Broadband subs per 100 pop.	25.6
Hindu	5.2	Internet hosts per 1,000 pop.	377.0

SLOVAKIA

Area	49,035 sq km	Capital	Bratislava
Arable as % of total land	28.9	Currency	Euro (€)

People

Population	5.5m	Life expectancy: men	71.9 yrs
Pop. per sq km	112.2	women	79.5 yrs
Total growth		Adult literacy	...
in pop. 2000–10	1.1%	Fertility rate (per woman)	1.5
Pop. under 15	15.2%	Urban population	54.7%
Pop. over 60	17.7%		per 1,000 pop.
No. of men per 100 women	94.6	Crude birth rate	11.0
Human Development Index	84.0	Crude death rate	9.9

The economy

GDP	€69.1bn	GDP per head	$17,780
GDP	$96.0bn	GDP per head in purchasing	
Av. ann. growth in real		power parity (USA=100)	50.1
GDP 2006–11	3.7%	Economic freedom index	68.7

Origins of GDP		**Components of GDP**	
	% of total		% of total
Agriculture	4	Private consumption	57
Industry, of which:	35	Public consumption	18
Manufacturing	21	Investment	22
Services	61	Exports	89
		Imports	-86

Structure of employment

	% of total		% of labour force
Agriculture	3	Unemployed 2011	13.5
Industry	37	Av. ann. rate 2000–11	15.2
Services	60		

Energy

	m TOE		
Total output	6.2	Net energy imports as %	
Total consumption	17.8	of energy use	65
Consumption per head,			
kg oil equivalent	3,280		

Inflation and finance

Consumer price		*av. ann. increase 2006–11*	
inflation 2012	3.6%	Euro area:	
Av. ann. inflation 2007–12	2.9%	Narrow money	5.3%
Deposit rate, h'holds, Dec. 2012	2.09%	Broad money	4.7%
		H'hold saving rate, Dec. 2012	4.8%

Exchange rates

	end 2012		2012
€ per $	0.76	Effective rates	2005 = 100
€ per SDR	1.16	– nominal	127.91
		– real	134.67

Trade

Principal exports		Principal imports	
	$bn fob		*$bn cif*
Machinery & transport equip.	42.4	Machinery & transport equip.	20.8
Intermediate & manuf. products	14.9	Intermediate manuf. products	11.2
Miscellaneous manuf. goods	4.8	Fuels	9.1
Chemicals	2.4	Chemicals	5.1
Total incl. others	**78.4**	Total incl. others	**74.6**

Main export destinations		Main origins of imports	
	% of total		*% of total*
Germany	20.4	Germany	19.5
Czech Republic	14.5	Czech Republic	18.8
Poland	7.5	Russia	11.6
Hungary	7.4	Hungary	7.1
EU27	84.8	EU27	73.2

Balance of payments, reserves and debt, $bn

Visible exports fob	78.4	Change in reserves	0.3
Visible imports fob	-75.1	Level of reserves	
Trade balance	3.3	end Dec.	2.4
Invisibles inflows	10.0	No. months of import cover	0.3
Invisibles outflows	-12.8	Official gold holdings, m oz	1.0
Net transfers	-0.5	Foreign debt[a]	32.0
Current account balance	0.0	– as % of GDP	37
– as % of GDP	0.0	– as % of total exports	42
Capital balance	5.2	Debt service ratio	7
Overall balance	0.1	Aid given	0.06
		– as % of GDP	0.09

Health and education

Health spending, % of GDP	8.7	Education spending, % of GDP	4.2
Doctors per 1,000 pop.	3.0	Enrolment, %: primary	101
Hospital beds per 1,000 pop.	6.4	secondary	90
Improved-water source access,		tertiary	55
% of pop.	100		

Society

No. of households	2.3m	Cost of living, Dec. 2012	
Av. no. per household	2.4	New York = 100	...
Marriages per 1,000 pop.	4.7	Cars per 1,000 pop.	313
Divorces per 1,000 pop.	2.1	Colour TV households, % with:	
Religion, % of pop.		cable	42.6
Christian	85.3	satellite	53.7
Non-religious	14.3	Telephone lines per 100 pop.	19.3
Muslim	0.2	Mobile telephone subscribers	
Other	0.1	per 100 pop.	109.4
Hindu	<0.1	Broadband subs per 100 pop.	13.7
Jewish	<0.1	Internet hosts per 1,000 pop.	251.7

a 2010

SLOVENIA

Area	20,253 sq km	Capital	Ljubljana
Arable as % of total land	8.5	Currency	Euro (€)

People

Population	2.0m	Life expectancy: men	76.1 yrs
Pop. per sq km	100.2	women	82.8 yrs
Total growth		Adult literacy	99.7%
in pop. 2000–10	2.2%	Fertility rate (per woman)	1.5
Pop. under 15	13.8%	Urban population	49.9%
Pop. over 60	22.4%		per 1,000 pop.
No. of men per 100 women	95.7	Crude birth rate	9.9
Human Development Index	89.2	Crude death rate	9.8

The economy

GDP	€35.6bn	GDP per head	$24,130
GDP	$49.5bn	GDP per head in purchasing	
Av. ann. growth in real		power parity (USA=100)	56.0
GDP 2006–11	0.7%	Economic freedom index	61.7

Origins of GDP		Components of GDP	
	% of total		% of total
Agriculture	2	Private consumption	57
Industry, of which:	32	Public consumption	21
manufacturing	21	Investment	22
Services	66	Exports	72
		Imports	-71

Structure of employment

	% of total		% of labour force
Agriculture	9	Unemployed 2011	8.2
Industry	33	Av. ann. rate 2000–11	6.1
Services	58		

Energy

	m TOE		
Total output	3.7	Net energy imports as %	
Total consumption	7.2	of energy use	49
Consumption per head,			
kg oil equivalent	3,520		

Inflation and finance

Consumer price		av. ann. increase 2006–11	
inflation 2012	2.6%	Euro area:	
Av. ann. inflation 2007–12	2.5%	Narrow money (M1)	5.3%
Money market rate, Dec. 2012	0.11%	Broad money	4.7%
		H'hold saving rate, Dec. 2012	3.4%

Exchange rates

	end 2012		2012
€ per $	0.76	Effective rates	2005 = 100
€ per SDR	1.16	– nominal	...
		– real	...

Trade

Principal exports		Principal imports	
	$bn fob		*$bn cif*
Machinery & transport equip.	8.9	Machinery & transport equip.	10.8
Manufactures	6.6	Manufactures	10.2
Chemicals	4.8	Mineral fuels & lubricants	5.0
Miscellaneous manufactures	3.0	Chemicals	4.4
Total incl. others	**28.9**	Total incl. others	**35.5**

Main export destinations		Main origins of imports	
	% of total		*% of total*
Germany	24.0	Germany	18.5
Italy	14.4	Italy	18.0
Austria	9.2	Austria	11.5
Croatia	7.6	Croatia	5.1
France	6.9	France	4.7
Hungary	4.8	China	4.6
EU27	71.0	EU27	67.7

Balance of payments, reserves and debt, $bn

Visible exports fob	29.6	Change in reserves	-0.1
Visible imports fob	-30.8	Level of reserves	
Trade balance	-1.2	end Dec.	1.0
Invisibles inflows	7.8	No. months of import cover	0.3
Invisibles outflows	-6.8	Official gold holdings, m oz	0.1
Net transfers	0.2	Foreign debt	...
Current account balance	0.0	– as % of GDP	...
– as % of GDP	0.0	– as % of total exports	...
Capital balance	-0.7	Debt service ratio	...
Overall balance	-0.1	Aid	1.27
		– as % of GDP	0.13

Health and education

Health spending, % of GDP	9.1	Education spending, % of GDP	5.7
Doctors per 1,000 pop.	2.5	Enrolment, %: primary	98
Hospital beds per 1,000 pop.	4.6	secondary	97
Improved-water source access,		tertiary	90
% of pop.	99		

Society

No. of households	0.7m	Cost of living, Dec. 2012	
Av. no. per household	2.7	New York = 100	...
Marriages per 1,000 pop.	3.2	Cars per 1,000 pop.	522
Divorces per 1,000 pop.	1.1	Colour TV households, % with:	
Religion, % of pop.		cable	69.8
Christian	78.4	satellite	9.5
Non-religious	18.0	Telephone lines per 100 pop.	42.9
Muslim	3.6	Mobile telephone subscribers	
Hindu	<0.1	per 100 pop.	106.6
Jewish	<0.1	Broadband subs per 100 pop.	24.3
Other	<0.1	Internet hosts per 1,000 pop.	207.8

SOUTH AFRICA

Area	1,225,815 sq km	Capital	Pretoria
Arable as % of total land	10.3	Currency	Rand (R)

People

Population	50.5m	Life expectancy: men	53.1 yrs
Pop. per sq km	41.2	women	54.1 yrs
Total growth		Adult literacy	88.7%
in pop. 2000–10	12.0%	Fertility rate (per woman)	2.4
Pop. under 15	30.3%	Urban population	62.0%
Pop. over 60	7.3%		per 1,000 pop.
No. of men per 100 women	98.1	Crude birth rate	20.5
Human Development Index	62.9	Crude death rate	14.3

The economy

GDP	R2,964bn	GDP per head	$8,070
GDP	$408bn	GDP per head in purchasing	
Av. ann. growth in real		power parity (USA=100)	22.8
GDP 2006–11	2.8%	Economic freedom index	61.8

Origins of GDP		Components of GDP	
	% of total		% of total
Agriculture	2	Private consumption	59
Industry, of which:	31	Public consumption	21
manufacturing	13	Investment	20
Services	67	Exports	29
		Imports	-29

Structure of employment

	% of total		% of labour force
Agriculture	5	Unemployed 2011	24.7
Industry	24	Av. ann. rate 2000–11	25.4
Services	71		

Energy

	m TOE		
Total output	162.4	Net energy imports as %	
Total consumption	136.9	of energy use	-19
Consumption per head,			
kg oil equivalent	2,738		

Inflation and finance

Consumer price		av. ann. increase 2006–11	
inflation 2012	5.7%	Narrow money (M1)	9.3%
Av. ann. inflation 2007–12	6.7%	Broad money	10.7%
Money market rate, Dec. 2012	4.78%		

Exchange rates

	end 2012		2012
			2005 = 100
R per $	8.64	Effective rates	
R per SDR	13.07	– nominal	67.6
R per €	11.33	– real	89.7

Trade

Principal exports		Principal imports	
	$bn fob		$bn cif
Platinum	11.0	Petrochemicals	14.0
Gold	10.3	Petroleum oils & other	5.7
Iron ores & concentrates	8.3	Cars & other vehicles	5.1
Coal	7.4	Motor vehicle components	3.7
Car & other components	4.4	Pharmaceutical products	2.2
Total incl. others	**90.9**	Total incl. others	**95.1**

Main export destinations		Main origins of imports	
	% of total		% of total
China	15.1	China	14.7
United States	9.1	Germany	11.5
Japan	7.9	United States	8.0
India	7.7	Saudi Arabia	6.0

Balance of payments, reserves and debt, $bn

Visible exports fob	102.9	Change in reserves	4.9
Visible imports fob	-100.4	Level of reserves	
Trade balance	2.5	end Dec.	48.8
Invisibles inflows	20.1	No. months of import cover	4.3
Invisibles outflows	-34.3	Official gold holdings, m oz	4.0
Net transfers	-2.0	Foreign debt	113.5
Current account balance	-13.7	– as % of GDP	18
– as % of GDP	-3.4	– as % of total exports	58
Capital balance	8.2	Debt service ratio	5
Overall balance	4.7		

Health and education

Health spending, % of GDP	8.5	Education spending, % of GDP	6.0
Doctors per 1,000 pop.	0.8	Enrolment, %: primary	102
Hospital beds per 1,000 pop.	...	secondary	94
Improved-water source access,		tertiary	...
% of pop.	91		

Society

No. of households	14.2m	Cost of living, Dec. 2012	
Av. no. per household	3.6	New York = 100	72
Marriages per 1,000 pop.	3.5	Cars per 1,000 pop.	113
Divorces per 1,000 pop.	0.6	Colour TV households, % with:	
Religion, % of pop.		cable	0.0
Christian	81.2	satellite	8.9
Non-religious	14.9	Telephone lines per 100 pop.	8.2
Muslim	1.7	Mobile telephone subscribers	
Hindu	1.1	per 100 pop.	126.8
Other	0.9	Broadband subs per 100 pop.	1.8
Jewish	0.1	Internet hosts per 1,000 pop.	94.3

SOUTH KOREA

Area	99,274 sq km	Capital	Seoul
Arable as % of total land	15.5	Currency	Won (W)

People

Population	48.4m	Life expectancy: men	77.3 yrs
Pop. per sq km	487.5	women	84.0 yrs
Total growth		Adult literacy	...
in pop. 2000–10	4.8%	Fertility rate (per woman)	1.5
Pop. under 15	16.2%	Urban population	83.2%
Pop. over 60	15.6%		per 1,000 pop.
No. of men per 100 women	99.4	Crude birth rate	10.0
Human Development Index	90.9	Crude death rate	5.9

The economy

GDP	W1,237trn	GDP per head	$22,420
GDP	$1,116bn	GDP per head in purchasing	
Av. ann. growth in real		power parity (USA=100)	62.0
GDP 2006–11	3.5%	Economic freedom index	70.3

Origins of GDP		Components of GDP	
	% of total		% of total
Agriculture	3	Private consumption	53
Industry, of which:	39	Public consumption	15
manufacturing	31	Investment	29
Services	58	Exports	56
		Imports	-54

Structure of employment

	% of total		% of labour force
Agriculture	7	Unemployed 2011	3.4
Industry	17	Av. ann. rate 2000–11	3.5
Services	76		

Energy

	m TOE		
Total output	44.9	Net energy imports as %	
Total consumption	250.0	of energy use	82
Consumption per head,			
kg oil equivalent	5,060		

Inflation and finance

Consumer price		av. ann. increase 2006–11	
inflation 2012	2.2%	Narrow money (M1)	7.6%
Av. ann. inflation 2007–12	3.3%	Broad money	10.3%
Money market rate, Dec. 2012	2.75%	H'hold saving rate, Dec. 2012	3.8%

Exchange rates

	end 2012		2012
W per $	1,076	Effective rates	2005 = 100
W per SDR	1,645	– nominal	...
W per €	1,412	– real	...

Trade

Principal exports		Principal imports	
	$bn fob		$bn cif
Information & communications		Crude petroleum	92.3
products	72.7	Machinery & equipment	60.3
Semiconductors	53.3	Chemicals & related products	44.6
Chemicals & related products	52.8	Semiconductors	43.5
Machinery & equipment	51.6		
Total incl. others	**555.2**	Total incl. others	**524.4**

Main export destinations		Main origins of imports	
	% of total		% of total
China	24.2	China	16.5
United States	10.1	Japan	13.0
Japan	7.1	United States	8.5
Hong Kong	5.6	Germany	3.2

Balance of payments, reserves and debt, $bn

Visible exports fob	551.8	Change in reserves	14.8
Visible imports fob	520.1	Level of reserves	
Trade balance	31.7	end Dec.	306.9
Invisibles inflows	113.0	No. months of import cover	5.8
Invisibles outflows	-115.9	Official gold holdings, m oz	1.8
Net transfers	-2.6	Foreign debt	449.6
Current account balance	26.1	– as % of GDP	40
– as % of GDP	2.3	– as % of total exports	68
Capital balance	-12.8	Debt service ratio	8
Overall balance	14.0	Aid given	1.33
		– as % of GDP	0.12

Health and education

Health spending, % of GDP	7.2	Education spending, % of GDP	5.0
Doctors per 1,000 pop.	2.0	Enrolment, %: primary	106
Hospital beds per 1,000 pop.	10.3	secondary	97
Improved-water source access,		tertiary	103
% of pop.	98		

Society

No. of households	18.4m	Cost of living, Dec. 2012	
Av. no. per household	2.7	New York = 100	106
Marriages per 1,000 pop.	6.5	Cars per 1,000 pop.	293
Divorces per 1,000 pop.	2.3	Colour TV households, % with:	
Religion, % of pop.		cable	85.6
Non-religious	46.4	satellite	14.4
Christian	29.4	Telephone lines per 100 pop.	60.9
Buddhist	22.9	Mobile telephone subscribers	
Other	1.0	per 100 pop.	108.5
Muslim	0.2	Broadband subs per 100 pop.	36.9
Jewish	<0.1	Internet hosts per 1,000 pop.	6.5

SPAIN

Area	504,782 sq km	Capital	Madrid
Arable as % of total land	25.1	Currency	Euro (€)

People

Population	46.5m	Life expectancy:	men	78.8 yrs
Pop. per sq km	92.1		women	84.8 yrs
Total growth		Adult literacy		97.7%
in pop. 2000–10	14.4%	Fertility rate (per woman)		1.5
Pop. under 15	14.9%	Urban population		77.4%
Pop. over 60	22.4%			per 1,000 pop.
No. of men per 100 women	97.5	Crude birth rate		10.0
Human Development Index	88.5	Crude death rate		8.7

The economy

GDP	€1,063bn	GDP per head	$31,990
GDP	$1,477bn	GDP per head in purchasing	
Av. ann. growth in real		power parity (USA=100)	66.7
GDP 2006–11	0.1%	Economic freedom index	68.0

Origins of GDP		Components of GDP	
	% of total		% of total
Agriculture	3	Private consumption	58
Industry, of which:	26	Public consumption	21
manufacturing	13	Investment	22
Services	71	Exports	30
		Imports	-31

Structure of employment

	% of total		% of labour force
Agriculture	4	Unemployed 2011	21.6
Industry	22	Av. ann. rate 2000–11	13.2
Services	74		

Energy

	m TOE		
Total output	34.2	Net energy imports as %	
Total consumption	127.7	of energy use	73
Consumption per head,			
kg oil equivalent	2,773		

Inflation and finance

Consumer price		av. ann. increase 2006–11	
inflation 2012	2.4%	Euro area:	
Av. ann. inflation 2007–12	2.2%	Narrow money (M1)	5.3%
Money market rate, Dec. 2012	0.18%	Broad money	4.7%
		H'hold saving rate[a], Dec. 2012	8.2%

Exchange rates

	end 2012		2012
€ per $	0.76	Effective rates	2005 = 100
€ per SDR	1.16	– nominal	103.0
		– real	96.6

Trade

Principal exports	$bn fob	Principal imports	$bn cif
Machinery & transport equip.	33.7	Machinery & transport equip.	98.6
Chemicals & related products	40.0	Mineral fuels & lubricants	77.1
Food, drink & tobacco	39.9	Chemicals & related products	52.3
Mineral fuels & lubricants	22.5	Food, drink & tobacco	34.4
Total incl. others	**298.6**	Total incl. others	**363.0**

Main export destinations	% of total	Main origins of imports	% of total
France	17.7	Germany	12.5
Germany	10.1	France	11.4
Portugal	7.9	Italy	6.8
Italy	7.8	China	5.9
EU27	66.6	EU27	56.9

Balance of payments, reserves and aid, $bn

Visible exports fob	304.3	Overall balance	13.6
Visible imports fob	-359.7	Change in reserves	14.8
Trade balance	-55.4	Level of reserves	
Invisibles inflows	201.8	end Dec.	46.7
Invisibles outflows	-190.0	No. months of import cover	1.0
Net transfers	-8.2	Official gold holdings, m oz	9.1
Current account balance	-51.9	Aid given	4.17
– as % of GDP	-3.5	– as % of GDP	0.29
Capital balance	70.8		

Health and education

Health spending, % of GDP	9.4	Education spending, % of GDP	5.0
Doctors per 1,000 pop.	4.0	Enrolment, %: primary	106
Hospital beds per 1,000 pop.	3.2	secondary	125
Improved-water source access,		tertiary	78
% of pop.	100		

Society

No. of households	17.9m	Cost of living, Dec. 2012	
Av. no. per household	2.6	New York = 100	100
Marriages per 1,000 pop.	3.4	Cars per 1,000 pop.	475
Divorces per 1,000 pop.	2.2	Colour TV households, % with:	
Religion, % of pop.		cable	13.7
Christian	78.6	satellite	14.5
Non-religious	19.0	Telephone lines per 100 pop.	42.8
Muslim	2.1	Mobile telephone subscribers	
Jewish	0.1	per 100 pop.	113.2
Other	0.1	Broadband subs per 100 pop.	23.8
Hindu	<0.1	Internet hosts per 1,000 pop.	90.9

a Gross.

SWEDEN

Area	449,964 sq km	Capital	Stockholm
Arable as % of total land	6.4	Currency	Swedish krona (Skr)

People

Population	9.4m	Life expectancy: men	79.7 yrs
Pop. per sq km	20.9	women	83.7 yrs
Total growth		Adult literacy	...
in pop. 2000–10	5.9%	Fertility rate (per woman)	1.9
Pop. under 15	16.5%	Urban population	85.2%
Pop. over 60	25.0%		per 1,000 pop.
No. of men per 100 women	99.2	Crude birth rate	12.0
Human Development Index	91.6	Crude death rate	9.6

The economy

GDP	Skr3,503bn	GDP per head	$57,110
GDP	$540bn	GDP per head in purchasing	
Av. ann. growth in real		power parity (USA=100)	86.2
GDP 2006–11	1.5%	Economic freedom index	72.9

Origins of GDP		Components of GDP	
	% of total		% of total
Agriculture	2	Private consumption	48
Industry, of which:	26	Public consumption	26
manufacturing	16	Investment	20
Services	72	Exports	50
		Imports	-44

Structure of employment

	% of total		% of labour force
Agriculture	2	Unemployed 2011	7.5
Industry	20	Av. ann. rate 2000–11	6.3
Services	78		

Energy

	m TOE		
Total output	33.5	Net energy imports as %	
Total consumption	51.3	of energy use	35
Consumption per head,			
kg oil equivalent	5,468		

Inflation and finance

		av. ann. increase 2006–11	
Consumer price			
inflation 2012	0.9%	Narrow money (M1)	5.6%
Av. ann. inflation 2007–12	1.6%	Broad money	6.1%
Repurchase rate, Dec. 2012	1.50%	H'hold saving rate, Dec. 2012	11.4%

Exchange rates

	end 2012		2012
Skr per $	6.59	Effective rates	2005 = 100
Skr per SDR	10.00	– nominal	106.6
Skr per €	8.65	– real	100.6

Trade

Principal exports		Principal imports	
	$bn fob		*$bn cif*
Machinery & transport equip.	73.3	Machinery & transport equip.	64.3
Chemicals & related products	19.3	Fuels & lubricants	24.5
Mineral fuels & lubricants	14.6	Chemicals & related products	19.5
Raw materials	12.4	Food, drink & tobacco	14.2
Total incl. others	**186.9**	Total incl. others	**177.0**

Main export destinations		Main origins of imports	
	% of total		*% of total*
Germany	9.9	Germany	18.1
Norway	8.8	Denmark	8.1
United Kingdom	7.0	Norway	7.7
Denmark	6.1	Netherlands	5.9
Finland	6.1	United Kingdom	5.8
EU27	56.0	EU27	68.2

Balance of payments, reserves and aid, $bn

Visible exports fob	189.1	Overall balance	0.9
Visible imports fob	-174.3	Change in reserves	2.0
Trade balance	14.8	Level of reserves	
Invisibles inflows	137.0	end Dec.	50.2
Invisibles outflows	-103.0	No. months of import cover	2.1
Net transfers	-7.2	Official gold holdings, m oz	4.0
Current account balance	41.7	Aid given	5.60
– as % of GDP	7.7	– as % of GDP	1.02
Capital balance	-46.9		

Health and education

Health spending, % of GDP	9.4	Education spending, % of GDP	7.0
Doctors per 1,000 pop.	3.8	Enrolment, %: primary	101
Hospital beds per 1,000 pop.	2.7	secondary	99
Improved-water source access,		tertiary	74
% of pop.	100		

Society

No. of households	4.6m	Cost of living, Dec. 2012	
Av. no. per household	2.1	New York = 100	104
Marriages per 1,000 pop.	5.1	Cars per 1,000 pop.	467
Divorces per 1,000 pop.	2.5	Colour TV households, % with:	
Religion, % of pop.		cable	56.9
Christian	67.2	satellite	19.0
Non-religious	27.0	Telephone lines per 100 pop.	48.7
Muslim	4.6	Mobile telephone subscribers	
Other	0.8	per 100 pop.	118.6
Hindu	0.2	Broadband subs per 100 pop.	31.8
Jewish	0.1	Internet hosts per 1,000 pop.	636.0

SWITZERLAND

Area	41,293 sq km	Capital	Berne
Arable as % of total land	10.1	Currency	Swiss franc (SFr)

People

Population	7.7m	Life expectancy:	men	80.2 yrs
Pop. per sq km	186.5		women	84.7 yrs
Total growth		Adult literacy		...
in pop. 2000–10	6.9%	Fertility rate (per woman)		1.5
Pop. under 15	15.2%	Urban population		73.7%
Pop. over 60	23.3%			per 1,000 pop.
No. of men per 100 women	96.7	Crude birth rate		10.0
Human Development Index	91.3	Crude death rate		8.3

The economy

GDP	SFr587bn	GDP per head	$83,330
GDP	$659bn	GDP per head in purchasing	
Av. ann. growth in real		power parity (USA=100)	106.5
GDP 2006–11	1.8%	Economic freedom index	81.0

Origins of GDP		**Components of GDP**	
	% of total		% of total
Agriculture	1	Private consumption	57
Industry, of which:	26	Public consumption	11
manufacturing	18	Investment	21
Services	73	Exports	51
		Imports	-40

Structure of employment

	% of total		% of labour force
Agriculture	3	Unemployed 2011	4.1
Industry	21	Av. ann. rate 2000–11	3.7
Services	76		

Energy

	m TOE		
Total output	12.6	Net energy imports as %	
Total consumption	26.2	of energy use	52
Consumption per head,			
kg oil equivalent	3,349		

Inflation and finance

Consumer price		av. ann. increase 2006–11	
inflation 2012	-0.7%	Narrow money (M1)	13.6%
Av. ann. inflation 2007–12	0.4%	Broad money	6.3%
Money market rate, Dec. 2012	-0.02%	H'hold saving rate, Dec. 2012	14.1%

Exchange rates

	end 2012		2012
SFr per $	0.92	Effective rates	2005 = 100
SFr per SDR	1.41	– nominal	127.0
SFr per €	1.21	– real	112.9

Trade

Principal exports		Principal imports	
	$bn fob		*$bn cif*
Chemicals	84.1	Chemicals	42.2
Precision instruments, watches & jewellery	46.5	Machinery, equipment & electronics	34.6
Machinery, equipment & electronics	41.6	Precision instruments, watches & jewellery	20.4
Metals & metal manufactures	14.7	Motor vehicles	19.0
Total incl. others	**223.3**	Total incl. others	**196.9**

Main export destinations		Main origins of imports	
	% of total		*% of total*
Germany	21.2	Germany	34.1
United States	10.8	Italy	11.0
Italy	8.1	France	9.1
France	7.5	United States	5.2
United Kingdom	5.0	Austria	4.6
China	4.5	Netherlands	4.6
Hong Kong	4.0	United Kingdom	3.6
EU27	56.9	EU27	78.1

Balance of payments, reserves and aid, $bn

Visible exports fob	345.6	Overall balance	54.7
Visible imports fob	-320.4	Change in reserves	60.3
Trade balance	25.2	Level of reserves	
Invisibles inflows	178.2	end Dec.	330.6
Invisibles outflows	-154.4	No. months of import cover	8.4
Net transfers	-13.1	Official gold holdings, m oz	33.4
Current account balance	35.9	Aid given	3.08
– as % of GDP	5.4	– as % of GDP	0.45
Capital balance	22.1		

Health and education

Health spending, % of GDP	10.0	Education spending, % of GDP	5.4
Doctors per 1,000 pop.	4.1	Enrolment, %: primary	103
Hospital beds per 1,000 pop.	5.0	secondary	95
Improved-water source access, % of pop.	100	tertiary	55

Society

No. of households	3.6m	Cost of living, Dec. 2012	
Av. no. per household	2.2	New York = 100	124
Marriages per 1,000 pop.	5.3	Cars per 1,000 pop.	528
Divorces per 1,000 pop.	2.2	Colour TV households, % with:	
Religion, % of pop.		cable	90.5
Christian	81.3	satellite	15.4
Non-religious	11.9	Telephone lines per 100 pop.	59.9
Muslim	5.5	Mobile telephone subscribers	
Other	0.6	per 100 pop.	131.4
Hindu	0.4	Broadband subs per 100 pop.	40.0
Jewish	0.3	Internet hosts per 1,000 pop.	688.5

TAIWAN

Area	36,179 sq km	Capital	Taipei
Arable as % of total land	...	Currency	Taiwan dollar (T$)

People

Population	23.2m	Life expectancy:[a] men		75.7 yrs
Pop. per sq km	641.3		women	81.5 yrs
Total growth		Adult literacy		96.1%
in pop. 2000–10	4.2%	Fertility rate (per woman)		1.1
Pop. under 15	16.7%	Urban population		...
Pop. over 60	14.5%			per 1,000 pop.
No. of men per 100 women	101	Crude birth rate		9.0
Human Development Index	...	Crude death rate[a]		7.1

The economy

GDP	T$13,745bn	GDP per head	$19,980
GDP	$464bn	GDP per head in purchasing	
Av. ann. growth in real		power parity (USA=100)	78.1
GDP 2006–11	3.9%	Economic freedom index	72.7

Origins of GDP		**Components of GDP**	
	% of total		% of total
Agriculture	2	Private consumption	60
Industry, of which:	31	Public consumption	12
manufacturing	26	Investment	21
Services	67	Exports	76
		Imports	-69

Structure of employment

	% of total		% of labour force
Agriculture	5	Unemployed 2011	4.4
Industry	37	Av. ann. rate 2000–11	4.6
Services	59		

Energy

	m TOE		
Total output	...	Net energy imports as %	
Total consumption	...	of energy use	...
Consumption per head,			
kg oil equivalent	...		

Inflation and finance

Consumer price		*av. ann. increase 2006–11*	
inflation 2012	1.9%	Narrow money (M1)	7.5%
Av. ann. inflation 2007–12	1.4%	Broad money (M2)	4.8%
Interbank rate, Dec. 2012	0.41%		

Exchange rates

	end 2012		2012
T$ per $	29.02	Effective rates	2005 = 100
T$ per SDR	44.67	– nominal	...
T$ per €	38.39	– real	...

Trade

Principal exports		Principal imports	
	$bn fob		$bn cif
Electronic products	85.4	Intermediate goods	216.4
Basic metals	30.2	Capital goods	39.4
Information & communications		Consumer goods	24.8
products	18.4		
Textiles	11.1		
Total incl. others	**291.9**	Total	**280.6**

Main export destinations		Main origins of imports	
	% of total		% of total
China	28.8	Japan	18.6
Hong Kong	13.7	China	15.5
United States	12.5	United States	9.2
Japan	6.2	South Korea	6.4

Balance of payments, reserves and debt, $bn

Visible exports fob	307.1	Change in reserves	3.6
Visible imports fob	-279.4	Level of reserves	
Trade balance	27.7	end Dec.	386.3
Invisibles inflows	71.0	No. months of import cover	13.9
Invisibles outflows	-53.7	Official gold holdings, m oz	0.0
Net transfers	-3.7	Foreign debt	122.5
Current account balance	41.3	– as % of GDP	26
– as % of GDP	8.9	– as % of total exports	32
Capital balance	-31.7	Debt service ratio	5
Overall balance	6.2	Aid given	0.04
		– as % of GDP	0.09

Health and education

Health spending, % of GDP	...	Education spending, % of GDP	...
Doctors per 1,000 pop.	...	Enrolment, %: primary	...
Hospital beds per 1,000 pop.	...	secondary	...
Improved-water source access,		tertiary	...
% of pop.	...		

Society

No. of households	7.8m	Cost of living, Dec. 2012	
Av. no. per household	3.0	New York = 100	85
Marriages per 1,000 pop.	5.3	Cars per 1,000 pop.	250
Divorces per 1,000 pop.	2.5	Colour TV households, % with:	
Religion, % of pop.		cable	84.2
Other	81.8	satellite	0.4
Non-religious	12.7	Telephone lines per 100 pop.	72.7
Christian	5.5	Mobile telephone subscribers	
Hindu	<0.1	per 100 pop.	124.1
Jewish	<0.1	Broadband subs per 100 pop.	23.7
Muslim	<0.1	Internet hosts per 1,000 pop.	270.3

a 2012 estimate.

THAILAND

Area	513,115 sq km	Capital	Bangkok
Arable as % of total land	30.8	Currency	Baht (Bt)

People

Population	69.5m	Life expectancy: men	71.1 yrs
Pop. per sq km	135.4	women	78.8 yrs
Total growth		Adult literacy	93.5%
in pop. 2000–10	9.4%	Fertility rate (per woman)	1.5
Pop. under 15	21.5%	Urban population	34.1%
Pop. over 60	11.7%		per 1,000 pop.
No. of men per 100 women	96.7	Crude birth rate	11.5
Human Development Index	69.0	Crude death rate	9.5

The economy

GDP	Bt10,540bn	GDP per head	$4,970
GDP	$346bn	GDP per head in purchasing	
Av. ann. growth in real		power parity (USA=100)	18.0
GDP 2006–11	2.6%	Economic freedom index	64.1

Origins of GDP		Components of GDP	
	% of total		% of total
Agriculture	12	Private consumption	56
Industry, of which:	41	Public consumption	13
manufacturing	36	Investment	27
Services	46	Exports	77
		Imports	-72

Structure of employment

	% of total		% of labour force
Agriculture	39	Unemployed 2011	0.7
Industry	21	Av. ann. rate 2000–11	1.5
Services	40		

Energy

	m TOE		
Total output	70.6	Net energy imports as %	
Total consumption	117.4	of energy use	40
Consumption per head,			
kg oil equivalent	1,699		

Inflation and finance

		av. ann. increase 2006–11	
Consumer price			
inflation 2012	3.0%	Narrow money	9.2%
Av. ann. inflation 2007–12	2.9%	Broad money	9.6%
Money market rate, Dec. 2012	2.69%		

Exchange rates

	end 2012		2012
Bt per $	30.64	Effective rates	2005 = 100
Bt per SDR	47.08	– nominal	...
Bt per €	40.20	– real	...

Trade

Principal exports		Principal imports	
	$bn fob		$bn cif
Machinery, equip. & supplies	84.4	Machinery, equip. & supplies	74.7
Food	29.4	Fuel & lubricants	43.8
Manufactured goods	27.1	Manufactured goods	39.2
Chemicals	22.6	Chemicals	23.7
Total incl. others	**220.2**	Total incl. others	**229.1**

Main export destinations		Main origins of imports	
	% of total		% of total
China	12.3	Japan	18.4
Japan	10.8	China	13.4
United States	9.8	United States	6.3
Hong Kong	7.4	United Arab Emirates	5.9

Balance of payments, reserves and debt, $bn

Visible exports fob	219.1	Change in reserves	2.9
Visible imports fob	-202.1	Level of reserves	
Trade balance	17.0	end Dec.	174.9
Invisibles inflows	48.7	No. months of import cover	7.7
Invisibles outflows	-70.5	Official gold holdings, m oz	4.9
Net transfers	10.7	Foreign debt	80.0
Current account balance	5.9	– as % of GDP	25
– as % of GDP	1.7	– as % of total exports	32
Capital balance	-5.3	Debt service ratio	4
Overall balance	1.2	Aid given	0.74
		– as % of GDP	0.01

Health and education

Health spending, % of GDP	4.1	Education spending, % of GDP	5.8
Doctors per 1,000 pop.	0.3	Enrolment, %: primary	91
Hospital beds per 1,000 pop.	2.1	secondary	79
Improved-water source access,		tertiary	48
% of pop.	96		

Society

No. of households	20.8m	Cost of living, Dec. 2012	
Av. no. per household	3.4	New York = 100	84
Marriages per 1,000 pop.	4.7	Cars per 1,000 pop.	63
Divorces per 1,000 pop.	1.1	Colour TV households, % with:	
Religion, % of pop.		cable	9.6
Buddhist	93.2	satellite	4.8
Muslim	5.5	Telephone lines per 100 pop.	9.6
Christian	0.9	Mobile telephone subscribers	
Non-religious	0.3	per 100 pop.	111.6
Hindu	0.1	Broadband subs per 100 pop.	5.0
Jewish	<0.1	Internet hosts per 1,000 pop.	48.9

TURKEY

Area	779,452 sq km	Capital	Ankara
Arable as % of total land	27.8	Currency	Turkish Lira (YTL)

People

Population	73.6m	Life expectancy: men	72.0 yrs
Pop. per sq km	94.4	women	76.6 yrs
Total growth		Adult literacy	90.8%
in pop. 2000–10	14.3%	Fertility rate (per woman)	2.0
Pop. under 15	26.4%	Urban population	71.5%
Pop. over 60	9.0%		per 1,000 pop.
No. of men per 100 women	99.5	Crude birth rate	16.9
Human Development Index	72.2	Crude death rate	5.5

The economy

GDP	YTL1,298bn	GDP per head	$10,520
GDP	$775bn	GDP per head in purchasing	
Av. ann. growth in real		power parity (USA=100)	35.6
GDP 2006–11	3.5%	Economic freedom index	62.9

Origins of GDP		Components of GDP	
	% of total		% of total
Agriculture	9	Private consumption	71
Industry, of which:	28	Public consumption	14
manufacturing	19	Investment	24
Services	63	Exports	24
		Imports	-33

Structure of employment

	% of total		% of labour force
Agriculture	24	Unemployed 2011	9.8
Industry	27	Av. ann. rate 2000–11	10.2
Services	49		

Energy

	m TOE		
Total output	32.2	Net energy imports as %	
Total consumption	105.1	of energy use	69
Consumption per head,			
kg oil equivalent	1,445		

Inflation and finance

Consumer price		av. ann. increase 2006–11	
inflation 2012	8.9%	Narrow money (M1)	17.6%
Av. ann. inflation 2007–12	8.1%	Broad money	17.2%
Money market rate, Dec. 2012	5.00%		

Exchange rates

	end 2012		2012
YTL per $	1.78	Effective rates	2005 = 100
YTL per SDR	2.74	– nominal	...
YTL per €	2.34	– real	...

Trade

Principal exports		Principal imports	
	$bn fob		*$bn cif*
Agricultural products	24.6	Fuels	34.4
Iron & steel	17.1	Chemicals	33.2
Transport equipment	17.0	Mechanical machinery	21.2
Textiles & clothing	14.0	Transport equipment	20.0
Total incl. others	**134.9**	Total incl. others	**240.8**

Main export destinations		Main origins of imports	
	% of total		*% of total*
Germany	10.3	Russia	9.9
Iraq	6.2	Germany	9.5
United Kingdom	6.0	China	9.0
Italy	5.8	United States	6.7
France	5.0	Italy	5.6
EU27	46.2	EU27	37.8

Balance of payments, reserves and debt, $bn

Visible exports fob	143.5	Change in reserves	2.0
Visible imports fob	-232.5	Level of reserves	
Trade balance	-89.0	end Dec.	87.9
Invisibles inflows	42.9	No. months of import cover	4.0
Invisibles outflows	-32.6	Official gold holdings, m oz	6.3
Net transfers	0.7	Foreign debt	307.0
Current account balance	-77.0	– as % of GDP	40
– as % of GDP	-9.9	– as % of total exports	170
Capital balance	66.6	Debt service ratio	30
Overall balance	1.0	Aid given	1.27
		– as % of GDP	0.16

Health and education

Health spending, % of GDP	6.7	Education spending, % of GDP	...
Doctors per 1,000 pop.	1.7	Enrolment, %: primary	104
Hospital beds per 1,000 pop.	2.5	secondary	82
Improved-water source access,		tertiary	55
% of pop.	100		

Society

No. of households	18.9m	Cost of living, Dec. 2012	
Av. no. per household	3.9	New York = 100	92
Marriages per 1,000 pop.	8.0	Cars per 1,000 pop.	111
Divorces per 1,000 pop.	1.6	Colour TV households, % with:	
Religion, % of pop.		cable	13.9
Muslim	98.0	satellite	46.1
Non-religious	1.2	Telephone lines per 100 pop.	20.7
Christian	0.4	Mobile telephone subscribers	
Other	0.3	per 100 pop.	88.7
Hindu	<0.1	Broadband subs per 100 pop.	10.3
Jewish	<0.1	Internet hosts per 1,000 pop.	96.4

UKRAINE

Area	603,700 sq km	Capital	Kiev
Arable as % of total land	56.1	Currency	Hryvnya (UAH)

People

Population	45.2m	Life expectancy: men		63.5 yrs
Pop. per sq km	74.9		women	74.6 yrs
Total growth		Adult literacy		99.7%
in pop. 2000–10	-7.0%	Fertility rate (per woman)		1.5
Pop. under 15	13.9%	Urban population		68.9%
Pop. over 60	20.9%			per 1,000 pop.
No. of men per 100 women	85.2	Crude birth rate		11.0
Human Development Index	74.0	Crude death rate		16.2

The economy

GDP	UAH1,317bn	GDP per head	$3,620
GDP	$165bn	GDP per head in purchasing	
Av. ann. growth in real		power parity (USA=100)	15.0
GDP 2006–11	0.5%	Economic freedom index	46.3

Origins of GDP		**Components of GDP**	
	% of total		% of total
Agriculture	10	Private consumption	66
Industry, of which:	32	Public consumption	18
manufacturing	16	Investment	21
Services	59	Exports	54
		Imports	-59

Structure of employment

	% of total		% of labour force
Agriculture	16	Unemployed 2011	7.9
Industry	23	Av. ann. rate 2000–11	8.5
Services	61		

Energy

	m TOE		
Total output	76.0	Net energy imports as %	
Total consumption	117.4	of energy use	40
Consumption per head,			
kg oil equivalent	1,699		

Inflation and finance

Consumer price		av. ann. increase 2006–11	
inflation 2012	0.6%	Narrow money (M1)	20.3%
Av. ann. inflation 2007–12	11.5%	Broad money	21.3%
Money market rate, Dec. 2012	8.32%		

Exchange rates

	end 2012		2012
UAH per $	7.99	Effective rates	2005 = 100
UAH per SDR	12.28	– nominal	65.6
UAH per €	10.48	– real	98.2

Trade

Principal exports		Principal imports	
	$bn fob		*$bn cif*
Non-precious metals	22.1	Fuels and mineral products	30.0
Food & agricultural produce	12.8	Machinery & equipment	20.0
Machinery & equipment	11.9	Chemicals	8.0
Fuels & mineral products	10.3	Food & agricultural produce	6.3
Chemicals	5.4		
Total incl. others	**68.4**	**Total incl. others**	**82.6**

Main export destinations		Main origins of imports	
	% of total		*% of total*
Russia	26.9	Russia	28.7
Turkey	5.8	Germany	8.4
Italy	4.6	China	8.3
Poland	3.8	Poland	5.0
China	3.7	Belarus	4.7

Balance of payments, reserves and debt, $bn

Visible exports fob	62.4	Change in reserves	-2.8
Visible imports fob	-80.4	Level of reserves	
Trade balance	-18.0	end Dec.	31.8
Invisibles inflows	26.8	No. months of import cover	3.8
Invisibles outflows	-22.7	Official gold holdings, m oz	0.9
Net transfers	3.7	Foreign debt	134.5
Current account balance	-10.2	– as % of GDP	88
– as % of GDP	-6.2	– as % of total exports	167
Capital balance	6.8	Debt service ratio	31
Overall balance	-2.5		

Health and education

Health spending, % of GDP	7.2	Education spending, % of GDP	5.3
Doctors per 1,000 pop.	3.5	Enrolment, %: primary	100
Hospital beds per 1,000 pop.	8.7	secondary	94
Improved-water source access,		tertiary	82
% of pop.	98		

Society

No. of households	20.0m	Cost of living, Dec. 2012	
Av. no. per household	2.3	New York = 100	72
Marriages per 1,000 pop.	7.8	Cars per 1,000 pop.	153
Divorces per 1,000 pop.	2.8	Colour TV households, % with:	
Religion, % of pop.		cable	22.5
Christian	83.8	satellite	14.5
Non-religious	14.7	Telephone lines per 100 pop.	28.1
Muslim	1.2	Mobile telephone subscribers	
Jewish	0.1	per 100 pop.	122.3
Other	0.1	Broadband subs per 100 pop.	7.0
Hindu	<0.1	Internet hosts per 1,000 pop.	48.1

UNITED ARAB EMIRATES

Area	83,600 sq km	Capital	Abu Dhabi
Arable as % of total land	0.6	Currency	Dirham (AED)

People

Population	7.9m	Life expectancy: men		76.0 yrs
Pop. per sq km	94.5	women		78.0 yrs
Total growth		Adult literacy		90.0%
in pop. 2000–10	147.6%	Fertility rate (per woman)		1.7
Pop. under 15	19.1%	Urban population		84.4%
Pop. over 60	2.0%		per 1,000 pop.	
No. of men per 100 women	228.3	Crude birth rate		12.3
Human Development Index	81.8	Crude death rate		1.4

The economy

GDP	AED1,323bn	GDP per head	$45,650
GDP	$360bn	GDP per head in purchasing	
Av. ann. growth in real		power parity (USA=100)	99.6
GDP 2006–11	2.6%	Economic freedom index	71.1

Origins of GDP		Components of GDP	
	% of total		% of total
Agriculture	1	Private consumption	57
Industry, of which:	56	Public consumption	8
manufacturing	10	Investment	25
Services	44	Exports	78
		Imports	-69

Structure of employment

	% of total		% of labour force
Agriculture	8	Unemployed 2008	4.0
Industry	22	Av. ann. rate 2000–08	2.9
Services	70		

Energy

			m TOE
Total output	176.3	Net energy imports as %	
Total consumption	62.1	of energy use	-184
Consumption per head,			
kg oil equivalent	8,271		

Inflation and finance

Consumer price		av. ann. increase 2006–11	
inflation 2012	0.7%	Narrow money (M1)	17.1%
Av. ann. inflation 2007–12	3.1%	Broad money	15.6%
Interbank rate, Dec. 2011	1.52%		

Exchange rates

	end 2012		2012
AED per $	3.67	Effective rates	2005 = 100
AED per SDR	5.64	– nominal	97.6
AED per €	4.81	– real	...

Trade

Principal exports		Principal imports	
	$bn fob		*$bn cif*
Re-exports	107.9	Machinery & electrical equip.	34.2
Crude oil	90.6	Precious stones & metals	33.1
Gas	15.9	Vehicles & other transport	
		equipment	17.5
		Base metals & related products	13.1
Total incl. others	**281.6**	Total incl. others	**229.7**

Main export destinations		Main origins of imports	
	% of total		*% of total*
Japan	16.1	India	19.8
South Korea	14.0	China	13.9
Iran	10.9	United States	8.2
India	5.5	Germany	4.6

Balance of payments, reserves and debt, $bn

Visible exports fob	281.6	Change in reserves	-5.5
Visible imports fob	-202.1	Level of reserves	
Trade balance	79.5	end Dec.	37.3
Invisibles, net	-36.8	No. months of import cover	1.8
Net transfers	-12.0	Official gold holdings, m oz	0.0
Current account balance	30.7	Foreign debt	156.3
– as % of GDP	8.5	– as % of GDP	46
Capital balance	-16.4	– as % of total exports	50
Overall balance	4.5	Debt service ratio	8
		Aid given	0.74
		– as % of GDP	0.22

Health and education

Health spending, % of GDP	3.3	Education spending, % of GDP	...
Doctors per 1,000 pop.	1.9	Enrolment, %: primary	...
Hospital beds per 1,000 pop.	1.9	secondary	...
Improved-water source access,		tertiary	...
% of pop.	100		

Society

No. of households	1.6m	Cost of living, Dec. 2012	
Av. no. per household	5.1	New York = 100	75
Marriages per 1,000 pop.	1.8	Cars per 1,000 pop.	249
Divorces per 1,000 pop.	0.5	Colour TV households, % with:	
Religion, % of pop.		cable	51.6
Muslim	76.9	satellite	98.3
Christian	12.6	Telephone lines per 100 pop.	23.1
Hindu	6.6	Mobile telephone subscribers	
Other	2.8	per 100 pop.	148.6
Non-religious	1.1	Broadband subs per 100 pop.	11.0
Jewish	<0.1	Internet hosts per 1,000 pop.	42.8

UNITED KINGDOM

Area	242,534 sq km	Capital	London
Arable as % of total land	24.7	Currency	Pound (£)

People

Population	62.4m	Life expectancy: men		78.3 yrs
Pop. per sq km	257.3	women		82.4 yrs
Total growth		Adult literacy		...
in pop. 2000–10	5.4%	Fertility rate (per woman)		1.9
Pop. under 15	17.4%	Urban population		79.6%
Pop. over 60	22.7%			per 1,000 pop.
No. of men per 100 women	96.8	Crude birth rate		12.1
Human Development Index	87.5	Crude death rate		9.4

The economy

GDP	£1,516bn	GDP per head	$48,110
GDP	$2,445bn	GDP per head in purchasing	
Av. ann. growth in real		power parity (USA=100)	74.0
GDP 2006–11	0.2%	Economic freedom index	74.8

Origins of GDP		**Components of GDP**	
	% of total		% of total
Agriculture	1	Private consumption	64
Industry, of which:	22	Public consumption	22
manufacturing	11	Investment	15
Services	78	Exports	32
		Imports	-34

Structure of employment

	% of total		% of labour force
Agriculture	1	Unemployed 2011	7.8
Industry	19	Av. ann. rate 2000–11	5.8
Services	80		

Energy

	m TOE		
Total output	148.8	Net energy imports as %	
Total consumption	202.5	of energy use	27
Consumption per head,			
kg oil equivalent	3,252		

Inflation and finance

Consumer price		av. ann. increase 2006–11	
inflation 2012	2.8%	Narrow money	...
Av. ann. inflation 2007–12	3.3%	Broad money	6.3%
Money market rate, Dec. 2012	0.45%	H'hold saving rate[a], Dec. 2012	7.1%

Exchange rates

	end 2012		2012
£ per $	0.62	Effective rates	2005 = 100
£ per SDR	1.03	– nominal	82.2
£ per €	0.81	– real	90.1

Trade

Principal exports		Principal imports	
	$bn fob		*$bn cif*
Machinery & transport equip.	160.4	Machinery & transport equip.	205.1
Chemicals & related products	83.1	Mineral fuels & lubricants	89.2
Mineral fuels & lubricants	64.7	Chemicals & related products	78.2
Food, drink & tobacco	28.4	Food, drink & tobacco	56.7
Total incl. others	**479.2**	Total incl. others	**639.8**

Main export destinations		Main origins of imports	
	% of total		*% of total*
Germany	10.6	Germany	12.5
United States	9.6	China	8.2
Netherlands	7.6	Netherlands	7.0
France	7.1	United States	5.8
Ireland	5.8	France	5.7
EU27	50.5	EU27	48.6

Balance of payments, reserves and aid, $bn

Visible exports fob	479.2	Overall balance	10.9
Visible imports fob	-639.8	Change in reserves	12.2
Trade balance	-160.7	Level of reserves	
Invisibles inflows	605.8	end Dec.	94.5
Invisibles outflows	-444.3	No. months of import cover	1.0
Net transfers	-35.1	Official gold holdings, m oz	10.0
Current account balance	-34.3	Aid given	13.83
– as % of GDP	-1.4	– as % of GDP	0.56
Capital balance	31.5		

Health and education

Health spending, % of GDP	9.3	Education spending, % of GDP	5.6
Doctors per 1,000 pop.	2.8	Enrolment, %: primary	107
Hospital beds per 1,000 pop.	3.0	secondary	105
Improved-water source access,		tertiary	60
% of pop.	100		

Society

No. of households	27.6m	Cost of living, Dec. 2012	
Av. no. per household	2.3	New York = 100	112
Marriages per 1,000 pop.	5.0	Cars per 1,000 pop.	434
Divorces per 1,000 pop.	2.4	Colour TV households, % with:	
Religion, % of pop.		cable	14.4
Christian	71.1	satellite	39.4
Non-religious	21.3	Telephone lines per 100 pop.	53.3
Muslim	4.4	Mobile telephone subscribers	
Other	1.4	per 100 pop.	130.8
Hindu	1.3	Broadband subs per 100 pop.	32.7
Jewish	0.5	Internet hosts per 1,000 pop.	129.9

a Gross.

UNITED STATES

Area	9,372,610 sq km	Capital	Washington DC
Arable as % of total land	17.5	Currency	US dollar ($)

People

Population	313.1m	Life expectancy:	men	76.2 yrs
Pop. per sq km	33.4		women	81.3 yrs
Total growth		Adult literacy		...
in pop. 2000–10	0.85%	Fertility rate (per woman)		2.1
Pop. under 15	20.2%	Urban population		82.4%
Pop. over 60	18.2%			per 1,000 pop.
No. of men per 100 women	97.4	Crude birth rate		13.7
Human Development Index	93.7	Crude death rate		8.3

The economy

GDP	$14,991bn	GDP per head	$48,110
Av. ann. growth in real		GDP per head in purchasing	
GDP 2006–11	0.5%	power parity (USA=100)	100
		Economic freedom index	76.0

Origins of GDP		**Components of GDP**	
	% of total		% of total
Agriculture	1	Private consumption	72
Industry, of which:	20	Public consumption	17
manufacturing	13	Non-government investment	15
Services[a]	79	Exports	14
		Imports	-18

Structure of employment

	% of total		% of labour force
Agriculture	2	Unemployed 2011	8.9
Industry	17	Av. ann. rate 2000–11	6.2
Services	81		

Energy

	m TOE		
Total output	1,725	Net energy imports as %	
Total consumption	2,216	of energy use	22
Consumption per head,			
kg oil equivalent	7,164		

Inflation and finance

Consumer price		av. ann. increase 2006–11	
inflation 2012	2.1%	Narrow money (M1)	9.7%
Av. ann. inflation 2007–12	2.1%	Broad money	4.8%
Fed funds rate, Dec. 2012	0.16%	H'hold saving rate, Dec. 2012	3.9%

Exchange rates

	end 2012		2012
$ per SDR	1.54	Effective rates	2005 = 100
$ per €	1.31	– nominal	88.6
		– real	89.1

Trade

Principal exports	$bn fob	Principal imports	$bn fob
Industrial supplies	500.3	Industrial supplies	755.8
Capital goods, excl. vehicles	493.0	Consumer goods, excl. vehicles	514.1
Consumer goods, excl. vehicles	175.0	Capital goods, excl. vehicles	510.7
Vehicles & products	133.1	Vehicles & products	254.6
Total incl. others	**1,480.4**	Total incl. others	**2,207.8**

Main export destinations	% of total	Main origins of imports	% of total
Canada	19.0	China	18.9
Mexico	13.3	Canada	14.5
China	7.0	Mexico	12.0
Japan	4.5	Japan	6.0
United Kingdom	3.8	Germany	4.5
Germany	3.1	South Korea	2.7
EU27	18.2	EU27	16.6

Balance of payments, reserves and aid, $bn

Visible exports fob	1,501	Overall balance	16
Visible imports fob	-2,236	Change in reserves	48.3
Trade balance	-735	Level of reserves	
Invisibles inflows	1,355	end Dec.	537.3
Invisibles outflows	-953	No. months of import cover	2.0
Net transfers	-133	Official gold holdings, m oz	261.5
Current account balance	-466	Aid given	30.92
– as % of GDP	-3.1	– as % of GDP	0.20
Capital balance	571		

Health and education

Health spending, % of GDP	17.9	Education spending, % of GDP	5.6
Doctors per 1,000 pop.	2.4	Enrolment, %: primary	102
Hospital beds per 1,000 pop.	3.0	secondary	96
Improved-water source access,		tertiary	95
% of pop.	99		

Society

No. of households	118.7m	Cost of living, Dec. 2012	
Av. no. per household	2.6	New York = 100	100
Marriages per 1,000 pop.	6.7	Cars per 1,000 pop.	436
Divorces per 1,000 pop.	3.5	Colour TV households, % with:	
Religion, % of pop.		cable	58.2
Christian	78.3	satellite	29.0
Non-religious	16.4	Telephone lines per 100 pop.	46.6
Other	2.0	Mobile telephone subscribers	
Jewish	1.8	per 100 pop.	92.7
Muslim	0.9	Broadband subs per 100 pop.	27.4
Hindu	0.6	Internet hosts per 1,000 pop.[b]	1,722.8

a Including utilities.
b Includes all hosts ending ".com", ".net" and ".org" which exaggerates the numbers.

VENEZUELA

Area	912,050 sq km	Capital	Caracas
Arable as % of total land	2.9	Currency	Bolivar (Bs)

People

Population	29.4m	Life expectancy:	men	71.8 yrs
Pop. per sq km	32.2		women	77.7 yrs
Total growth		Adult literacy		95.5%
in pop. 2000–10	19.0%	Fertility rate (per woman)		2.4
Pop. under 15	29.5%	Urban population		93.5%
Pop. over 60	8.6%			per 1,000 pop.
No. of men per 100 women	100.7	Crude birth rate		19.8
Human Development Index	74.8	Crude death rate		5.2

The economy

GDP	Bs1,358bn	GDP per head	$10,810
GDP	$316bn	GDP per head in purchasing	
Av. ann. growth in real		power parity (USA=100)	26.5
GDP 2006–11	2.6%	Economic freedom index	36.1

Origins of GDP		**Components of GDP**	
	% of total		% of total
Agriculture	6	Private consumption	55
Industry, of which:	52	Public consumption	12
manufacturing	14	Investment	23
Services	42	Exports	30
		Imports	-20

Structure of employment

	% of total		% of labour force
Agriculture	8	Unemployed 2011	8.3
Industry	22	Av. ann. rate 2000–11	11.4
Services	70		

Energy

	m TOE		
Total output	192.7	Net energy imports as %	
Total consumption	76.9	of energy use	-150
Consumption per head,			
kg oil equivalent	2,669		

Inflation and finance

			av. ann. increase 2006–11
Consumer price			
inflation 2012	21.1%	Narrow money	34.6%
Av. ann. inflation 2007–12	27.4%	Broad money	32.8%
Money market rate, Dec. 2012	0.33%		

Exchange rates

	end 2012		2012
		Effective rates	2005 = 100
Bs per $	4.29		
Bs per SDR	6.59	– nominal	46.0
Bs per €	5.63	– real	189.2

Trade

Principal exports		Principal imports	
	$bn fob		*$bn cif*
Oil	88.0	Intermediate goods	16.7
Non-oil	4.8	Capital goods	7.7
		Consumer goods	7.1
Total	**92.8**	Total	**38.3**

Main export destinations		Main origins of imports	
	% of total		*% of total*
United States	43.0	United States	35.4
Netherlands Antilles	11.3	Colombia	18.7
China	6.5	Brazil	13.2
Colombia	3.4	Mexico	4.4

Balance of payments, reserves and debt, $bn

Visible exports fob	92.6	Change in reserves	-1.7
Visible imports fob	-46.2	Level of reserves	
Trade balance	46.5	end Dec.	27.9
Invisibles inflows	4.1	No. months of import cover	4.9
Invisibles outflows	-22.7	Official gold holdings, m oz	11.8
Net transfers	-0.5	Foreign debt	67.9
Current account balance	27.3	– as % of GDP	15
– as % of GDP	8.6	– as % of total exports	65
Capital balance	-27.6	Debt service ratio	6
Overall balance	-4.0		

Health and education

Health spending, % of GDP	5.2	Education spending, % of GDP	3.6
Doctors per 1,000 pop.	...	Enrolment, %: primary	102
Hospital beds per 1,000 pop.	0.9	secondary	83
Improved-water source access,		tertiary	78
% of pop.	...		

Society

No. of households	6.7m	Cost of living, Dec. 2012	
Av. no. per household	4.4	New York = 100	126
Marriages per 1,000 pop.	3.3	Cars per 1,000 pop.	117
Divorces per 1,000 pop.	0.8	Colour TV households, % with:	
Religion, % of pop.		cable	28.6
Christian	89.3	satellite	5.6
Non-religious	10.0	Telephone lines per 100 pop.	24.9
Muslim	0.3	Mobile telephone subscribers	
Other	0.3	per 100 pop.	97.8
Hindu	<0.1	Broadband subs per 100 pop.	6.2
Jewish	<0.1	Internet hosts per 1,000 pop.	34.5

VIETNAM

Area	331,114 sq km	Capital	Hanoi
Arable as % of total land	20.8	Currency	Dong (D)

People

Population	88.8m	Life expectancy: men	73.4 yrs
Pop. per sq km	268.2	women	77.4 yrs
Total growth		Adult literacy	93.2%
in pop. 2000–10	11.5%	Fertility rate (per woman)	1.8
Pop. under 15	25.1%	Urban population	31.0%
Pop. over 60	6.7%		per 1,000 pop.
No. of men per 100 women	97.7	Crude birth rate	15.9
Human Development Index	61.7	Crude death rate	5.2

The economy

GDP	D2,535trn	GDP per head	$1,407
GDP	$124bn	GDP per head in purchasing	
Av. ann. growth in real		power parity (USA=100)	7.1
GDP 2006–11	6.5%	Economic freedom index	51.0

Origins of GDP		Components of GDP	
	% of total		% of total
Agriculture	22	Private consumption	63
Industry, of which:	41	Public consumption	6
manufacturing	19	Investment	35
Services	37	Exports	87
		Imports	-91

Structure of employment

	% of total		% of labour force
Agriculture	48	Unemployed 2011	2.0
Industry	22	Av. ann. rate 2000–11	2.3
Services	30		

Energy

	m TOE		
Total output	65.9	Net energy imports as %	
Total consumption	59.2	of energy use	-11
Consumption per head,			
kg oil equivalent	681		

Inflation and finance

Consumer price		av. ann. increase 2006–11	
inflation 2011	9.1%	Narrow money (M1)	18.6
Av. ann. inflation 2007–12	13.2%	Broad money	27.0
Treasury bill rate, Nov. 2012	6.96%		

Exchange rates

	end 2012		2012
D per $	20,477	Effective rates	2005 = 100
D per SDR	26,149	– nominal	...
D per €	27,086	– real	...

Trade

Principal exports		Principal imports	
	$bn fob		*$bn cif*
Textiles & garments	14.0	Machinery & equipment	15.2
Crude oil	7.3	Petroleum products	9.9
Footwear	6.5	Textiles	6.8
Fisheries products	6.1	Steel	6.3
Total incl. others	**95.4**	Total incl. others	**104.2**

Main export destinations		Main origins of imports	
	% of total		*% of total*
United States	17.6	China	30.7
Japan	11.0	South Korea	14.3
China	10.6	Singapore	10.8
South Korea	4.8	Japan	10.1
Germany	4.4	Thailand	7.4
Australia	3.1	Hong Kong	6.3
Malaysia	3.0	United States	4.6

Balance of payments, reserves and debt, $bn

Visible exports fob	96.9	Change in reserves	1.1
Visible imports fob	-97.4	Level of reserves	
Trade balance	-0.5	end Dec.	14.0
Invisibles inflows	9.3	No. months of import cover	1.5
Invisibles outflows	-17.3	Official gold holdings, m oz	...
Net transfers	8.7	Foreign debt	57.8
Current account balance	0.2	– as % of GDP	35
– as % of GDP	0.2	– as % of total exports	43
Capital balance	6.4	Debt service ratio	3
Overall balance	1.2		

Health and education

Health spending, % of GDP	6.8	Education spending, % of GDP	6.6
Doctors per 1,000 pop.	1.2	Enrolment, %: primary	106
Hospital beds per 1,000 pop.	2.2	secondary	77
Improved-water source access,		tertiary	24
% of pop.	95		

Society

No. of households	20.5m	Cost of living, Dec. 2012	
Av. no. per household	4.3	New York = 100	71
Marriages per 1,000 pop.	5.3	Cars per 1,000 pop.	19
Divorces per 1,000 pop.	0.2	Colour TV households, % with:	
Religion, % of pop.		cable	16.4
Other	62.0	satellite	18.6
Non-religious	29.6	Telephone lines per 100 pop.	11.5
Christian	8.2	Mobile telephone subscribers	
Muslim	0.2	per 100 pop.	143.4
Hindu	<0.1	Broadband subs per 100 pop.	4.3
Jewish	<0.1	Internet hosts per 1,000 pop.	2.1

ZIMBABWE

Area	390,759 sq km	Capital	Harare
Arable as % of total land	10.6	Currency	Zimbabwe dollar (Z$)

People

Population	12.8m	Life expectancy: men	54.0 yrs
Pop. per sq km	32.8	women	52.7 yrs
Total growth		Adult literacy	92.2%
in pop. 2000–10	0.5%	Fertility rate (per woman)	3.1
Pop. under 15	39.5%	Urban population	38.6%
Pop. over 60	5.8%		per 1,000 pop.
No. of men per 100 women	97.2	Crude birth rate	28.7
Human Development Index	39.7	Crude death rate	11.7

The economy

GDP[a]	$9.7bn	GDP per head[a]	$760
Av. ann. growth in real		GDP per head in purchasing	
GDP 2006–11	0.9%	power parity (USA=100)[a]	1.1
		Economic freedom index	28.6

Origins of GDP		Components of GDP	
	% of total		% of total
Agriculture	16	Private consumption	92
Industry, of which:	37	Public consumption	24
manufacturing	17	Investment	23
Services	47	Exports	49
		Imports	-88

Structure of employment

	% of total		% of labour force
Agriculture	...	Unemployed 2011	...
Industry	...	Av. ann. rate 2000–11	...
Services	...		

Energy

	m TOE		
Total output	8.6	Net energy imports as %	
Total consumption	9.6	of energy use	10
Consumption per head,			
kg oil equivalent	764		

Inflation[a] and finance

Consumer price			av. ann. increase 2006–11
inflation 2012	5.0%	Narrow money (M1)	...
Av. ann. inflation 2007–12	3.3%	Broad money	...
Treasury bill rate, Dec. 2010	7.5%		

Exchange rates

	end 2012		2012
Z$ per $	...	Effective rates	2005 = 100
Z$ per SDR	...	– nominal	...
Z$ per €	...	– real	...

Trade

Principal exports		Principal imports	
	$bn fob		*$bn cif*
Gold	0.7	Machinery & transportation	
Platinum	0.6	equipment	0.5
Tobacco	0.5	Fuels & energy	0.4
Ferro-alloys	0.4	Manufactures	0.3
		Chemicals	0.2
Total incl. others	**2.9**	**Total incl. others**	**4.5**

Main export destinations		Main origins of imports	
	% of total		*% of total*
South Africa	17.3	South Africa	55.1
China	16.9	China	9.1
Congo-Kinshasa	11.7	Zambia	3.5
Botswana	10.5	India	3.3
Italy	6.0	Botswana	3.2

Balance of payments[a], reserves[a] and debt, $bn

Visible exports fob	4.5	Change in reserves	-0.1
Visible imports fob	-7.6	Level of reserves	
Trade balance	-3.1	end Dec.	0.7
Invisibles, net	-1.2	No. months of import cover	0.9
Net transfers	1.0	Official gold holdings, m oz	0.0
Current account balance	-3.2	Foreign debt	6.3
– as % of GDP	-33.3	– as % of GDP[b]	69
Capital balance	1.5	– as % of total exports	153
Overall balance	-0.8	Debt service ratio[ab]	...

Health and education

Health spending, % of GDP	...	Education spending, % of GDP	2.5
Doctors per 1,000 pop.	0.1	Enrolment, %: primary	...
Hospital beds per 1,000 pop.	1.7	secondary	...
Improved-water source access,		tertiary	6
% of pop.	80		

Society

No. of households	3.2m	Cost of living, Dec. 2012	
Av. no. per household	4.0	New York = 100	...
Marriages per 1,000 pop.	...	Cars per 1,000 pop.	202
Divorces per 1,000 pop.	...	Colour TV households, % with:	
Religion, % of pop.		cable	...
Christian	87.0	satellite	...
Non-religious	7.9	Telephone lines per 100 pop.	2.8
Other	4.2	Mobile telephone subscribers	
Muslim	0.9	per 100 pop.	72.1
Hindu	<0.1	Broadband subs per 100 pop.	0.3
Jewish	<0.1	Internet hosts per 1,000 pop.	2.4

a Estimates.
b 2008

EURO AREA[a]

Area	2,578,704 sq km	Capital	–
Arable as % of total land	24.4	Currency	Euro (€)

People

Population	331.3m	Life expectancy: men	79.5 yrs
Pop. per sq km	128.5	women	85.1 yrs
Total growth		Adult literacy	...
in pop. 2000–10	8.5%	Fertility rate (per woman)	1.6
Pop. under 15	15.4%	Urban population	75.4%
Pop. over 60	23.8%		per 1,000 pop.
No. of men per 100 women	96.1	Crude birth rate	10.0
Human Development Index	89.3	Crude death rate	9.9

The economy

GDP	€18,195bn	GDP per head	$39,290
GDP	$13,080bn	GDP per head in purchasing	
Av. ann. growth in real		power parity (USA=100)	73.3
GDP 2006–11	0.5%	Economic freedom index	67.1

Origins of GDP

Components of GDP

	% of total		% of total
Agriculture	2	Private consumption	57
Industry, of which:	26	Public consumption	22
manufacturing	16	Investment	20
Services	72	Exports	44
		Imports	-42

Structure of employment

	% of total		% of labour force
Agriculture	4	Unemployed 2010	9.3
Industry	25	Av. ann. rate 2000–11	9.1
Services	71		

Energy

	m TOE		
Total output	478.2	Net energy imports as %	
Total consumption	1,205.8	of energy use	60
Consumption per head,			
kg oil equivalent	3,633		

Inflation and finance

		av. ann. increase 2006–11	
Consumer price			
inflation 2012	2.5%	Narrow money (M1)	5.3%
Av. ann. inflation 2007–12	2.1%	Broad money	4.7%
Interbank rate, Dec. 2012	0.07%	H'hold saving rate, Dec. 2012	7.2%

Exchange rates

	end 2012		2012
€ per $	0.76	Effective rates	2005 = 100
€ per SDR	1.16	– nominal	99.32
		– real	92.71

Trade[b]

Principal exports		Principal imports	
	$bn fob		*$bn cif*
Machinery & transport equip.	905.1	Mineral fuels & lubricants	680.9
Manufactures	493.5	Machinery & transport equip.	617.6
Chemicals	356.1	Manufactures	559.0
Food, drink & tobacco	106.4	Chemicals	215.8
Mineral fuels & lubricants	140.6	Food, drink & tobacco	127.2
Raw materials	62.5	Raw materials	119.6
Total incl. others	**2,169.6**	Total incl. others	**2,396.1**

Main export destinations		Main origins of imports	
	% of total		*% of total*
United States	16.9	China	17.0
China	8.7	Russia	11.6
Switzerland	9.0	United States	11.1
Russia	6.9	Norway	5.4
Turkey	4.7	Switzerland	5.4
Norway	3.0	Japan	4.0

Balance of payments, reserves and aid, $bn

Visible exports fob	2,469	Overall balance	-35
Visible imports fob	-2,457	Change in reserves	59.7
Trade balance	12	Level of reserves	
Invisibles inflows	1,537	end Dec.	847.7
Invisibles outflows	-1,385	No. months of import cover	2.6
Net transfers	-148	Official gold holdings, m oz	346.9
Current account balance	16	Aid given[c]	51.19
– as % of GDP	0.1	– as % of GDP[c]	0.39
Capital balance	80		

Health and education

Health spending, % of GDP	10.8	Education spending, % of GDP	5.5
Doctors per 1,000 pop.	3.6	Enrolment, %: primary	105
Hospital beds per 1,000 pop.	5.8	secondary	107
Improved-water source access,		tertiary	60
% of pop.	100		

Society

No. of households	142.6	Colour TV households, % with:	
Av. no. per household	2.32	cable	...
Marriages per 1,000 pop.	4.1	satellite	...
Divorces per 1,000 pop.	1.9	Telephone lines per 100 pop.	42.7
Cost of living, Dec. 2012		Mobile telephone subscribers	
New York = 100	...	per 100 pop.	121.1
Cars per 1,000 pop.	508	Broadband subs per 100 pop.	25.5
		Internet hosts per 1,000 pop.	405.9

a Data generally refer to the 17 EU members that have adopted the euro: Austria,
   Belgium, Cyprus, Estonia, Finland, France, Germany, Greece, Ireland, Italy,
   Luxembourg, Malta, Netherlands, Portugal, Slovakia, Slovenia and Spain.
b EU27, excluding intra-trade.   c Excluding Cyprus and Malta.

WORLD

Area	148,698,382 sq km	Capital	...
Arable as % of total land	10.7	Currency	...

People

Population	6,974.0m	Life expectancy: men	67.1 yrs
Pop. per sq km	46.9	women	71.6 yrs
Total growth		Adult literacy	83.7%
in pop. 2000–10	12.6%	Fertility rate (per woman)	2.5
Pop. under 15	26.9%	Urban population	52.1%
Pop. over 60	11.0%		per 1,000 pop.
No. of men per 100 women	101.7	Crude birth rate	20.0
Human Development Index	69.4	Crude death rate	8.2

The economy

GDP	$70.0trn	GDP per head	$9,510
Av. ann. growth in real		GDP per head in purchasing	
GDP 2006–11	3.3%	power parity (USA=100)	24.1
		Economic freedom index	57.1

Origins of GDP		Components of GDP	
	% of total		% of total
Agriculture	3	Private consumption	62
Industry, of which:	26	Public consumption	19
manufacturing	17	Investment	20
Services	71	Exports	29
		Imports	-30

Structure of employment[a]

	% of total		% of labour force
Agriculture	...	Unemployed 2010	8.6
Industry	...	Av. ann. rate 2000–11	7.1
Services	...		

Energy

	m TOE		
Total output	12,738	Net energy imports as %	
Total consumption	12,324	of energy use	-3
Consumption per head,			
kg oil equivalent	1,851		

Inflation and finance

Consumer price		av. ann. increase 2006–11	
inflation 2012	3.6%	Narrow money (M1)[a]	7.1%
Av. ann. inflation 2007–12	3.9%	Broad money[a]	6.5%
LIBOR $ rate, 3-month, Dec. 2012	0.31%	H'hold saving rate, Dec. 2012[a]	5.6%

Trade

World exports

	$bn fob		$bn fob
Manufactures	12,232	Ores & minerals	913
Fuels	2,556	Agricultural raw materials	365
Food	1,461	Total incl. others	**18,257**

Main export destinations

Main origins of imports

	% of total		% of total
United States	11.6	China	11.6
China	8.3	Germany	7.9
Germany	6.7	United States	7.8
France	4.1	Japan	4.7
Japan	4.3	Netherlands	3.4
United Kingdom	3.7	France	3.3

Balance of payments, reserves and aid, $bn

Visible exports fob	17,885	Overall balance[c]	0
Visible imports fob	-17,535	Change in reserves	1,134
Trade balance	350	Level of reserves	
Invisibles inflows	7,643	end Dec.	12,173
Invisibles outflows	-7,445	No. months of import cover	6
Net transfers	-149	Official gold holdings, m oz	998
Current account balance	399	Aid given[b]	114.19
– as % of GDP	0.6	– as % of GDP[b]	0.24
Capital balance[c]	-249		

Health and education

Health spending, % of GDP	10.4	Education spending, % of GDP	...
Doctors per 1,000 pop.	1.4	Enrolment, %: primary	107
Hospital beds per 1,000 pop.	...	secondary	68
Improved-water source access,		tertiary	27
% of pop.	88		

Society

No. of households	...	Cost of living, Dec. 2012	
Av. no. per household	...	New York = 100	...
Marriages per 1,000 pop.	...	Cars per 1,000 pop.	...
Divorces per 1,000 pop.	...	Colour TV households, % with:	
Religion, % of pop.		cable	...
Christian	31.5	satellite	...
Muslim	23.2	Telephone lines per 100 pop.	22.4
Non-religious	16.3	Mobile telephone subscribers	
Hindu	15.0	per 100 pop.	91.0
Other	13.8	Broadband subs per 100 pop.	19.8
Jewish	0.2	Internet hosts per 1,000 pop.	105.9

a   OECD countries.
b   OECD, non-OECD Europe and Middle East countries.
c   2009

Glossary

Balance of payments The record of a country's transactions with the rest of the world. The **current account** of the balance of payments consists of: visible trade (goods); "invisible" trade (services and income); private transfer payments (eg, remittances from those working abroad); official transfers (eg, payments to international organisations, famine relief). Visible imports and exports are normally compiled on rather different definitions to those used in the trade statistics (shown in principal imports and exports) and therefore the statistics do not match. The **capital account** consists of long- and short-term transactions relating to a country's assets and liabilities (eg, loans and borrowings). The **current and capital accounts**, plus an errors and omissions item, make up the **overall balance. Changes in reserves** include gold at market prices and are shown without the practice often followed in balance of payments presentations of reversing the sign.

Big Mac index A light-hearted way of looking at exchange rates. If the dollar price of a burger at McDonald's in any country is higher than the price in the United States, converting at market exchange rates, then that country's currency could be thought to be over-valued against the dollar and vice versa.

Body-mass index A measure for assessing obesity – weight in kilograms divided by height in metres squared. An index of 30 or more is regarded as an indicator of obesity; 25 to 29.9 as over-weight. Guidelines vary for men and for women and may be adjusted for age.

CFA Communauté Financière Africaine. Its members, most of the francophone African nations, share a common currency, the CFA franc, pegged to the euro.

Cif/fob Measures of the value of merchandise trade. Imports include the cost of "carriage, insurance and freight" (cif) from the exporting country to the importing. The value of exports does not include these elements and is recorded "free on board" (fob). Balance of payments statistics are generally adjusted so that both exports and imports are shown fob; the cif elements are included in invisibles.

Crude birth rate The number of live births in a year per 1,000 population. The crude rate will automatically be relatively high if a large proportion of the population is of childbearing age.

Crude death rate The number of deaths in a year per 1,000 population. Also affected by the population's age structure.

Debt, foreign Financial obligations owed by a country to the rest of the world and repayable in foreign currency. The **debt service ratio** is debt service (principal repayments plus interest payments) expressed as a percentage of the country's earnings from exports of goods and services.

Debt, household All liabilities that require payment of interest or principal in the future.

Economic Freedom Index The ranking includes data on labour and business freedom as well as trade policy, taxation, monetary policy, the banking system, foreign-investment rules, property rights, government spending, regulation policy, the level of corruption and the extent of wage and price controls.

Effective exchange rate The nominal index measures a currency's depreciation (figures below 100) or appreciation (figures over 100) from a base date against a trade-weighted basket of the currencies of the country's main trading partners. The real effective exchange rate reflects adjustments for relative movements in prices or costs.

EU European Union. Members are: Austria, Belgium, Bulgaria, Cyprus, Czech Republic, Denmark, Estonia, Finland, France, Germany, Greece, Hungary, Ireland, Italy, Latvia, Lithuania, Luxembourg, Malta, Netherlands, Poland, Portugal, Romania, Slovakia, Slovenia, Spain, Sweden and the United Kingdom. Croatia joined on July 1 2013.

Euro area The 17 euro area members of the EU are Austria, Belgium, Cyprus, Estonia, Finland, France, Germany, Greece, Ireland, Italy, Luxembourg, Malta, Netherlands, Portugal, Slovakia, Slovenia and Spain. Their common currency is the euro, which first came into circulation on January 1 2002.

Fertility rate The average number of children born to a woman who completes her childbearing years.

G7 Group of seven countries: United States, Japan, Germany, United Kingdom, France, Italy and Canada.

GDP Gross domestic product. The sum of all output produced by economic activity within a country. GNP (gross national product) and GNI (gross national income) include net income from abroad eg, rent, profits.

Household saving rate Household savings as % of disposable household income.

Import cover The number of months of imports covered by reserves ie, reserves ÷ $\frac{1}{12}$ annual imports (visibles and invisibles).

Inflation The annual rate at which prices are increasing. The most common measure and the one shown here is the increase in the consumer price index.

Internet hosts Websites and other computers that sit permanently on the internet.

Life expectancy The average length of time a baby born today can expect to live.

Literacy is defined by UNESCO as the ability to read and write a simple sentence, but definitions can vary from country to country.

Median age Divides the age distribution into two halves. Half of the population is above and half below the median age.

Money supply A measure of the "money" available to buy goods and services. Various definitions exist. The measures shown here are based on definitions used by the IMF and may differ from measures used nationally. Narrow money (M1) consists of cash in circulation and demand deposits (bank deposits that can be withdrawn on demand). "Quasi-money" (time, savings and foreign currency deposits) is added to this to create broad money.

OECD Organisation for Economic Co-operation and Development. The "rich countries" club was established in 1961 to promote economic growth and the expansion of world trade. It is based in Paris and now has 34 members.

Official reserves The stock of gold and foreign currency held by a country to finance any calls that may be made for the settlement of foreign debt.

Opec Organisation of Petroleum Exporting Countries. Set up in 1960 and based in Vienna, Opec is mainly concerned with oil pricing and production issues. Members are: Algeria, Angola, Ecuador, Iran, Iraq, Kuwait, Libya, Nigeria, Qatar, Saudi Arabia, United Arab Emirates and Venezuela.

PPP Purchasing power parity. PPP statistics adjust for cost of living differences by replacing normal exchange rates with rates designed to equalise the prices of a standard "basket"of goods and services. These are used to obtain PPP estimates of GDP per head. PPP estimates are shown on an index, taking the United States as 100.

Real terms Figures adjusted to exclude the effect of inflation.

SDR Special drawing right. The reserve currency, introduced by the IMF in 1970, was intended to replace gold and national currencies in settling international transactions. The IMF uses SDRs for book-keeping purposes and issues them to member countries. Their value is based on a basket of the US dollar (with a weight of 41.9%), the euro (37.4%), the Japanese yen (9.4%) and the pound sterling (11.3%).

List of countries

Wherever data is available, the world rankings consider 198 countries: all those which had (in 2011) or have recently had a population of at least 1m or a GDP of at least $1bn. Here is a list of them.

	Population	GDP	GDP per head	Area '000 sq	Median age
	m, 2011	$bn, 2011	$PPP, 2011	km	yrs, 2011
Afghanistan	32.4	19.2	1,140	652	16.6
Albania	3.2	13.0	8,870	29	30.0
Algeria	36.0	188.7	8,660	2,382	26.2
Andorra	0.09	3.6	36,460[b]	0.4	40.0
Angola	19.6	104.3	5,920	1,247	16.6
Antigua & Barbuda	0.09	1.1	18,490	0.4	30.0
Argentina	40.8	446.0	16,000[a]	2,767	30.4
Armenia	3.1	10.2	5,790	30	32.1
Aruba	0.11	2.7	24,790[b]	0.2	38.3
Australia	22.6	1,379.4	41,970	7,682	36.9
Austria	8.4	417.7	42,170	84	41.8
Azerbaijan	9.3	63.4	10,060	87	29.5
Bahamas	0.3	7.8	31,980	14	30.9
Bahrain	1.3	22.9[a]	23,640[a]	0.7	30.1
Bangladesh	150.5	111.9	1,780	144	24.2
Barbados	0.3	3.7	19,320[a]	0.4	37.5
Belarus	9.6	55.1	14,940	208	38.3
Belgium	10.8	513.7	38,720	31	41.2
Belize	0.3	1.4	6,670	23	21.8
Benin	9.1	7.3	1,620	113	17.9
Bermuda	0.07	5.8[a]	84,280[b]	0.1	42.4
Bhutan	0.7	1.7	5,850	47	24.6
Bolivia	10.1	23.9	5,100	1,099	21.7
Bosnia	3.8	18.1	9,080	51	39.4
Botswana	2.0	17.3	14,750	581	22.9
Brazil	196.7	2,476.7	11,640	8,512	29.1
British Virgin Islands	0.03	0.9	41,450[ab]	0.2	29.5
Brunei	0.4	16.4	51,760	6	28.9
Bulgaria	7.4	53.5	15,080	111	41.6
Burkina Faso	17.0	10.4	1,300	274	17.1
Burundi	8.6	2.3	600	28	20.2
Cambodia	14.3	12.8	2,360	181	22.9
Cameroon	20.0	25.2	2,360	475	19.3
Canada	34.3	1,736.1	40,420	9,971	39.9
Cape Verde	0.5	1.9	4,090	4	22.8
Cayman Islands	0.05	3.3	43,800[ab]	0.3	38.7
Central African Republic	4.5	2.2	810	622	19.4
Chad	11.5	10.6	1,500	1,284	17.1
Channel Islands	0.16	11.5[a]	51,960[ab]	0.2	42.6
Chile	17.3	248.6	17,270	757	32.1
China	1,347.6	7,318.5	8,400	9,561	34.5
Colombia	46.9	333.4	10,030	1,142	26.8

	Population	GDP	GDP per head	Area '000 sq	Median age
	m, 2011	$bn, 2011	$PPP, 2011	km	yrs, 2011
Congo-Brazzaville	4.1	14.4	4,360	342	19.6
Congo-Kinshasa	67.8	15.7	370	2,345	16.7
Costa Rica	4.7	40.9	12,160	51	28.4
Côte d'Ivoire	20.2	24.1	1,790	322	19.2
Croatia	4.4	62.5	19,490	57	41.5
Cuba	11.3	68.7	10,000[ab]	111	38.4
Cyprus	1.1	24.7	32,250	9	34.2
Czech Republic	10.5	217.0	26,330	79	39.4
Denmark	5.6	333.6	40,930	43	40.6
Djibouti	0.9	1.3	2,300[a]	23	21.4
Dominican Republic	10.1	55.6	9,800	48	25.1
Ecuador	14.7	65.9	8,670	272	25.5
Egypt	82.5	229.5	6,280	1,000	24.4
El Salvador	6.2	23.1	6,830	21	23.2
Equatorial Guinea	0.7	19.8	36,200	28	20.3
Eritrea	5.4	2.6	580	117	19.0
Estonia	1.3	22.2	22,000	45	39.7
Ethiopia	84.7	30.2	1,110	1,134	18.7
Faroe Islands	0.05	2.2[a]	30,500[ab]	1	35.6
Fiji	0.9	3.8	4,760	18	26.4
Finland	5.4	263.0	37,460	338	42.0
France	63.1	2,773.0	35,250[c]	544	39.9
French Guiana	0.2	4.8[a]	17,290[a]	90	24.3
French Polynesia	0.3	6.7[a]	22,000[ab]	3	29.1
Gabon	1.5	17.1	15,850	268	21.6
Gambia, The	1.8	0.9	1,810	11	17.8
Georgia	4.3	14.4	5,470	70	37.3
Germany	82.2	3,600.8	39,460	358	44.3
Ghana	25.0	39.2	1,870	239	20.5
Greece	11.4	289.6	25,860	132	41.4
Greenland	0.06	2.4	37,400[ab]	2,176	29.6
Guadeloupe	0.4	11.0[a]	20,220[a]	2	36.8
Guam	0.16	4.6[ab]	28,130[ab]	0.5	29.2
Guatemala	14.8	46.9	4,930	109	18.9
Guinea	10.2	5.1	1,120	246	18.3
Guinea-Bissau	1.5	1.0	1,270	36	19.0
Guyana	0.8	2.6	3,440[a]	215	23.8
Haiti	10.1	7.3	1,170	28	21.5
Honduras	7.8	17.4	4,050	112	21.0
Hong Kong	7.1	248.6	50,550	1	41.8
Hungary	10.0	140.0	21,660	93	39.8
Iceland	0.3	14.0	36,480	103	34.8
India	1,241.5	1,872.8	3,650	3,287	25.1
Indonesia	242.3	846.8	4,640	1,904	27.8
Iran	74.8	429.0[a]	11,510[a]	1,648	27.1
Iraq	32.7	115.4	3,860	438	18.3
Ireland	4.5	217.3	40,870	70	34.7

	Population	GDP	GDP per head	Area '000 sq	Median age
	m, 2011	$bn, 2011	$PPP, 2011	km	yrs, 2011
Israel	7.6	242.9	28,810	21	30.1
Italy	60.8	2,194.0	32,670	301	43.2
Jamaica	2.8	14.4	8,710[a]	11	27.0
Japan	126.5	5,867.2	33,670	378	44.7
Jordan	6.3	28.8	5,970	89	20.7
Kazakhstan	16.2	188.0	13,100	2,717	29.0
Kenya	41.6	33.6	1,710	583	18.5
Kosovo	1.8	6.5	6,570[b]	11	28.7
Kuwait	2.8	176.6	54,280	18	28.2
Kyrgyzstan	5.4	6.2	2,400	199	23.8
Laos	6.3	8.3	2,790	237	21.5
Latvia	2.2	28.3	18,950	64	40.2
Lebanon	4.3	40.1	14,610	10	29.1
Lesotho	2.2	2.4	1,690	30	20.3
Liberia	4.1	1.5	590	111	18.2
Libya	6.4	71.7[a]	16,900[a]	1,760	25.9
Liechtenstein	0.04	6.2	89,400[ab]	160	40.0
Lithuania	3.3	42.7	21,480	65	39.3
Luxembourg	0.5	59.2	88,800	3	38.9
Macau	0.6	36.4	77,080	0.02	37.6
Macedonia	2.1	10.4	11,560	26	35.9
Madagascar	21.3	9.9	970	587	18.2
Malawi	15.4	5.6	890	118	16.9
Malaysia	28.9	287.9	16,050	333	26.0
Maldives	0.3	2.1	8,530	0.3	24.6
Mali	15.8	10.8	1,090	1,240	16.3
Malta	0.4	8.9	27,500	0.3	39.5
Martinique	0.4	11.2[a]	24,870[a]	1	39.4
Mauritania	3.5	4.2	2,530	1,031	19.8
Mauritius	1.3	11.3	14,420	2	32.4
Mexico	114.8	1,153.3	16,590	1,973	26.6
Moldova	3.5	7.0	3,370	34	35.2
Monaco	0.03	6.1	69,290[b]	2	45.0
Mongolia	2.8	8.8	4,740	1,565	25.4
Montenegro	0.6	4.5	13,430	14	35.9
Morocco	32.3	100.2	4,950	447	26.3
Mozambique	23.9	12.8	980	799	17.8
Myanmar	48.3	55.3	1,320[b]	677	28.2
Namibia	2.3	12.5	6,800	824	21.2
Nepal	30.5	18.9	1,250	147	21.4
Netherlands	16.7	836.1	42,780	42	40.7
New Caledonia	0.3	9.9	37,700[ab]	19	30.3
New Zealand	4.4	159.7	31,080	271	36.6
Nicaragua	5.9	9.3	3,810	130	22.1
Niger	16.1	6.0	730	1,267	15.5
Nigeria	162.5	244.0	2,530	924	18.5
North Korea	24.5	12.4	1,760[b]	121	32.9

	Population	GDP	GDP per head	Area '000 sq	Median age
	m, 2011	$bn, 2011	$PPP, 2011	km	yrs, 2011
Norway	4.9	485.8	60,390	324	38.7
Oman	2.8	71.8	28,680	310	25.3
Pakistan	176.7	210.2	2,740	804	21.7
Panama	3.6	26.8	15,590	77	27.3
Papua New Guinea	7.0	12.9	2,680	463	20.4
Paraguay	6.6	23.8	5,500	407	23.1
Peru	29.4	176.9	10,230	1,285	25.6
Philippines	94.9	224.8	4,120	300	22.2
Poland	38.3	514.5	21,080	313	38.0
Portugal	10.7	237.4	25,560	89	41.0
Puerto Rico	3.7	96.3[a]	15,970[ab]	9	34.4
Qatar	1.9	173.0	88,310	11	31.6
Réunion	0.8	22.1[a]	22,080[a]	3	29.9
Romania	21.4	189.8	15,980	238	38.5
Russia	142.8	1,857.8	21,920	17,075	37.9
Rwanda	10.9	6.4	1,280	26	18.7
St Lucia	0.2	1.3	11,600	0.6	27.4
San Marino	0.03	2.0	36,200[ab]	60	42.0
Saudi Arabia	28.1	576.8	24,270	2,200	25.9
Senegal	12.8	14.3	1,970	197	17.8
Serbia	9.9	45.8	11,890	88	37.6
Seychelles	0.09	1.1	25,790	460	32.0
Sierra Leone	6.0	3.0	1,130	72	18.4
Singapore	5.2	239.7	60,690	0.6	37.6
Slovakia	5.5	96.0	24,090	49	36.9
Slovenia	2.0	49.5	26,940	20	41.7
Somalia	9.6	1.1	590[b]	638	17.5
South Africa	50.5	408.2	10,960	1,226	24.9
South Korea	48.4	1,116.2	29,830	99	37.9
South Sudand	10.1	19.2	2,210[b]	644	18.0
Spain	46.5	1,476.9	32,090	505	40.1
Sri Lanka	21.0	59.2	5,580	66	30.7
Sudan	33.6	64.1[e]	2,330	1,862	19.7
Suriname	0.5	4.3	8,350	164	27.6
Swaziland	1.2	4.1	6,050	17	19.5
Sweden	9.4	539.7	41,480	450	40.7
Switzerland	7.7	659.3	51,230	41	41.4
Syria	20.8	59.1[a]	5,250[a]	185	21.1
Taiwan	23.2	464.0	37,570	36	38.0
Tajikistan	7.0	6.5	2,320	143	20.4
Tanzania	46.2	23.9	1,510	945	17.5
Thailand	69.5	345.7	8,650	513	34.2
Timor-Leste	1.2	1.1	1,580	15	16.6
Togo	6.2	3.6	1,050	57	19.7
Trinidad & Tobago	1.3	22.5	25,070	5	30.8
Tunisia	10.6	46.4	9,320	164	28.9
Turkey	73.6	775.0	17,110	779	28.3

	Population	GDP	GDP per head	Area '000 sq	Median age
	m, 2011	$bn, 2011	$PPP, 2011	km	yrs, 2011
Turkmenistan	5.1	28.1	9,420	488	24.5
Uganda	34.5	16.8	1,340	241	15.7
Ukraine	45.2	165.2	7,210	604	39.3
United Arab Emirates	7.9	360.2	47,890	84	30.1
United Kingdom	62.4	2,445.4	35,600	243	39.8
United States	313.1	14,991.3	48,110	9,373	36.9
Uruguay	3.4	46.7	15,080	176	33.7
Uzbekistan	27.8	45.4	3,290	447	24.2
Venezuela	29.4	316.5	12,750	912	26.1
Vietnam	88.8	123.6	3,410	331	28.2
Virgin Islands (US)	0.11	1.6[ab]	14,500[ab]	0.4	38.8
West Bank and Gaza	4.2	8.0[b]	2,900[ab]	6	18.1
Yemen	24.8	33.8	2,330	528	17.4
Zambia	13.5	19.2	1,620	753	16.7
Zimbabwe	12.8	9.7	530[b]	391	19.3
Euro area (17)	331.3	13,079.9	35,280	2,497	41.8
World	6,974.0	70,020.4	11,620	148,698	29.2

a Latest available year.
b Estimate.
c Including French Guiana, Guadeloupe, Martinique and Réunion.
d South Sudan became an independent state in July 2011.
e Data include South Sudan.

Sources

AFM Research
Airports Council International, *Worldwide Airport Traffic Report*
Art Newspaper, *The*

Bloomberg
BP, *Statistical Review of World Energy*
Business Software Alliance

CAF, *The World Giving Index*
CBRE, *Prime Office Occupancy Costs*
Central banks
Central Intelligence Agency, *The World Factbook*
Clarkson Research, *World Fleet Monitor*
Corporate Resources Group, *Quality of Living Report*

The Economist
www.economist.com
Economist Intelligence Unit, *Cost of Living Survey; Country Forecasts; Country Reports; Democracy index; Global Outlook - Business Environment Rankings*
ERC Statistics International, *World Cigarette Report*
Euromonitor, *International Marketing Data and Statistics; European Marketing Data and Statistics*
Eurostat, *Statistics in Focus*

Facebook
Finance ministries
Food and Agriculture Organisation

The Heritage Foundation, *Index of Economic Freedom*

IFPI
IMD, *World Competitiveness Yearbook*

IMF, *International Financial Statistics; World Economic Outlook*
International Centre for Prison Studies, *World Prison Brief*
International Cocoa Organisation, *Quarterly Bulletin of Cocoa Statistics*
International Coffee Organisation
International Cotton Advisory Committee, *March Bulletin*
International Diabetes Federation, *Diabetes Atlas*
International Grains Council
International Institute for Strategic Studies, *Military Balance*
International Labour Organisation
International Rubber Study Group, *Rubber Statistical Bulletin*
International Sugar Organisation, *Statistical Bulletin*
International Telecommunication Union, *ITU Indicators*
International Union of Railways
Internet Systems Consortium
Inter-Parliamentary Union

Johnson Matthey

McDonald's

National statistics offices
Nobel Foundation

OECD, *Development Assistance Committee Report; Economic Outlook; Environmental Data; Government at a Glance; OECD.Stat; Revenue Statistics*
www.olympic.org

Pew Research Centre, *The Global Religious Landscape*

Reporters Without Borders, *Press Freedom Index*
Reuters Thomson

Standard & Poor's *Global Stock Markets Factbook*
Sovereign Wealth Fund Institute
Stockholm International Peace Research Institute

Taiwan Statistical Data Book
The Times, *Atlas of the World*
Transparency International

UN, *Demographic Yearbook*; *Global Refugee Trends*; *National Accounts*; *State of World Population Report*; *Survey on Crime Trends*; *World Contraceptive Use*; *World Population Database*; *World Population Prospects*; *World Urbanisation Prospects*
UNAIDS, *Report on the Global AIDS Epidemic*
UNCTAD, *Review of Maritime Transport*; *World Investment Report*
UNCTAD/WTO International Trade Centre

UN Development Programme, *Human Development Report*
UNESCO, Institute for Statistics
US Census Bureau
US Department of Agriculture

Visionofhumanity.org

WHO, *Global Immunisation Data*; *World Health Statistics Annual*
World Bank, *Doing Business*; *Global Development Finance*; *Migration and Remittances Factbook*; *World Development Indicators*; *World Development Report*
World Bureau of Metal Statistics, *World Metal Statistics*
World Economic Forum/Harvard University, *Global Competitiveness Report*
World Resources Institute, *World Resources*
World Tourism Organisation, *Yearbook of Tourism Statistics*
World Trade Organisation, *Annual Report*